HAUNTED PLACES IN
THE AMERICAN SOUTH

HAUNTED PLACES IN THE AMERICAN SOUTH

Alan Brown

University Press of Mississippi Jackson

www.upress.state.ms.us

∞

Library of Congress Cataloging-in-Publication Data

Brown, Alan, 1950 Jan. 12–
    Haunted places in the American South / Alan Brown.
        p.   cm.
    Includes bibliographical references and index.
    ISBN 1-57806-476-7 (cloth : alk. paper) — ISBN 1-57806-477-5
(pbk. : alk. paper)
        1. Ghosts—Southern States.   2. Apparitions—Southern States.
    3. Haunted houses—Southern States.   I. Title.
    BF1472.U6 B743   2002
    133.1'0975—dc21   2002000635

British Library Cataloging-in-Publication Data available

To Marilyn, my sheltering spirit

CONTENTS

Acknowledgments xi
Preface xiii
Introduction xv

ALABAMA
Linn Henley Building 5
Marengo 9
McCandless Hall 15
The Sloss Furnaces 19
Sturtivant Hall 25
ARKANSAS
The Allen House 33
Crescent Hotel 36
Gurdon Lights 40
Pea Ridge National Military Park 44
FLORIDA
Fort Zachary Taylor 51
The Jameson Inn of Crestview 54
Kingsley Plantation 59
Lilian Place 63
Old Leon County Jail 66
GEORGIA
Davenport House 71
The Juliette Gordon Low Girl Scout Center 73

The Pirate's House 77
Telfair Museum of Art 80
KENTUCKY
Bobby Mackey's Music World 85
Headless Woman Rock 91
Liberty Hall 94
Van Meter Auditorium 98
LOUISIANA
The *Delta Queen* 105
Griffon House 109
The Myrtles 113
Oak Alley 119
MISSISSIPPI
The Ell Davis Woods 125
King's Tavern 129
Magnolia Hall 134
The *Meridian Star* Building 140
Peavey Melody Music 143
The Pigford Building 146
Waverley 150
NORTH CAROLINA
Fort Fisher 163
Gimghoul Castle 166
New Hanover County Public Library 170
The Vander Lights 173
SOUTH CAROLINA
Hagley Landing 179
The Ladd House 184
St. Philip's Protestant Episcopal Church Graveyard 188
Wedgefield Plantation 191
TENNESSEE
Brinkley Female College 197

Carter House 203
The Orpheum Theater 207
St. Mary's Catholic Church 209
The Woodruff-Fontaine House 213
TEXAS
The Alamo 219
Driskill Hotel 226
The Houston Public Library 230
The Texas Governor's Mansion 232
The Villa Main Railroad Crossing 236
VIRGINIA
Eppington 241
Lee's Boyhood Home 245
Physic Hill 248
Ramsay House 252

Bibliography 255
Index 265

ACKNOWLEDGMENTS

I am deeply indebted to the following librarians who responded to my request for information: Trudy Bazemore from the Georgetown County Library System (Georgetown, South Carolina); Marianne Cawley from the Charleston County Public Library (Charleston, South Carolina); Don Paul Crook from the St. Mary Parish Library (Franklin, Louisiana); Glen Emery from the Jacksonville Main Library (Jacksonville, Florida); Laura Garcia from the Corpus Christi Public Library (Corpus Christi, Texas); L. Hatchet from the Texas Genealogy Department (San Antonio, Texas); Rita Holtz from the Alexandria Library (Alexandria, Virginia); Michael Maurin from the St. John the Baptist Parish Library (La Place, Louisiana); Donna Stephens from the St. Augustine Historical Society (St. Augustine, Florida); Beverly Tetterton from the New Hanover County Public Library (Wilmington, North Carolina); Fred G. Turner from the Olivia Raney Library (Raleigh, North Carolina); Cynthia Vise from the State Library of Florida (Tallahassee, Florida); and Doug Weiskopf from the Houston Public Library (Houston, Texas).

I would also like to thank Joyce Brannan, Pattie Grady, Scott Honeycutt, Ruth Jacob, Kenneth Reynolds, Christopher Shelton, and Troy Taylor, who served as consultants for this project. Finally I am grateful to the UWA University Research Grants Committee for providing me with funding for this project.

PREFACE

The idea for this book came about as a result of my interest in storytelling. After moving to Meridian, Mississippi, from Springfield, Illinois, in 1986, I discovered that one thing southerners love even more than football, bass fishing, and fried chicken is talking. Most southerners seem to be willing to take the time to tell tales and to listen to them as well. My first five books are, in fact, a celebration of southern storytelling. In all of my previous books, I adopted the folklorist's approach to oral narratives and transcribed the stories exactly as I heard them. No matter what the informants were talking about—outlaws or sharecropping or ghosts—their individual voices came through.

After the publication of my last book of folklore—*Shadows and Cypress: Southern Ghost Stories* (2000)—I decided to look at ghost legends from an entirely different angle. Taking my cue from such established storytellers as Kathryn Tucker Windham and Nancy Roberts, I paraphrased many of the tales I received from informants and from published accounts. Although I did attempt, now and then, to add a few literary flourishes to my rewritten versions, I did not consciously add any fictional elements for the sake of drama or suspense. Most of the stories, I felt, were already so incredible that they did not need embellishment.

A project as ambitious as this one has turned out to be could not have been completed without the assistance of many other individuals. Dennis William Hauck's *Haunted Places: The National*

Directory (1996) proved to be an indispensable tool as I set about collecting the stories for this book. All of my informants are listed in the bibliography. Most of these people (local historians, curators of historic homes, and others) were very familiar with the history and lore of the haunted places. I also relied very heavily on librarians from all over the South. All of these people graciously took the time to comb their vertical files for obscure clippings from newspapers and magazines. After completing my book, I had ample proof that southern hospitality is still alive and well.

INTRODUCTION

Have you ever wondered why so many ghosts seem to favor houses? I came to this conclusion in 1996 and again in 2000 when I completed two collections of oral ghost narratives. Of all the places given by my informants as settings for their tales, houses far outnumbered other locales. The reason for this is clear. Houses are places where human beings spend many of the most meaningful times of their lives. For generations, people were born in the home, and many have died there as well, sometimes under very tragic circumstances. For many people, the home is their entire world, the place that gives them their identity. It is small wonder, then, that in some cases, the home ties are so strong that they continue to be a powerful attraction, even after death. Not surprisingly, the majority of the haunted places mentioned in this book are houses.

By the same reasoning, though, any location that has been frequented by people has the potential of being haunted. The list includes other types of buildings, such as factories, libraries, and hotels. It can also include outdoor settings, such as forests, gorges, and railroad crossings. Even modes of transportation, such as steamboats, have been known to harbor spirits. In other words, ghosts can be found anyplace where people can be found.

Several criteria were used in selecting the places included in this book, other than the presence of ghosts at some point in their history. Like any collector of legends, I gave preference to those stories that have never been published before in book form. These stories include places such as Peavey Melody Music in Meridian, Mississippi; the Vander Lights in Vander, North Carolina; and the Governor's Mansion in Austin, Texas. I was also interested in updating stories that are much better known, such as Waverley in West Point, Mississippi, and the Myrtles in St. Francisville, Louisiana. Most, but not all, of the places featured in this book are open to the public. I selected private residences for inclusion in the book only if the stories were too good to pass up. All of the buildings except for two are still in existence.

Most of the stories in *Haunted Places in the American South* are legends, meaning that they are tales based in fact but which have been embellished over the years through various retellings. Most of these stories are very old, reflecting the history of the places they describe. The longest, and often the best, stories are those told by people who have had actual brushes with the supernatural. From the standpoint of the folklorists, first-hand accounts are not legends until they have been told to someone else, who then passes the story on with his own little touches. A few of the stories in this book, such as "Headless Woman Rock" in Leitchfield, Kentucky, and "the Ell Davis Woods" near Eudora, Mississippi, are so fanciful that they almost qualify as folk tales, stories that both the storyteller and the audience recognize as being fictional. I kept the number of folk tales to a bare minimum because most people seem to favor those tales that call for a position of belief or disbelief. We seem to be drawn to stories that make us question our view of reality, of what could happen under the right circumstances.

To make the book more accessible to the general reader, I have presented the stories in a very conventional way. Each tale begins with the history of the haunted place, then moves on to the information that can neither be proved or disproved because it deals with the supernatural. In the story of the haunting of Magnolia Hall in Natchez, Mississippi, I attempted to present my own encounter with the uncanny in an objective manner. After finishing the story, I realized how difficult it is to describe un-explained phenomena without sacrificing one's desire to sound rational. Because of my visit to Magnolia Hall, I gained more respect for those people whose emotions seem to get the best of them as they relate their own unnerving experiences in haunted places.

So as you begin reading about some of the South's most haunted places, prepare to be enlightened and entertained. Briefly suspend your skepticism and enjoy the book for what it is: a collection of good stories. Possibly, after reading several of the tales, you might even find yourself wondering, "Can such things really be?"

HAUNTED PLACES IN THE AMERICAN SOUTH

ALABAMA

Linn Henley Building

ike many older libraries, the Linn Henley Building is architecturally suited for a haunting. Built in 1927, this neoclassical stone structure served as the original Birmingham Public Library until the early 1980s when the new library was built across the street on Twenty-first Street. The Linn Henley Building now houses the archives, interlibrary loan services, government documents, the southern history department, and administrative offices. Despite some modifications, the building looks much like it did when it was first built. And, if the tales told by librarians for the past thirty years can be believed, the ghost of a former librarian, Fant Thornley, feels so much at home there that he still walks the marble hallways and prowls around the dimly lit stacks.

Fant Thornley was born in Pickens, South Carolina, in 1901. Fant was educated at Presbyterian College in Clinton, South Carolina. After serving in the United States Marine Corps from 1943 to 1945, he began his career as a librarian in the Richland County Public Library in Columbia, South Carolina. In 1949, Fant moved to Alabama, where he started out as assistant director of the Birmingham Public Library. He became the director when Mrs. Emily M. Danton retired in 1953. During his tenure as director, he not only greatly expanded the library's physical plant and services, but he also implemented the integration of black and white libraries in 1963. In addition to his duties as director of the Birmingham Public Library, Fant served as president of the Bostick & Thornley publishing firm located in Charleston, South Carolina. His best-known publication is *Boot,* an illustrated, interpretive account of the U.S. Military Corps in World War II. By the time Fant Thornley died of a heart attack in his southside apartment in 1970, the library was circulating more than 2.4 million books per year.

Fant Thornley's dedication to supervising the everyday operation of the Birmingham Public Library has apparently survived beyond death itself. People say that the smell of cigarette smoke, which had always announced his presence during his twenty years at the library, can still be detected in certain sections of the building when no one else is present. Marvin Whiting, the recently retired director of archives at the library, had a particularly disturbing experience in October of 1977. Whiting was at his desk working after hours on a catalog of newspapers. At 11:30, he heard the sound of the elevator rising to the third floor. Whiting just naturally assumed that the security guard was coming up to see him for some reason because he was the only other person in the building at the time. He heard the elevator come up and stop and its doors open and close. As the door to the room where Whiting was working swung open, he turned around to see what the security guard wanted. To his amazement, nobody was there. He stood up and started for the door, but it swung shut before he could reach it. Then he heard the sound of the elevator going back down to the first floor. The familiar odor of Chesterfield cigarettes, Thornley's favorite brand, suggested to Whiting that he may have had a visitation from "the other side." Filled with a sudden desire for human company, Whiting immediately went down to the first floor to talk to the security guard. After he explained what had happened, the guard was visibly shaken. He told Whiting that he heard the elevator rise, even though he knew that he and the archivist were the only two people in the library at the time. Baffled by what had just occurred, Whiting decided to stop working and go home. The next day, Whiting told his co-workers that he had encountered the ghost of Fant Thornley.

The ghost of the Linn Henley Building remained dormant for twelve years. Then in 1989, another person had an unnerving experience in the building. An electrician who had been working in the stacks came running into the archives. Trying to catch his breath, the man said that he had been working in the section where government papers and other documents are kept when he sensed that someone had come up behind him. He turned around and saw the figure of a man who appeared not to be real. The staff produced a picture of Fant Thornley and asked him if this was the man he saw. After the electrician said that it was, they told him that Mr. Thornley had died nineteen years before. Later, the staff reported that the electrician was so frightened that he refused to return to the stacks unless someone went with him.

Eight years later, a young woman who works in the archives also had a chance meeting with Fant Thornley's ghost. Jim Baggett, the current archivist in the Linn Henley Building, says that she was in the kitchen area of the auditorium on the third floor setting up refreshments for a reception: "She said that it was late in the day, and she was alone. She looked up, and there was a man in a 1950s-era suit standing in the kitchen door. As she stood there looking at him, he vanished." Knowing full well that no one could have entered the kitchen without being seen, she became so scared that she ran out of the room. "The next day, we showed her some photographs and tried to do a line-up with her. I showed her a picture of Fant and some other people, but she wasn't able to pick him out of the group."

The haunting of the Linn Henley Building eventually received national attention, largely because of coverage by the *Birmingham News* and the *Birmingham Post-Herald* in the 1980s and 1990s. In December 1997, a representative of *Fate* magazine contacted Jim Baggett and asked him if he would like to participate in a paranormal investigation of the archives. Thinking that the results produced by legitimate researchers might put to rest the fears of some of the library personnel, Baggett agreed. However, Baggett's hopes were dashed in January 1998 when the investigators turned out to be two professional wrestlers, Johnny Peoples and "the Great Kaiser," accompanied by a reporter from the magazine: "Both wrestlers arrived in full makeup and joined me in the elevator. After a few seconds, the elevator stopped on the second floor. The door opened, and a little boy stood in the doorway with his mouth wide open, staring at the two wrestlers. I thought I was going to 'lose it' right on the spot. After seeing Johnny Peoples and 'the Great Kaiser,' the little boy changed his mind about taking the elevator and took off running. The door closed, and we continued to the third floor. We went up to the auditorium where Fant had last been seen, and when we got up there, the Great Kaiser put on his mask and sat down in a chair in the middle of the room. It was never explained to me why he did this. Then Peoples took out a copy of the Koran and a Hopi Indian doll, and he said that first he had to show these spirits that he was not malevolent. Then he laid these things in a triangle in the doorway to the kitchen. He went into the kitchen and came out and told me that he had in fact seen the ghost. Then the reporter started asking questions of Fant Thornley as to why he was there." Supposedly, the investigators learned that Thornley considered the auditorium to be his own private domain. Thornley indicated that he liked to go to the auditorium occasionally to recover from the stress of patrolling the stacks and other parts of the building. The investigators also learned that Thornley was pleased with the way the library was being run. When Baggett asked Peoples if Thornley was ready to "go to the light," he replied that Thornley had not been summoned to the light but that he would go when he is called. The investigators also took photographs throughout the building. Baggett says, "They kept taking pictures in the hope that Fant would materialize. I tried my best not to get in any of the pictures. They wanted to take one in front of a picture of George Washington. Johnny Peoples kept saying that he wanted me in the picture. I said no, but he took it anyway. This picture is also on their Web site, by the way. My reputation is ruined!"

To get to the Linn Henley Building, take the 22nd Street North Exit off Interstate 20/59. The library is located at 2100 Park Place, Birmingham, Alabama; phone: 205-226-3600.

Marengo

LOWNDESBORO

Lowndesboro, Alabama, is a living time capsule, a relic from the nineteenth century. The two-lane road that winds through this little town is lined with a series of antebellum houses, mansions, and churches. According to legend, the source

9

for this town's miraculous survival in the midst of the catastrophic destruction of the Civil War is concealed within the history of one of the town's best-preserved houses, Marengo.

Marengo was built by Dr. John Howard in Autauga country across the Alabama River, north of Lowndesboro. Soon, he became dissatisfied with the location of his house, so he decided to move it to Lowndesboro, where the prospects of enlarging his practice were much better. He had slaves dismantle the house, float it on rafts across the Alabama River, and rebuild it on the other side. Except for converting a window into a door leading into one of the front rooms, Dr. Howard preserved the home's original appearance. Conflicting accounts place the year at 1843 and 1847.

By the time of the Civil War, ownership of Dr. Howard's home had passed to another physician, Dr. Charles Edwin Reese. On a fateful April day in 1865, Dr. Reese was in his office treating a patient with a severe rash when he received word that General James T. Wilson's army was camped just outside of town. Concerned that Lowndesboro would suffer the same fate as Selma had when Wilson's army destroyed the foundry there, Dr. Reese devised a ruse to save his town. He and his patient climbed into Dr. Reese's buggy and headed out to General Wilson's camp. Dr. Reese's heart raced as he and his patient entered Wilson's tent. The stone-faced general listened intently while the doctor explained that an epidemic of smallpox had taken a heavy toll on the citizenry of Lowndesboro, and he displayed the lesions of his patient's face and arms as proof. Dr. Reese went on to say that the general would be exposing his troops to great risk if they passed through Lowndesboro on their way to Montgomery. Staring at the patient's repulsive-looking lesions, General Wilson agreed with the doctor that bypassing Lowndesboro would be the most prudent course of action. In the next few days, Montgomery fell to Wilson's army, but Lowndesboro remained virtually untouched by the Yankees. If the legend is to be believed, Lowndesboro owes its very existence to a lie told by a doctor almost a century and a half ago.

Dr. Reese may have spared his town needless suffering, but the same cannot be said of his own house. His wife, Sarah Dudley Reese, was a nervous soul who hated being left in the house alone when he was out on house calls, so he bought her a large brass lock to put her mind at rest. The story goes that she was so afraid that someone would find the door key that she took the key to a local gypsy and had a curse put on it so that the key would burn anyone who touched it except Sarah and her husband. Sarah carried the key with her at all times and occasionally locked her husband out of the house after an argument. After Mrs. Reese died in 1924, the house was purchased by L. James Powell in 1925. He named the house "Marengo" after the county where his wife grew up. As soon as his son, L. James Powell Jr., inherited the property in 1959, he set about to restore the house to its former splendor. In 1960, James spent $250,000 to renovate the house. His wife, Kathleen, was an invalid who spent most of her time in a wheelchair. Like Mrs. Reese before her, Kathleen feared being in the house by herself, so her husband bought her a pistol for self-defense and taught her how to use it. After a party in 1961, James Powell left Marengo to take the help home in his pickup truck. When he returned, he was horrified to find that his wife had been shot in her bed with her own pistol. The authorities concluded that Kathleen's death was a suicide, even though her crutches were on one side of the room and the gun was kept on the other side.

Marengo passed through several hands until Colonel Jerry Doherty bought it in 1974. He and his wife, Allison, converted the house into the Marengo Tea House and began catering private parties. While they were refinishing the house, they occasionally heard the laughter of a woman coming from one of the rooms. When they rushed into the room to see who was laughing, they found no one there. In the fall of 1975, the Dohertys were entertaining a group from Maxwell Air Force Base. One of the members of the group was a psychic from New York named Sylvia C. While they were relaxing in the bar, Sylvia announced that Jerry and Sarah were sharing their home with the spirit of a woman named Kathleen who was pleased with their efforts to maintain the beauty of her home. The psychic also said that the spirit of Kathleen, who was born in February and died in February, would leave Marengo in February. Later that evening, after Colonel Doherty produced a large key from his pocket and placed it on the bar, the psychic recoiled in fright, claiming that it possessed an "evil charge" and that it belonged to a woman who was very unhappy during her stay in the house. When the Dohertys returned from a vacation to Hawaii and California in February of 1976, they sensed that the spirit of Kathleen had departed. Never again were they bothered by any sort of paranormal activity in Marengo.

By the early 1990s, Marengo had become a bed and breakfast operated by Mark Moody and his father. Although he had heard that the house had a haunted history, Mark did not take any of the stories very seriously until May 1994 when he was visiting with a friend in the tavern area in the basement: "I noticed that as I was talking to him, my attention was diverted to an area of the room that has a round mirror hanging on the wall. For the life of me, I could not understand why my attention was being directed that way. It must have been more of a subconscious kind of thing. But all of a sudden, there was a woman that appeared. She was standing in the front of the stairs. She had on black boots, a charcoal-gray skirt, a wool-looking skirt with pleats in the front, [and] a blouse that was high around her neck. Her hair was piled up on top of her head. She was an attractive woman around thirty-five or forty years old. She appeared to have recognized me, but she also had a look about her that was between sadness and bewilderment. I could see every expression on that woman's face. I could see when she blinked her eyes. I could see when she moved her hands. I could see everything about her clothes. I didn't say anything to the friend of mine who was with me, and I asked him if he would like anything to drink. At that point, I got up to get us something to drink, and he screamed. I knew that he had seen her. The hair on his arm was standing up, and water was coming out of his eyes, and he was stuttering. He said, 'You will not believe what I just saw!' and I said, 'Well, I might.' And he described the same thing that I had seen."

Later that same month, another psychic visited Marengo, and she confirmed Mark's suspicions that his house was haunted: "A lady from Birmingham who helps the Birmingham police department solve missing children cases and various crimes through means of psychic use came here for dinner for the first time. She had a date with her. And when they came in here, the first thing she said to my parents was, 'Do you know who the lady sitting on the front porch with the black boots and the charcoal-gray skirt and the blouse that's high on her neck and the hair on top of her head is?' We said, 'No, we don't know who she is, but we know who you're talking about.'"

The psychic agreed to come back at another time and go through the house with a small tape recorder to try to recap some of the events that had taken place in this house over the years. Mark said, "She seemed to feel that the woman was the wife of the doctor who originally moved the house across the river, Dr. Howard. She thought that perhaps he might have had an abusive tendency, that he may have struck her in a fit of rage perhaps, and this may have led to her early death." When she was in the room to the left of the front door, she indicated that the doctor at that time had placed valuables or documents in the trunk that he did not want her to see. The psychic added that she had felt something like a horse crop strike her across the back when she was in that room, like she was being beaten. She could even feel the blood running down her back from the cuts inflicted by the whip. Before she left, the psychic said that no one who has lived in Marengo has ever been happy.

Mark has also heard the same kind of ghostly laughter that terrified the Dohertys: "I had a situation where I woke up early one morning because someone was outside my bedroom door calling my name. I said, 'Who is it?' I got up and went all through the house. Every door in the house was locked. There was no way that someone could have gotten in there, but there was someone standing outside my door calling my name."

Other people have also sensed a spectral presence in the house, especially in a particular spot in the tavern where Mark first saw the ghost of the woman: "We have a specific area in the tavern in the basement where somebody will come up to you and sort of catch you by the arm and will say, 'Has anything ever happened in this room in this particular area right here?' and we'll say, 'Why do you ask?' and they'll say, 'Whenever I stand on this particular spot, I get an uneasy, frightened feeling.' We might go a month or so, and no one will feel anything at all down there, and then the same thing will occur, and it is always in that same room, in that same spot, and that is that area down in that little bar in the basement. So my guess is that this is where something traumatic perhaps happened to this woman, and I think that this might be what's causing those people to have those feelings of discomfort."

Apparently, the haunting has not hurt business at Marengo.

In fact, Mark believes that the house's haunted reputation seems to attract people to the bed and breakfast: "A lot of people from the military bases travel to Europe and tell people about the ghosts at Marengo. We were contacted one time by a lady and her husband who were writing a book. They had studied visual phenomenon in Graceland as it related to sightings of Elvis Presley in and around the property. They had heard about Marengo and decided to check it out. How they heard about it, I don't know." Even though Mark is convinced that Marengo is haunted by the ghosts of distraught women, he does not agree with the psychic that everyone who lives in the house becomes miserable after a while: "I don't know if there is a cloud hanging over Marengo that has caused people to be unhappy. I have lived here many years, and I can't say that I'm an unhappy fellow."

Marengo is located approximately twenty-five miles west of Montgomery, Alabama, on Highway 80; phone: 334-278-4442.

McCandless Hall

ATHENS STATE UNIVERSITY

ATHENS

Athens State University is the oldest institution of higher education in the state of Alabama. It was founded in 1822 by a group of local citizens who bought five acres of land, erected a building, and began Athens Female Academy. The school has undergone several different incarnations and name changes over the years, largely as a result of changes in ownership and affiliation. In 1889, the name was changed to Athens Female College after being transferred to the Conference of Methodist Churches. When the school became coed in 1931, its name was changed to Athens College. In 1975, the school was named Athens State College when it became part of the state educational system. The last name change occurred in 1998 when a bill passed by the state legislature renamed the school Athens State University.

The history of Athens State University is punctuated with a series of tragic occurrences. The university was almost destroyed when the Union army under the command of Colonel Ivan Vasilevitch Turchinov sacked Athens on May 1–2, 1862. Turchinov had every intention of burning Athens Female Academy but was prevented from doing so by the headmistress, Madame Jane Hamilton Childs, who presented the colonel a letter from Abraham Lincoln ordering him to spare the school. Several students died at the school from freak accidents and illness in the nineteenth century. One of these was a young woman who was rooming at Founder's Hall, the oldest building on campus. While rushing down the stairs for a midnight meeting with her boyfriend, the candle she was holding set fire to her nightgown, causing her to burn to death. In late October and early November of 1909, four young girls died in a typhoid epidemic, along with Florence Brown, the only faculty member who stayed at the institution to care for the sick.

Many of these tragic incidents have generated ghost stories. The best known of Athens State University's ghost stories, and an integral part of the university's fabled past, is the sad tale of Abigail Burns. According to the legend, she was a beautiful twenty-two-year-old opera singer who performed *La Traviata* one stormy night in 1914 at the dedication of McCandless Hall, a beautiful Greek Revival auditorium that housed the music, drama, and art departments. The audience was so taken with her performance that she was called out for several encores. For her last curtain call, Abigail, dressed in a white gown and holding a bouquet of red roses, promised to return. After blowing a final kiss to the crowd, she left the building and climbed into the carriage that was to take her to her next booking. Around midnight, the troupe was caught in a terrible thunderstorm several miles outside of the city. Just as the carriage was about to cross a bridge, a bolt of lightning and a clap of thunder split the night sky. The frightened horses reared on their hind legs, causing the carriage to disengage from the harness and plummet over the side of the bridge and crash on the rocks below. When her colleagues clambered down the embankment to save Abigail, they found her struggling to extricate herself from the wreckage. By the time they reached her, she had collapsed on the ground. Abigail Burns died at the scene, still clutching her bouquet of red roses. The academic community was so shaken by the tragic death of the young woman that a beech tree was planted near the side entrance of McCandless Hall to commemorate her last performance. The beech tree is still there.

During the winter following the death of the opera singer, several students saw the image of a woman in a white dress standing in the third-floor window of McCandless Hall. She was holding a bouquet of red roses. On many occasions, students have sensed her presence through the smell of her flowers. Sometimes, the figure is bathed in an eerie light. Sandra Cooke, an administrative secretary in Brown Hall, said that she first heard the stories about Abigail's ghost when she was a student at Athens State College. She added that the stories are not told as much these days as they were in the 1960s and 1970s, but some students still claim to have seen her standing in the third-floor window, fulfilling the promise she made back in 1914 to return to McCandless Hall.

Although there are many people living on campus and in the surrounding community who fervently believe the legend of Abigail Burns, the facts of the story do not stand up to close scrutiny. While it is true that an opera singer did perform at what was then known as the Music Hall in 1914, the performer was a male named Enrico Aresoni. The announcement of the dedication of the new music hall in the *Alabama Courier* of October 21, 1914, made no mention of Abigail Burns. In addition, a state death certificate search conducted by Forest E. Ludden, state registrar, turned up no record of the death of Abigail Burns between 1908 and 1922. No newspapers from that time period have been found that carried either an announcement of a performance by Abigail Burns or her obituary.

The story's lack of credibility did not discourage an investigation by Joe Slate's parapsychology class in the 1980s. Employing an investigative procedure called the *Omega Quest,* the students joined hands to form inner and outer circles in the art studio at McCandless Hall. Soon, the smell of roses was detected in the room, followed by the sudden flaring of the candle flame. As a strange yellow glow bathed the room, the fragrance of roses intensified. The leader of the group, a twenty-two-year-old male, made contact with what he claimed was the spirit of Abigail Burns. She told him that she had been trained in Philadelphia and was touring to prepare her for a career as an opera singer. The spirit indicated that she had fallen in love not only with the city of Athens but with a certain young man as well. After performing in a neighboring Alabama city, she had planned to return to Athens to be reunited with her lover, the son of a wealthy landowner. After her death, the young man continued to visit the art studio to mourn his loss. After a while, he stopped coming to the studio altogether, but Abigail never forgot him. She ended the session by vowing never to leave the building where her love for the young man had blossomed. As soon as Abigail's spirit left the studio, the group leader revealed that in a past life, he had been the object of Abigail's affections. During the session, he felt the deep love that he had had for her over a half century before.

The legend of Abigail Burns is so deeply embedded in the fabric of Athens State University that her spirit will probably never leave the school or the city entirely. On May 12, 1987, the area's deep affection for its resident ghost was manifested in a special performance of *La Traviata* by the Huntsville Opera Theater. The event was promoted as being held in memory of Abigail Burns. Of the three hundred guests who attended the performance at McCandless Hall, only a "past-life hypnotist" from New Orleans claimed to have seen her ghost. He said that she was surrounded by an unearthly glow. When the performance ended, she waved goodbye to the audience. One gets the impression that this is not the last time that the ghost of Abigail Burns makes an appearance at McCandless Hall.

To find Athens State University, take the Highway 99 Exit off Interstate 65. The university is located at 300 North Beaty Street, Athens, Alabama; phone: 1-800-522-0272.

The Sloss Furnaces

BIRMINGHAM

The Sloss furnaces are all that is left of Jefferson County's once thriving iron industry. When an Irish farmer's son from northern Alabama named James Withers Sloss rode into the village of Birmingham in 1876, the iron industry was beginning to resurrect itself. The Oxmoor furnaces had resumed operations in the winter of 1873 for the first time since they were destroyed by General James T. Wilson's Raiders in 1865. For a while, it seemed as if the new furnaces would go out of business because all of the hardwood forests in the area had been cut down to produce the charcoal used in the pig iron-making process. Then on February 28, 1876, Levin S. Goodrich successfully made pig iron with coke instead of charcoal at the Oxmoor furnaces. Coal, which was used to make coke, was plentiful in Jefferson County, as were iron ore and limestone. So to entrepreneurs like James Withers Sloss, Birmingham appeared to be an ideal location for new furnaces.

Sloss founded the Sloss Furnace Company in 1881. On April 12, 1882, the first of Sloss's two 70-ton furnaces was blown in. The Sloss furnaces were very similar to the Alice furnaces built only two years earlier by Henry DeBardeleben on Birmingham's western flank. In 1886 Sloss retired and sold his company to a group of financiers. One of the financiers, Joseph Forney Johnston, became president of the reorganized Sloss Iron and Steel Company. The two new furnaces were built in north Birmingham, and extensive coal and ore lands were purchased. Under the leadership of Thomas O. Seddon, who became president in 1888, the Sloss Iron and Steel Company bought twelve smaller companies, including several ore and coal suppliers and three furnaces in northern Alabama, making it the second-largest company in the Birmingham district. In 1899, the company became the Sloss-Sheffield Steel and Iron Company.

The original Sloss furnaces also experienced a period of regrowth at the turn of the century. The furnaces were rebuilt, and a new blowing engine house and additional stoves and boilers were added. Between 1927 and 1931, the original furnaces were dismantled and replaced by new furnaces that incorporated such improvements as a mechanical loading system for raw materials. Electrical power was also introduced. These furnaces are still standing.

In 1952, the Sloss-Sheffield Steel and Iron Company was purchased by the United States Pipe and Foundry Company, which continued to produce pig iron. United States Pipe and Foundry was acquired by the Jim Walter Corporation in 1969. Then in 1971, the furnaces standing along the First Avenue North Viaduct were closed for good. The Jim Walter Corporation deeded the Sloss furnaces property to the Alabama State Fair Authority in the hope that it would be transformed into a museum of industrial history. A group of citizens who called themselves the Sloss Furnace Association waged a successful campaign for the preservation of the Sloss furnaces. The efforts of the Sloss Furnace Association gained national attention, and the Sloss furnaces were eventually designated as a National Historic Landmark by the United States Department of the Interior. The Sloss Furnaces National Historical Landmark is the only museum of its kind in the world, and the only National Historical Landmark to represent twentieth-century technology.

Many of the company owners lived up on the mountains surrounding Birmingham, safe from the smoke produced by the furnaces. The people who worked at the furnaces were not as fortunate. Most of them lived in little shanties close to the furnaces, making it impossible for them to escape the sulfurous fumes emitted by the huge smokestacks. One of the men who worked there said, "Boy, from all the smoke and pollution, and all the fires and the sulfur smell, we felt like we were in hell." Another veteran of the furnaces complained, "The only difference between working here in summer and winter is that in the summer, you were burned all over. In the winter, you were burned on one side and froze on the other."

Iron was very dangerous in the nineteenth century, and quite a few died in the furnaces. For some reason, though, only two of them have returned as ghosts. One of these is the spirit of a young girl who came to the Sloss furnaces in the early 1900s. The girl was unmarried and pregnant. She most likely felt like an outcast because becoming pregnant out of wedlock was considered to be a terrible taboo at that time. She sneaked through the gate and walked over to one of the furnaces. The men were so busy pouring iron into the sows that they did not see her climb the ladder to the top of the furnace. When they finally caught sight of her, it was too late. She jumped off the ladder and plummeted into the molten iron. Shortly after the girl's suicide, an official ceremony was being held at the furnaces. Local politicians and company executives sitting side by side were listening to a speech given by a company official when their attention was diverted by what appeared to be a white deer running through the crowd. Soon, rumors spread that the deer was the spirit of the young woman who had jumped into one of the furnaces. For many years, the deer continued to disrupt big events, usually those featuring dignitaries of some sort.

The most famous ghost at the Sloss furnaces is the spirit of Theophilus Calvin Jowers. Jowers came to Jones Valley from his father's plantation shortly after the Civil War. On August 11, 1870, he married a twenty-three-year-old girl named Sarah Latham in Irondale. To support his wife and family, Jowers took a job at the Cahaba Iron Works at Cahaba. He learned how to make charcoal, how to prepare the sand molds that shaped the molten metal, and how to handle the mules that pulled the loaded ore cars up the pine track to the top of the furnace hill. After W. S. McElwain sold the Irondale furnace in 1873, Jowers decided to work for the Eureka Mining and Transportation Company at the Oxmoor furnaces, where he perfected his skills as a furnaceman. In the spring of 1887, he was offered the job as assistant foundryman at the Alice Furnace No. 1 on First Avenue North in Birmingham. By emphasizing the advantages that living in Birmingham would offer them and their five children, his wife agreed to the move, although she secretly wished that he would take a safer job.

During the first week of September, Sarah's worst fears were finally realized. Jowers was assigned to a crew that was given the task of removing the old bell of Alice Furnace No. 1, dropping the bell into the furnace, and replacing it with a new bell. Jowers was standing close to the top of the furnace holding the rope which was to release the old bell when he lost his footing. He and the bell went down into the furnace together. The bell turned as it fell, and Jowers landed on top of it. The intense heat and molten iron reduced his body to ashes almost instantly. According to an article appearing on the front page of the Saturday morning edition of the *Birmingham Age* on September 10, 1887, the workers attached a piece of sheet iron to a length of gas pipe in an attempt to retrieve Jowers's remains. All that they were able to fish out of the molten iron were his head, bowels, two hip bones, and a few ashes. Sarah was not entirely surprised when a representative from the company knocked on her door with the bad news. Over the years, she had accepted the possibility that her husband would someday meet his end at the furnaces.

Sarah knew that she and her children would make do after the death of her husband because iron men always took care of their own. She was given a job selling lunches to her husbands' co-workers from her home. Before long, she began hearing stories about her husband's ghost. Furnace workers reported experiencing a cold feeling when they stood on the bridge at the Alice

Furnace No. 1. Others told of seeing a figure moving around in the shimmering heat. After Alice No. 1 was torn down in 1905, Jowers's ghost apparently moved to Alice No. 2 until it was closed in 1927. The Oxmoor furnaces closed the same year. This meant that the only remaining furnaces in the Birmingham area were the Sloss furnaces. Then in 1927, Calvin Jowers's son, John Jowers, was driving over the viaduct by the Sloss furnaces in a Model-T Ford with his son Leonard. John stopped the engine of the car so that he and Leonard could watch the workers tap the Sloss. All at once, John grabbed his son's arm and pointed to what appeared to a man walking though the sparks. The iron was too hot for a real human being to be standing that close to it, so John believed that it must be a ghost. John saw the ghost on subsequent trips to Sloss furnaces, and he eventually concluded that the apparition was the ghost of his father. Jowers's ghost became a fixture at the Sloss furnaces until they were finally closed in 1970. Perhaps, his ghostly appearances were a fulfillment to a promise he made to his wife: "As long at there's a furnace in Jefferson County, I will be there."

While it is true that only two ghosts have ever been seen at the Sloss furnaces, other types of ghostly activity have been reported at the site. Many people have had unnerving experiences at the Blowing Engine Building. Built in 1902, it is the oldest building still standing at the Sloss furnaces. Workers say that when they place an object like a coffee cup in a certain spot and leave, they find that the object has been moved to a new location when they return. Workers have also seen doors opening and closing by themselves. People walking on the cat-walk have caught the sight of a glowing, human-like shape with no recognizable features standing at the other end. One of these workers, Ron Bates, admits that he is baffled by some of the strange happenings at the Sloss furnaces: "I've been here eleven years, and I can't say that I believe all of the stories that I've heard about this place, but I do think that something is here. I can't explain it. It's like a force or something. I'll be walking around here by myself and see something out of the corner of my eye, something like the shape of a person. It will be there for a minute, then it will be gone. I can't explain it."

To get to the Sloss furnaces, take Interstate 20/59 to the First Avenue North Exit. The furnaces are located at First Avenue North and 32nd Street, Birmingham, Alabama; phone: 205-324-1911.

Sturtivant Hall

SELMA

turtivant Hall in Selma, Alabama, is one of the finest examples of antebellum architecture in the entire Black Belt. It was constructed in 1852–1853. It took two architects to complete the massive project. In 1864, the mansion was purchased by the president of the First National Bank of Selma, a man named John McGee Parkman, for $64,000. The three years that he lived here with his wife and his two daughters, Emily Norris Parkman and Maria Hunter Parkman, were the happiest days of his life. As members of one of the most prominent families in Selma, John and his wife enjoyed the privileges that accompany money and social position.

However, the good life ended for John Parkman and his family in 1866. That same year, he invested heavily in cotton futures, using the bank's money. A few weeks later, the price of cotton dropped from $.30 to $.35 per pound to $.15 to $.18 per pound. Unfortunately for Parkman, the Federal army occupying Selma at the time had deposited a considerable sum of money at Parkman's bank. When General Wager Swayne learned of Parkman's failed business venture, he had Parkman placed under arrest. Parkman was taken to Cahaba and held prisoner at Castle Morgan, and he died soon thereafter.

The story of John Parkman's final days is shrouded in mystery. According to one story, his friends devised a scheme to help him escape. After securing the warden's cooperation with bribes, they arranged for a steamer to be waiting at the Cahaba wharf to pick him up. To create a diversion, his friends arranged for a group of musicians to march up and down in front of the stockade. Meanwhile, Parkman walked out of his cell, which had been left unlocked by the warden, climbed over the wall, and ran down the bluff. By this time, some of the guards had detected the fleeing figure, and they began firing into the darkness. Some people say that Parkman was shot as he dived into the river. Others maintain that he was crushed by the huge paddle wheel of a passing steamboat. Another version of the story holds that Parkman was shot by his own friends to cover up their participation in the bank scandal. Only one thing is certain: John McGee Parkman died during his attempted escape from the prison in Cahaba. Afterward, Mrs. Parkman was forced to sell her beloved home for a mere $12,000. She and her daughters left Selma in disgrace for parts unknown.

Sturtivant Hall is now open to the general public. Hundreds of people from all over the world visit Sturtivant Hall each year, attracted by the structure's antebellum grandeur and by its haunted reputation. The stories about Sturtivant Hall have been perpetuated by locals, by tour guides, and by Selma resident Kathryn Tucker Windham, who first wrote the story of Selma's ruined banker in *13 Alabama Ghosts and Jeffrey*. Busloads of schoolchildren visit the old mansion each year, eager to catch a glimpse of the ghosts in Ms. Windham's book, which traces the earliest stories of the hauntings to servants who began seeing Parkman's spirit shortly after the house was sold to Emile Gillman. According to Ms. Windham's account, they believed that Parkman's restless spirit was sighted staring out of a cupola window and leaning against the iron grillwork railing on the side portico because he was buried under a fig tree near the scuppernong arbor. They held to their story, even when told that John Parkman was actually buried at Live Oak Cemetery and that his tombstone is there for all to see.

Long-time tour guide Pat Tate is very familiar with the history of the house and with the strange things that have happened there. As a rule, the ghostly activity is restricted to the sound of footsteps or the opening and closing of doors. Occasionally, though, the disturbances are much more dramatic: "John Parkman has mostly been sighted upstairs, and several times people have said that they have seen little flashes of light. We have had a lot of students who have sighted him up in the cupola, too. He has not been seen outside of the house, though. A year ago [1997], we were having a 'battle ball' here for the reenactment of the battle of Selma. They always have guards posted in the study so that children would not go upstairs, which was off limits. Well, I noticed that one of the guards was missing, so when he came back, I questioned him, and he said that he had three people tell him that they had seen children upstairs looking out the window. He had gone up to check, and there were no children anywhere.

"The Orkin man came here one time. The ladies [tour guides] were downstairs, and he was upstairs spraying in the cupola. All at once, he came running down the stairs. He was so scared that he left all of his equipment up there. He swore that he was never coming back because someone had pushed him on those stairs. We never saw him again."

The upstairs room where Parkman's little girls have made an appearance was their bedroom. The small furniture and antique dolls give the impression that they have just stepped out for a moment. Sometimes, it appears that they are still using the bedroom. On more than one occasion, a maid has made the bed and returned later on to find the impression of a small child on the blanket. Ms. Tate says that in 1997 something happened upstairs that suggests that these little spirits are still playing pranks: "Several months ago, we had a group of young people standing in the hall. We had a tremendous painting sitting on an easel. Nobody was standing near it. Suddenly, it just jumped off and broke into a hundred pieces. The children screamed, and then everybody was really quiet. They could not be convinced that it was not Mr. Parkman or his little girls who had knocked it off."

As to the legend concerning Mr. Parkman's supposed burial under the fig tree, Ms. Tate maintains a healthy skepticism. She adds this interesting footnote to Ms. Windham's account: "Adolf was an elderly black man who worked here when they first started restoring Sturtivant in the 1950s, cleaning it up and painting it. He told the story that his grandfather plowed in the garden after the Parkmans left. And Adolf's grandfather said that the mule would come to a sudden place in the yard and would rare up and would not go forward. Adolf claimed that that was the spot where Mr. Parkman had been buried. He was convinced that he was there. And when Adolf worked here, he would never, never go out in that garden."

Despite the large number of stories that Ms. Tate has heard over the years, she says that she has never been afraid at Sturtivant Hall, not even upstairs where most of the strange occurrences have taken place. In fact, she and the other tour guides frequently make light of the ghostly phenomena: "Whenever we hear somebody walking around upstairs or when the doors open and close, we politely say, 'Good evening, Mr. Parkman.'" If his spirit has indeed returned to Sturtivant Hall, she says that it is because he loved his house so much. It was his refuge from the world that had wronged him so deeply.

Sturtivant Hall is located at 713 Mabry Street in Selma, Alabama; phone: 334-872-5626.

ARKANSAS

the attic have disturbed the sleep of many occupants over the years. On two occasions, terrified tenants called the police to investigate the unmistakable sounds of footsteps coming from an upstairs room. Both times, the police were called out to the house, but the source of the noises was never found. One tenant said she took small comfort in the possibility that squirrels could have been the culprits.

In the late 1960s, one of the tenants might actually have photographed the ghost. One day, Dr. Stacy Clanton photographed his wife standing in front of a mirror. When the picture was developed, a milky-white human shape was clearly visible in the background. Dr. Clanton admitted that the weird image could have been produced by a trick of light, but he did not rule out the possibility that he had captured a genuine ghost on film. For months after leaving the Allen House, Dr. Clanton had nightmares, most of which centered around the mirror and the strange noises from the attic area.

The identity of the ghost has not been determined to everyone's satisfaction. In fact, many Monticellonians believe that there are two ghosts in the Allen House. Allen Bonner, a son of Ladelle Allen Bonner, is said to be the ghost who haunts the attic tower, which was his special study area. Ladelle is said to be the ghost who is heard pacing back and forth regularly. Before the Paintons bought the Allen House, they were told that Ladelle Allen's spirit haunts the apartment house because she disapproves of her former home being used for commercial purposes.

While some former tenants say they had unnerving experiences during their stay at the Allen House, one renter may have actually benefited from the building's haunted reputation. Some Monticellonians are certain that the writer Carolyn Wilson was inspired by the ghost to write her novel *Scent of Lilacs*. Not surprisingly, her book is set in a haunted house.

Monticello, Arkansas, is in the southeast portion of the state on U.S. Highway 425. The house is a private residence located at 705 North Main Street.

Crescent Hotel

Victorian-era hotels have a way of exciting the imagination. Thanks to books and movies like *The Shining,* the general public has come to associate opulent, nineteenth-century hotels with supernatural activity. The Crescent Hotel in Eureka Springs, Arkansas, certainly belongs in this category. Situated at the north end of West Mountain on a majestic location, the Crescent Hotel appears at first glance to be an ideal setting for ghosts. This is one case where looks are not deceiving.

The Crescent Hotel was built between 1884 and 1886 in Eureka Springs by Powell Clayton and his associates, the Eureka Springs Improvement Company, and the Frisco Railroad. It was designed by the Missouri architect Isaac Taylor, who is probably best known for designing the Rialto Building and the Liggett and Meyers Office Building and the Tobacco Building in St. Louis. Specially constructed wagons transported huge pieces of magnesium limestone from a quarry on the White River. Stone masons from Ireland fitted the huge stone blocks without the use of mortar. The interior was furnished with Edison lamps, electric bells, and a hydraulic elevator. The grand opening of the Crescent Hotel on March 20, 1886, was celebrated with a grand ball featuring Harry Barton and his orchestra. Four hundred people were in attendance, including Governor James G. Blaine, the Republican presidential nominee.

In its first fifteen years of operation, the Crescent Hotel catered to the "carriage set." Its upper-class clientele were brought into the tiny town of Eureka Springs on a specially built spur line of the Frisco Railroad. Although the curative powers of the nearby springs were billed as the hotel's main attractions, visitors were also drawn to the Crescent by its special accommodations. A stable with a hundred horses was provided for the guests' riding pleasure. During their stay, visitors were treated to dances in the afternoon and dance parties every evening with music provided by an in-house orchestra. Other leisure-time activities included picnics, hiking, streetcar rides, and rides to Sanitarium Lake in a large open coach called the "Tally ho."

In 1907, when it was discovered that the region's spring water possessed no real healing powers, the hotel fell into a period of decline. The railroad sold the Crescent to A. S. Maddox and J. S. Phillips, who opened the Crescent College and Conservatory for young women in 1908. The Crescent continued to operate as a hotel for tourists during the summer months, but the high cost of maintaining the huge building soon proved to be too much of a burden. The school closed in 1924 and then reopened as a junior college from 1930 to 1934. After the college closed, the Crescent was leased as a summer hotel by several different businesses.

Then in 1937, the Crescent Hotel entered the strangest phase in its entire history. Norman Baker, who had made a fortune with the invention of an organ called the Calliaphone, converted the old hotel into a hospital and "health resort." This self-proclaimed medical expert had been convicted in Iowa in 1936 of practicing medicine without a license. After Baker came into legal possession of the Crescent Hotel, he embarked on an ambitious $50,000 remodeling scheme, which consisted of tearing out the elegant balconies and replacing them with concrete porches. Much of the beautiful woodwork was painted over in garish colors. Baker's private room was a lavish penthouse suite decorated with purple furnishings. The miraculous cures that he promised his patients involved the drinking of the hotel's mineral water. After Baker was convicted again in 1940 and sentenced to serve fours years in Leavenworth Prison, the clinic closed down.

The Crescent was sealed up until 1946 when new investors bought the hotel and promoted it as a prepackaged destination spot. Despite extensive remodeling, the hotel had taken on a "run-down" appearance. In the 1950s and 1960s, guests eager to sample the hotel's nineteenth-century charm passed the time with horseback riding, swimming, and evening dances. After the railroad left Eureka Springs, the hotel fell upon hard times once again in the 1970s and early 1980s. Then in the mid-1980s, new investors offered the capital to begin refurbishing the Crescent Hotel. Under a five-year restoration plan put into place by the hotel's present owners, the Crescent Hotel and Spa entered the millennium with the promise of regaining much of its lost luster by 2002.

Like many buildings where a tragic death has occurred, the Crescent Hotel is said to be a very haunted place. One of the Crescent's most common ghostly manifestations is the spirit of a muscular young Swede named Michael who was killed in 1884 in a construction accident on the site. According to reports, Michael seems to be far more interested in teasing staff members and guests than he is in scaring them. On one occasion, a maid who was trying to remove a laundry cart from a storeroom felt something pulling on the other handle. After several unsuccessful attempts to remove the cart, the maid exclaimed,

"Michael, let go!" Almost instantly, whatever was holding onto the cart released its grip.

Much of the ghostly activity in the Crescent seems to be centered around two rooms. In Room 414, a family was watching television when a shapeless "thing" walked through the outside door, crossed the room, and entered the bathroom. Frantically, they called down to the desk, complaining that their room was haunted. They were promptly given a room in another local hotel. Room 218 has been given the title "the ghost room" because of the large number of guests who have experienced supernatural phenomena there. Visitors have reported hearing strange sounds in Room 218 at night. One time, a bellboy had just opened the door when, suddenly, it slammed right in his face. One guest said he could not sleep in the room because something was shaking him awake.

The most commonly seen ghost in the Crescent Hotel is a distinguished-looking man wearing a beard and formal clothing. He has been seen in Room 218, but he usually appears in the lobby and bar area. In the early 1990s, an auditor entered the bar after closing hours to get a drink of water. He clearly saw a bearded man sitting on a bar stool. The auditor tried to talk to him, but the strange man did not answer back. The auditor left the bar to get his partner. When he returned, the strange figure was gone. One of the auditors went to the lobby to look for the man. As he stood at the foot of the ornate staircase, the auditor saw the man from the bar staring down at him from the second-floor landing. The auditor began walking up the stairs but felt something pushing him back as he approached the second floor. He immediately reported the incident to the manager.

Two other spirits have been seen in the Crescent Hotel as well. In July 1987, a woman was leaving her hotel room when she saw a nurse pushing a gurney down the hallway in the middle of the night. When the nurse reached the wall, both she and the gurney vanished. Some people believe that the ghost of Dr. Baker wanders around the vicinity of the old recreation room near the foot of the stairs leading to the first floor. He always gives the appearance of being lost.

Once the Crescent Hotel began receiving recognition as one of Arkansas's most haunted locations, the management decided to make its haunted reputation part of its appeal. It now offers guided walking tours of the hotel, a historic cemetery, and Spring Street houses. Many guests at the Crescent Hotel, especially those in Rooms 414 and 218, have discovered the truth behind the hotel's promise to provide "unique accommodations."

The Crescent Hotel is located at 75 Prospect Street on the Highway 62 historic loop in Eureka Springs, Arkansas; phone: 501-253-9766.

Gurdon Lights

GURDON

Every fall since the mid-1950s, college freshmen from Henderson State University have walked the Missouri-Pacific railroad tracks of little Gurdon, Arkansas, at night in search of the fabled Gurdon Lights. The ghostly phenomenon has tantalized curiosity seekers in eastern Arkansas for generations, probably because it has not proven to be as easy to debunk as other popular legends have been, such as the disappearance of ships in the Bermuda Triangle. In the summer of 1980, a party of twelve professors, students, and visitors traveled to the famed railroad crossing to conduct a scientific investigation into the Gurdon Lights. Their goal was to determine whether or not there are other plausible explanations for the phenomenon.

The legend of the Gurdon Lights is similar to the stories that have cropped up over the years to explain other ghostly lights that seem to favor railroad tracks. Unlike many of these railroad legends, the tale behind the Gurdon Lights is based on a single historical incident. One dark night in 1931, a railroad employee was accused by the foreman of sabotaging the tracks in an attempt to wreck the Sunshine Special. An article in the December 10, 1931, edition of the *Southern Standard* reported that the workman inadvertently wrecked a freight train the day before. No one was injured in the accident except for a small group of hoboes. Alone on the tracks with the foreman, the workman picked up a shovel and swung it at the man, knocking him to the ground. The foreman struggled to his feet and ran a few yards along the track, only to trip in a depression made by a rotting tree stump. The enraged workman picked up a spike maul and walked over to the foreman, who had managed to rise up on his knees. He then struck the foreman with the maul, knocking him back on the ground. Thinking that he had finished off the foreman for good, the workman walked into Gurdon, where he was arrested for suspicious behavior. Under intense questioning by the sheriff, the workman finally confessed. Having secured the murderer's confession, the authorities then rushed to the scene of the crime. The blood trail indicated that the workman had not given them the complete story. Incredibly, the foreman had managed to crawl almost a quarter of a mile before collapsing for the final time. The workman was electrocuted for the murder of the foreman in February 1932. Ever since, the story goes, the victim has walked the railroad tracks, swinging his lantern.

The Gurdon Lights have served as a source of entertainment for thousands of area residents. Matt Barrett, who lived in the region as a teenager, has fond memories of the phenomenon: "There's a little road in Gurdon that cuts behind the high school just in the middle of nowhere. The railroad tracks run parallel to the road. About two miles down the road is a little cemetery, and the Gurdon Lights can be seen about a mile beyond that. The light looks like a train lantern dangling from a cord. It swings back and forth. I saw it many times. One time, I walked up to it, and it vanished. Then it reappeared in back of me. Most times, though, when you walk toward the light, it keeps getting farther and farther away. I've never been closer than 200 yards away from it. I was really scared the first time I saw the light, but I'm not anymore. I think it's probably something that occurs in nature, like swamp gas."

Prior investigations have suggested that the Gurdon Lights phenomenon cannot be explained away through more conventional theories, such as headlights of cars from the nearby highway. Dr. Charles Leming, a professor of physics at Henderson State University, admitted that he had no other explanation for the lights. The lights do not polarize when viewed through a filter, as mirages do. Galvanometers have traced no electromagnetic current. And the light appears at almost any time under any weather conditions.

On a hot June evening in 1980, just as the sun was starting to set, Dr. Leming led his small party of students and professors down the track connecting Gurdon to Okolona. The head of the investigation was Mike Clingan, a student who had seen the Gurdon Light many times on his own. As the group was crossing an old railroad trestle, an orange glow appeared down where the tracks converge on the horizon. The glow swung to the right and disappeared. A few seconds later, it swept a downward arc across the track, swept back, and disappeared. The orange glow seemed to wobble a little as it moved, causing it to look as if it were a lantern being swung by an unseen hand.

By the time the group had crossed the trestle, it was almost totally dark. The group moved faster, motivated, no doubt, by what they had just seen. Suddenly, the light appeared again; this time, it emitted a much redder glow. While taking a rest one and a half miles from their cars, the students tried to explain what they had just seen. If headlights from passing cars had caused the light, they would have had to be refracted up and over the nearby hill to be visible on the other side. Dr. Leming added, "If it's the interstate, it's not every car that goes by, because it doesn't appear that often." Clingan then shared his research with the group. He revealed that he had gauged the length of time it would take a car to cross the horizon point at a 45-degree angle. "Moving at about eighty feet per second," he explained, "the lights would be visible much longer than the second it takes for the Gurdon Light to appear and disappear." He also observed that the highway sounds never seem to coordinate with the appearance of the lights. Another student suggested that the lights could be caused by an inversion layer, formed when warm air bumps into a cushion of cooler air above. Clingan rejected the theory because inversion layers do not occur with the same frequency as the Gurdon Lights.

After seeing the light a couple more times, the group left the Missouri-Pacific railroad tracks just as baffled as they had been before the investigation. They concluded that there were several ways to solve the mystery that had never been tried. One way to isolate the light would be to string people along the length of track between the interstate and the crossing. The source could also be pinpointed by placing one person on the inter-state bridge and another on the track to compare, via walkie-talkie, the passing of a truck with the appearance of the light. Finally, no one has tried to compare the spectra of the Gurdon Light with the spectra of headlights. The group believes that no one has made a really serious effort to determine the source of the Gurdon Lights because doing so would rob us of one of the little mysteries that make life interesting.

The Gurdon Lights appear along the Missouri–Pacific rail-road tracks north of Gurdon between state highway 57 and Interstate 30.

Pea Ridge National Military Park

PEA RIDGE

Although the Battle of Pea Ridge is not one of the best-known battles of the Civil War, its outcome had severely cur-tailed the Confederacy's advance into Missouri. On March 2, Major General Earl Van Dorn, newly appointed commander of Confederate troops west of the Mississippi, combined forces with those of Major General Sterling Price and Brigadier General Benjamin McCulloch in preparation for an invasion of Missouri. Brigadier General Samuel Ryan Curtis, who had been instructed to drive Price out of Missouri, consolidated his 10,250 troops where the Telegraph Road crossed Little Sugar Creek, three miles south of Pea Ridge at a nearby inn called Elkhorn Tavern. During the night of March 6, Van Dorn's army, divided into two divisions led by Price and McCulloch, proceeded to envelop Curtis instead of attacking him in his fortifications. Price's division reached the Telegraph Road by midmorning on March 7 and turned south toward Elkhorn Tavern. However, McCulloch's army fell so far behind that it had to leave the detour and attack several miles west of Elkhorn Tavern.

As a result, the Battle of Pea Ridge was actually fought in two separate engagements. When Curtis learned of the Confederate maneuver on March 7, he completely reversed his troops so that they were facing south instead of north. He then attacked both Confederate divisions at Leetown and Elkhorn Tavern. The fighting at Leetown took place in three separate sectors by the vegetation, cultivated fields, and road system. At the first sector, Foster's farm, McCulloch's cavalry easily routed the cavalry and captured a Federal battery. In the fighting that occurred at the second sector, the cornfields of the Oberson and Mayfield farms, both McCulloch and his replacement, Brigadier General James McIntosh, were killed. At the third sector, an area of scrub timber and dense brush, Colonel Louis Hebert's 2,000 Confederates pushed the Federals back toward Leetown and captured two Federal cannons. Exhausted by their trek through the thick undergrowth, Hebert's troops, along with the remnants of McCulloch's division, were eventually repulsed by Colonel Jefferson C. Davis and captured as they retreated to the Bentonville detour in midafternoon.

The most intense fighting of the entire Battle of Pea Ridge occurred around Elkhorn Tavern and just to the east. Price's division, with Van Dorn at the head, encountered Colonel Eugene A. Carr's Fourth Division at the tavern. By the time darkness halted the fighting, Van Dorn's troops had pushed both of Carr's flanks back up a steep plateau. During the night of March 7, Curtis deployed the First, Second, Third, and Fourth Divisions

45

in numerical order, facing right. This was one of the few times in the entire war when an entire army was exposed from flank to flank. To cover the movement of Curtis's troops, Brigadier General Franz Sigel hammered the Confederate forces with twenty-one cannons. Without sufficient ammunition for their cannons, Van Dorn was forced to retreat around the entire Federal army.

The Confederate loss at Pea Ridge was devastating. Approximately 1,500 Confederates died in the battle, compared to a Federal loss of 1,384 men. The defeat of Van Dorn's army destroyed any hope of the Confederate conquest of Missouri. In addition, the battle opened the door for the Federal takeover of Arkansas.

Pea Ridge National Military Park is not nearly as popular with tourists as some of the better-known Civil War battlefields are, possibly because it is located in such a remote area. The small number of visitors might also explain why very few ghosts have ever been reported to the rangers. In fact, only two of the buildings in the park have ever been visited by ghosts. One of them is the Visitors' Center. In 1995, a volunteer worker named Joan Vaughn was taking her customary walk around the Visitors' Center shortly before closing time to see if anyone was still in the building. This had been a very slow visitation day, and Joan was fairly certain that no one besides her was in the building, but she dutifully made her rounds anyway. When she entered the museum section of the Visitors' Center, she was surprised to see a lean, bearded man approximately six feet tall wearing a kind of brown outfit with a pack. She was impressed by the authentic look of his clothing. The man was staring intently at the artifacts in one of the displays. Thinking that he might be one of the reenactors who had staged a battle on the park that day, she went up to him and said that the Visitors' Center would be closing soon and that he needed to be ready to leave. The man gave her a vacant stare and did not say a word. Puzzled by the man's strange behavior, Joan continued her circuit through the Visitors' Center. After she had completed her rounds, she resumed her place at her desk. When the rangers came to lock the doors, she told them about seeing the strange man in the museum. She believed that he was still in the museum because she had not seen him leave through the only exit in the Visitors' Center. Operating on a hunch that someone might be hiding in a corner of the Visitors' Center, the rangers made a thorough search but found no one. Upon hearing the news, Joan was so shaken that she left the building immediately and went home.

The second building where strange activity has been reported is the Elkhorn Tavern, which was reconstructed on the battlefield. The Elkhorn Tavern was a private residence that had served as a way station on the Butterfield Overland Mail Trail before the outbreak of the Civil War. The tavern was burned to the ground six months after the Battle of Pea Ridge. In recent years, maintenance people who have gone through the building and turned off the lights have exited the tavern and discovered that the lights have been turned back on. When they return inside the tavern, they find that the lights have been turned back off.

Pea Ridge National Military Park consists of 4,300 acres of historic battlefield. The park is twenty miles north of Fayetteville on Arkansas 71; phone: 501-451-8122.

FLORIDA

Fort Zachary Taylor

Back in the days when coastal forts were the first line of defense on the Gulf and the Atlantic Ocean, Fort Zachary Taylor in Key West, Florida, was state of the art. Construction of the fort began in 1845 shortly after Florida became a state and continued until 1866. It received its name in 1850, the year President Zachary Taylor died in office. The fort was built of bricks on a foundation of granite rocks. Because the foundation rests on a coral shoal twelve feet under the water, the fort appeared to be an island unto itself during the Civil War. It was connected to the mainland by a twelve-hundred-foot causeway, and its walls reached a height of fifty feet. Fort Taylor had sanitary facilities flushed by the tides and a desalination plant. Two hundred cannons with a range of three miles pointed menacingly from three tiers of gun rooms. Only the bravest or most foolish blockade runner dared run past the fort.

On the same night that Florida seceded from the Union, Fort Taylor was seized by a handful of Federal soldiers. As a result, Key West, Florida, became the only city south of the Mason-Dixon line to remain loyal to the Union. Through the fort, Union forces were able to strangle Confederate supply lines. More than three hundred Confederate ships were captured by Fort Taylor, mostly by intimidation. So impressive were the fort's defenses, in fact, that it was never attacked. Still, scores of soldiers guarding the fort died, but not from gunfire. Ironically, the soldiers' most formidable enemy turned out not to be Confederate warships but, rather, the tiny disease-carrying mosquito. Hundreds of soldiers fell victim to the yellow fever epidemics of 1862 and 1864. For months, the infirmary was filled with soldiers suffering from dizziness and bloody vomiting.

These days, Fort Taylor is but a shadow of its former self. In 1898, the top two tiers were removed by engineers who believed that the fort's immense bulk made it an easy target. The rubble, cannons, and remaining ammunitions were dumped in the gun rooms, which were then filled with sand to strengthen the fort's bastions. In the twentieth century, the fort was declared obsolete because brick forts could not withstand assaults from modern artillery. Eventually, Fort Taylor was deeded to the state of Florida for use as a historic site. It was placed on the National Registry of Historic Places in 1971. The Florida State Park Service opened it to the public in 1985. As of 1998, though, much of the fort was closed to the public to repair damage inflicted by the ravages of time. As repairs progress, portions of the fort will gradually be reopened. As a result of dredging operations that filled in the quarter mile that separated Fort Taylor from the mainland, it is no longer an island. A moat surrounding the structure suggests what the mighty fort might have looked like to Confederate captains thinking about challenging its defenses.

Fort Taylor's popularity with Civil War buffs and lovers of history is due at least in part to the fact that it houses the largest collection of Civil War cannons in the United States. The story of the recovery of the cannons involves an architect from Naval Air Station at Key West named Howard England and, quite possibly, the spirit of one of the long-dead defenders of the fort. Howard England began excavating the fort in 1968. One day, he was digging in one of the gun rooms looking for artifacts when he sensed an eerie presence. It was as if he were being watched by someone. The feeling that he was not alone stayed with England for the rest of the day. That night when he went to bed, he dreamed that a Union soldier appeared to him in his bedroom. The soldier identified himself as Wendell Gardiner, an artillery man at Fort Taylor during the Civil War. He asked England why he was digging in the gun rooms, and he replied that he was looking for the cannons that were buried during the Spanish American War. Gardiner's face lit up, and he said that England could find his cannon, "Old Betsy," in Gun Room 13. The next day, England dug in the spot that the ghost had indicated in his dream and, sure enough, he found "Old Betsy." A couple of years later, England met some people at the fort who claimed to be relatives of Wendell Gardiner. They told him that Wendell had died at the fort. They were amazed that England had felt the presence of their dead ancestor.

Another ghostly sighting at the fort was reported in 1980. A tour guide was walking through a gun room when, all of a sudden, he felt a cold blast. He started shivering, not just because the temperature lowered, but also because it was a very hot August day. An instant later, he caught sight of a figure in a dark, heavy-looking uniform walking down a corridor. There was not supposed to be anyone else around at the time because the fort was closed, so the tour guide shouted for him to stop. The man kept on walking, just as if he hadn't heard the shouting. The tour guide followed the figure down a dark passageway that came to a dead end. He turned around several times and looked back down the passageway but saw no one. The eerie feeling that the tour guide experienced initially intensified because there was no other way in or out past the guide. He still has no rational explanation for what happened that day.

Other people who have spent long hours working at the

fort have also witnessed ghosts, usually at sunset or during the early morning hours. Spectral figures have been seen walking around the latrine and in the dining room. According to park ranger Frank Ofeldt, the ghosts at Fort Taylor also make their presence known through sound: "Once, in the main gallery where the guns would be, I heard someone say, 'Attention'—a very faint voice. . . . I've heard voices, and I've heard whistling. I couldn't make it out exactly what they were saying."

If ghosts are actually haunting Fort Zachary Taylor, all evidence indicates that they are doing it out of a sense of duty. These may be the spirits of men who do not know that they are dead and who, therefore, are continuing to do those things that were part of their daily routine when they were alive. Most park officials agree, though, that it is more important to think of Fort Taylor, not as a haunted place, but as a memorial to the brave men who lived and died there to preserve the Union.

The fort is located at the Truman Annex at the southern end of Southard Street in Key West, Florida; phone: 305-292-6713.

The Jameson Inn of Crestview

CRESTVIEW

Most haunted hotels have a rich history, peopled with gangsters, suicides, and loyal employees. However, as all ghost investigators know, buildings do not have to be old to be haunted. The following is the transcript of an interview I conducted on March 7, 2001, with Dave Pearson, the general man-

ager of the Jameson Inn of Crestview, at the time a brand-new
hotel that had opened in April 2000. The following events are
rendered even more disturbing by the fact that no one knows
the identity of the hotel's permanent clients.

"Jameson Inn is an interior corridor hotel. We were built and
opened in April of this past year in an area just outside of an
expanding small southern town called Crestview. Crestview is
not known for anything extraordinary, but this area here adjoins
a military reservation of Eglin Air Force Base and it's only in
the last couple of years that development has spread to this area
here.

"When the hotel first opened, it was a twenty-four-hour
operation. The first indication that there might be something a
little bit odd happened when our night auditors, who work
from 11:00 P.M. to 7:00 A.M., began reporting hearing strange
noises—knocks, door slams, that sort of things. Well, since most
of them had never worked that shift, I chalked that up to hearing things in the night and also to the fact that this was a new
building settling in and there's going to be that sort of thing. So
everyone pretty much discounted it. The night auditors gave
the ghost the name of 'Fred,' for lack of anything better.

"We have electric sliding doors in the lobby, and they would
cycle at odd times, and that could be due to shadows. Our elevators would arrive on the first floor with nobody on them,
which is very unusual, because they have to be activated. You
would hear the activation chime sound in the lobby from whatever floor [the elevator] was activated on, and invariably, that
would occur on the second floor. We also have video camera
surveillance on all floors, and whenever that began to occur with
some regularity, the night auditors would look at the video monitor and not see anything. So the elevators are self-activating,
which the Otis people tell us is not supposed to be happening.

"The very first telekinetic episode occurred when a guest checked into Room 206 and laid his garments on a bed. He turned his back and found that his garments had been moved. The first time, he thought he didn't put them where he thought he did. He straightened his garments out, and they were moved again. He demanded another room, and he was a very happy camper after that. Later on, we got the story from him.

"We've had housekeepers report that a little plastic door on the air conditioner unit pops up and seemingly defies gravity. We have an ironing board sitting beside a wall-mounted mirror, and those doors have popped open in that room.

"We didn't have any apparitions until probably our fifth month. And then someone reported seeing a younger man in an athletic shirt or a tank top or something. And it was only a fleeting glimpse. Since then, we have seen distortions in our video camera surveillance that appear to be only momentary movement. We have smelled very sweet cigar smoke that has been almost overpowering in our nonsmoking lobby. We've had reports of that on the second floor in the vicinity of that room. We've also had odd reports in an adjoining room, Room 208, so it's moved around somewhat.

"The first-hand experience I've had with it [occurred when] my assistant general manager and I went to check smoke detectors in a room on the second floor. We have to check them monthly in the entire hotel. I would go into a room, press a button, it sounds, and then it goes off. Well, as we proceeded down the hall, rooms we had just inspected would sound, and by the time we got back there, they would shut off. It was very annoying. The second floor was the only floor it happened on. The systems are not linked together. They are independent smoke detectors.

"On Halloween, I decided to capitalize on what I thought were just odd little occurrences and do a Halloween promotion.

So they had a raffle and drawing for somebody to stay in the room. And you know how that can get out of hand. I purposely stayed off the property so that it would not taint what was going on. And they indicated that it was a great promotion because a lot of weird stuff happened. The radio station was thrilled.

"We have had a psychic investigator—a writer—stay in one of the rooms, and he brought a medium with him, and he said he wanted to do an article. He asked to be moved to a different room on the second floor, so we accommodated him. They were very pleased with the second room from a standpoint of investigative purposes, but he didn't really reveal to us what he found or didn't. He indicated that that would appear in a forthcoming article. He said he did investigate the county records and found that the woods adjacent us had been reported as being haunted. We've not had anybody corroborate that from the town or county, but quite frankly, we haven't explored it either.

"There is one odd occurrence on the grounds. We adjoin a woody area, a marshy area, and a lake. We've got a big eight-point buck that just comes out of the woods here. This is a big hunting town. Something like that just doesn't go 'un-nailed.' And there are deer tracks all over there, and that thing pops up, and nobody's been able to bag it. Every other truck has a gun rack on it and pictures of deer, and we've got one that wanders around like Bambi. It just defies the imagination. That is probably the most abnormal thing going on. I have had another psychic investigator say that animal occurrences like that [in haunted places] are somewhat commonplace. I can't comment on that. She said that she had had other incidents where animal sightings out of the ordinary were somehow linked.

"As far as we know, nobody was injured or killed on the construction of the building. We don't have any evidence of any missing persons in this area, but again, we have not investigated. This is a brand-new building, and as far as we know, nothing was leveled on the site of the building.

"Oh, here's another occurrence. In December [of 2000], we got very lucky. We closed a corporate contract with Bell Helicopter from Canada. We filled up our entire hotel for the last three months with French Canadians, including Rooms 206 and 208. And about that same time, we were really busy, and all apparitions stopped. Of course, it would be hard to tell with a full hotel, because any noises would be attributed to the comings and goings of guests, whereas in the fall, we had very low occupancy when a lot of these manifestations were going on. So we figured, 'O.K. Whatever it was is gone.' I was speaking with the psychic investigator, and one of the gentlemen who was our guest overheard me, and he mentioned it to the individual staying in Room 206. The next day, this guy's down at the front desk telling us in broken English that he had had a sense that somebody was in the room tugging on his blankets, and he'd keep waking up. Of course, he didn't say anything because he thought his buddies would rib him. He knew nothing about anything out of the ordinary going on in the hotel. I don't know if he was creating a story to make us happy or not.

"That's pretty much of what we've had. At the point that it got beyond just night nerves and fell into a regular pattern, I had to calm down the staff because they are by themselves, and that can be an odd shift. At that point, we started to document it, and my promotional mind said, 'Well, I'm going to capitalize on this for Halloween.' And that's when we assimilated all of the occurrences. So I interviewed everybody and said, 'What did you see?' It's pretty well accepted now. I don't have anybody who's uncomfortable going into Rooms 206 and 208.

"This is very odd, but it could be just coincidental. The room is a double. The bed sits on a box-frame base. About two months ago just before the Canadians moved in, I had a call from a guest who had stayed there. He said the bed had broken in there. I wondered how a bed frame could break. I went in there and found that the bed had been framed together with duct tape. Now I'm not bragging about Jameson Inn, but given the overall quality of the construction of this hotel, for somebody to duct tape a bed together when all they had to do was just put in some angle braces just defies the imagination. This is odd. What does it mean? I don't know. I'm not going to draw any conclusions."

The Jameson Inn of Crestview, Florida, is located at 151 Cracker Barrel Drive; phone: 850-683-1778.

Kingsley Plantation

FORT GEORGE ISLAND

The main house at Kingsley Plantation, located on Fort George Island along the northeast coast of Florida, is the oldest plantation house in Florida still standing. The twelve-acre plantation, which became a national park in 1991, consists of the main house, a detached kitchen house, a barn, and twenty-three slave cabins. The plantation house is a far cry from the splendid showplaces one might expect to find scattered throughout the Black Belt region of the South. The simple white frame house, built of longleaf pine, coquina blocks, and clay bricks, features a two-story portion with porches on the north and south sides. The house is anchored by four single-story corner rooms.

Wooden shingles cover the hipped roof. Although the main house may not look like the conventional southern mansion, it does possess one feature common to many of the old homes: it is haunted.

The two-story plantation house was built by John McQueen, who acquired Fort George through a Spanish land grant in 1792. After several years of poor crops, McQueen sold Fort George Island to John Houstoun McIntosh. In 1813, McIntosh rented the house and the surrounding land to Zephaniah Kingsley, who had been a slave trader and shipbuilder. He moved to Fort George Island after his Laurel Grove plantation was destroyed by Indians. Four years later, he bought the entire island for $7,000. Kingsley was, by most accounts, a freethinker who delighted in defying convention, particularly the widely held opinions of religion and race relations.

When he moved in, he was accompanied by Anna Madgigaine Jai Kingsley, a Senegalese slave whom he had freed and married, and their three children. A fourth child was born on the plantation. With the help of his wife, who bought and sold slaves, Kingsley transformed the plantation into a thriving enterprise. Kingsley's success was aided, no doubt, by his humane treatment of his slaves. Bone samples of fish and animals recovered in archaeological digs conducted in 1988 suggested that his slaves had more time to hunt and fish, going farther away from their quarters than did slaves at other plantations. Because Kingsley trusted his slaves, they experienced more variety in their diet.

Soon after Florida became part of the United States, Kingsley became increasingly concerned about the fate of his wife and children. Working on the erroneous assumption that freed slaves would incite the rest of the slave population to riot, the legislature started passing discriminatory laws. To ensure the safety of his wife, his family, and fifty of his former slaves, Kingsley sent them to a colony he had established in Haiti in 1837. Two years later, Kingsley sold the house to his nephew, Kingsley B. Gibbs, who then sold it to John F. Rollins in 1868. The plantation remained in the Rollins family until 1923, when it was sold to the Fort George Club. In 1955, the plantation was sold to the state of Florida.

Kingsley's reputation as a haunted house became established soon after it was opened as a national park. Many visitors have claimed to see the ghost of an errant slave called "Red Eyes," who was accused of raping and murdering several young girls on the property. He was hanged from an oak tree along the plantation's entrance road. Since 1978, visitors have seen his glowing red eyes peering at them from the dark reaches of the surrounding forest. In October 1993, Miss Tes Rais of Jacksonville was driving down the road with some friends one night when she saw Red Eyes in the headlights, staring at her from the bushes.

Most of the ghostly activity at the plantation cannot really be ascribed to a specific entity. Soon after volunteer tour guide Frances Duncan began working at the plantation, she observed something very strange in Kingsley's bedroom. One morning as she entered the room, she discovered that the bed had been moved out a foot or so from its normal position against the wall. Frances moved it back, only to find that it had been moved out again the next day. When she looked down at the floor, she found a series of grooves indicating that this had been going on for quite a while. Frances also recalled several occasions when people in her tour groups reported the smell of gingerbread coming from the warming kitchen.

According to Frances Duncan, some individual spirits do occasionally make their presence known in the house. One of the park rangers told her that he and his wife were sleeping in the house one night when he woke up to see the figure of a black man standing by his bed. He was wearing a turban and a pair of ragged pants tied up with a piece of rope. The ranger tried, unsuccessfully, to wake up his wife so that she could confirm what he thought he was seeing. By the time she woke up, the ghost had vanished.

Frances is convinced that one day she actually agitated the spirit of Zephaniah Kingsley. She had been told by the park rangers never to say "Goodnight, Mr. Kingsley" inside the house because something "bad" might happen. One night after checking upstairs, she was walking down the stairs when, on impulse, she said, "Goodnight, Mr. Kingsley." Immediately, she experienced a chilling feeling: "I felt as if someone had dumped a bucket of ice water on my head. I got goose pimples all over, and I got out of there." That was the last time Frances ever wished Mr. Kingsley goodnight.

Joyce Elson Moore, author of *Haunt Hunter's Guide to Florida,* believes that she had an encounter with the spirit of the mistress of Kingsley Plantation. On her first visit to the island, she shot a series of slides when nobody was around. After she had the slides developed, she saw nothing unusual. Several days later, Frances showed the slides to a local photographers' group. After several slides were projected on the wall, a woman sitting next to Joyce exclaimed, "Look at the ghost!" Joyce got out of her chair and looked closely at the slide. To her amazement, she could clearly make out the figure of a woman in a white dress standing near the warming kitchen. She is now convinced that her camera captured the restless spirit of Anna Jai.

The fifty thousand tourists who visit Kingsley Plantation are attracted by both the beauty of its natural setting and its historical significance. According to local legends, the original occupants of the plantation are also drawn there for various reasons. In the case of Anna Madgigaine Jai Kingsley, the return of

her ghost to Kingsley Plantation might reflect her lingering desire to remain at the place where she and her family had enjoyed so many happy years before being sent away to Haiti.
This is not to say, though, that everyone on Fort George Island
believes that the place is really haunted. Katy Tilford, a ranger
with the National Park Service, refuses to ascribe every strange
event on the plantation to ghosts: "I have had no experience
with anything supernatural out there." At least, not yet.

Kingsley Plantation is on Fort George Island, north of the
Mayport Ferry landing on Route A1A.

Lilian Place

DAYTONA BEACH

Laurence Thompson, the builder of Lilian Place, was one of
the founders of Daytona Beach. After the town was incorporated in 1876, Thompson served as the first clerk. In 1884,
Thompson and his wife, Mary Eliza, set about building a mansion that would reflect his status in the newly formed city. Their
house was to be the first to be built in the peninsula. Because
there were no bridges across the Halifax when Lilian Place was
built, materials had to be shipped from the mainland by boat.
Construction was completed later that year. Lilian Place was,
and still is, an impressive structure consisting of three stories, a
full ground-level basement, and a tower.

The Thompson family became a driving force in the business
sector of Daytona Beach. Starting with a general store, Laurence

Thompson moved on to form a real estate and insurance partnership called "Bingham and Thompson." Laurence's spinster daughter, Lilian, spent her entire life in the house that bears his name. Laurence's older son, Laurence, was the working partner in the family business. His other son, Harrison, owned the Dodge Plymouth Agency in town. Harrison, the "wilder" of the two brothers, smoke and drank, even during Prohibition. He ended up marrying a French woman named Lucy, a divorcée with a nine-year-old son. Harrison and Lucy had a son, Harrison Coffin Thompson Jr., nicknamed "Brutie," who lived in his grandparents' home after his parents divorced. In a few years, Brutie moved back with his father, who had remarried. After Lilian died, Laurence and Harry inherited the house. They sold it to a relative, Alice Dalton, who named the house "Lilian Place" in Lilian's memory. Later, Alice gave the house to her godchild, Patricia Thompson, who rented out some of the rooms. In the early 1980s, Patricia sold Lilian Place to the McDole family. Patricia moved into a nearby condominium.

Aside from being one of Daytona's premier homes, Lilian Place also played a prominent role in one of American literature's most dramatic footnotes. On New Year's Day, 1896, Stephen Crane, a war correspondent for the *New York Press,* sailed from Jacksonville, Florida, on the steamer *Commodore,* which was running arms to the Cuban insurgents. Not long after leaving port, the *Commodore* went down, possibly as a result of sabotage, and Crane, with three or four members of the crew, were cast adrift in a ten-foot dinghy. After thirty hours at sea, the open boat was swamped in the Florida surf. One crew member, the oiler, was drowned. After Crane was rescued, he spent some time recovering at Lilian Place. Upon returning to New York, Crane sent the Thompsons autographed copies of his novel *Red Badge of Courage* and the short story he wrote about his harrowing experi-

ence entitled "The Open Boat." By 1978, the Thompsons' autographed copy of *Red Badge of Courage* had disappeared from the
house.

For over forty years, Lilian Place was home to a mischievous
ghost. Tenants usually did not stay very long there. Some complained that their sleep was occasionally disturbed by the figure
of a woman who stared at them until they woke up. Several
tenants saw a female apparition pouring water into a glass. The
most startling incident occurred soon after Patricia's daughter
Vicki was born. One night, Patricia put the sleeping baby in
her crib. When she checked back on her a couple of hours later,
the infant was sleeping on the floor. No one ever found out
how she got there.

In the 1980s, Patricia Thompson Bennett wrote a fictional
story explaining the haunting of Lilian Place. According to Ms.
Bennett's pamphlet, some time in the 1920s, Harrison Thompson met a very pretty young woman named Lucille, who worked
at Woolworth's Five and Ten Cent Store. Lucille and her father
had moved to Florida a few months before to start a fernery in
Volusia County. Harrison went to Woolworth's every day to eat
lunch, but as his relationship with Lucy blossomed, he soon
discovered another reason for going there. Seventeen-year-old
Lucille was flattered when Daytona's most eligible bachelor asked
her to marry him. Even though she was fully aware of the handsome young man's reputation as a playboy who smoke and drank,
she accepted his proposal.

Harrison invited Lucille to stay in the Thompson house
with his sister Lilian while they planned the marriage. Lucille
quit her job at Woolworth's, began assembling her trousseau,
and planned her wedding at the Congregational Church. While
staying with her future in-laws, Lucille passed the time by reading the books in their living room, including the autographed

copy of *Red Badge of Courage*. In the next few weeks, Harrison's visits became shorter and less frequent. One day, he confessed to Lucy that he had fallen in love with a French divorcée, a woman who, coincidentally, was also named Lucy. Heartbroken, Lucy remained at Lilian Place, apparently even after her death.

Lilian Place is located at 12121 Silver Beach Avenue, Daytona Beach, Florida. It is a private residence.

Old Leon County Jail

TALLAHASSEE

Many of the haunted jails in the South are ancient buildings with long, sad histories, such as the Old Exchange Building in Charleston, South Carolina. By contrast, the Art Deco Building that housed the old Leon County Jail in Tallahassee, Florida, looks more like a bomb shelter. Built in the 1930s, it served as a jail for a fairly short time. In the 1950s, a larger jail was constructed closer to the police station, but prisoners continued to be housed in the old Leon County Jail until the 1960s, when it was taken over by the Florida State Archives. The building was used as a library facility until the Florida Department of Revenue moved in during the 1990s. Despite the fact that the building has undergone a series of transformations down through the years, the psychic vibrations resonating from the ceilings and walls provide constant reminders that it was once a place of great suffering.

The harsh punishment inflicted upon prisoners in the early years of the jail's history appears to have made a lasting impression on the structure. During this time, most of the prisoners were blacks and indigent whites. Operating on the belief that such people need a firm hand, some of the guards exercised brute force on a regular basis. As a result, the emotional trauma experienced by many of the prisoners may have been etched upon the very masonry of the building. Ed Fausel, a local archaeologist/anthropologist, says that people working in the building since 1970 have reported hearing strange sounds. Several night workers have reported hearing the slamming of nonexistent doors, a sound so disturbing that one employee at the archives in the 1970s refused to work there after dark. Others have heard voices in rooms formerly used as jail cells. In the 1980s, staff members heard a wide variety of sounds, such as footsteps walking through a room and the pounding of a sledgehammer behind an inner wall.

The number of bizarre occurrences at the old Leon County Jail peaked in the late 1980s, primarily because of a fantastic archaeological find. In 1622, the Spanish galleon *Nuestra Senora de Atocha* sank in a hurricane off the coast of Florida. It lay in its watery grave until June 20, 1985, when the treasure hunter Mel Fisher discovered the *Atocha* near the Marquesas Keys. No sooner had he and his crew begun their salvage operation than questions of the ownership of the treasure arose. While the courts deliberated over the rightful ownership of the treasure, it was stored in the old Leon County Jail, which was deemed to be a very secure place. By the time the courts ruled that Florida would receive only a representative share of the treasure, the former jail had acquired a reputation among archives employees and guards as being a very "spooky" place, especially at night. However, Ed Fausel does not believe that spirits from the *Atocha* were responsible for weird happenings at the old jail: "They had people there twenty-four hours a day instead of just the normal daytime hours. There was more use of the building, so, of course, there were more reports [of ghosts]."

While Fausel's explanation seems logical enough, it does not account for the most terrifying incident that occurred when the *Atocha*'s treasure was stored in the former jail. One night, an archaeologist walked some steps inside the building to look at some Key West treasures also being held there. All of a sudden, he felt two phantom hands pick him up and hurl him down the stairs. Nothing approaching the violence of this attack has taken place in the old Leon County Jail since then.

Improvements made in the building in the 1990s have softened its formidable appearance somewhat. Two wings were added to the rear of the jail, a superfluous carport was removed, and new parking spaces were added. In addition, landscapers planted a new garden, giving the former jail a more domestic look. Mr. Fausel says that the ghosts have quieted down since the Florida Department of Revenue moved in. "But then," he added, "the workers lock up and go home at five o'clock."

The old Leon County Jail is on Calhoun Street near its intersection with Pensacola Street in Tallahassee, Florida.

GEORGIA

Davenport House

The Georgian-style Davenport House was built by architect Isaiah Davenport around 1820. The house is known for its beautifully crafted plasterwork and woodwork. The master builder from Rhode Island lived in the house with his wife, six sons, and a daughter for many years. The house was occupied by a variety of tenants in the twentieth century. By the time the Historic Savannah Foundation selected it as the first of its restoration projects, it had suffered the ravages of time and neglect. The restoration of the Davenport House was so successful that the women who made up the Historic Savannah Foundation used it as their headquarters for many years. The historic old home is now a museum.

The Davenport House is unique among haunted houses in the South in that one of its resident ghosts is a cat. Savannah author Gerald Chan Seig first heard the story from her father, Robert Chung Chan, who had participated in the revolution against the Manchu Dynasty. Fearing for his life, Robert Chan left China for the relative tranquillity of Savannah, Georgia. Ironically, he arrived at the height of the 1889 Hogan's fire, which started at Hogan's Department Store on Broughton Street. The fire also initiated Chan's integration into Savannah society. As he was running around looking for shelter, the spire of the Independence Presbyterian Church suddenly burst into flames.

71

Chan took this as a sign that fate intended for him to become a Presbyterian.

After the turmoil caused by the fire subsided, Robert Chan rented an apartment at the Davenport House, which at that time had been converted into a boardinghouse for Chinese families. One afternoon, Robert Chan returned home from work and began walking up the front steps of the house. Without warning, a large yellow cat darted in front of him. Startled by the sudden appearance of a cat he had never seen before, Robert opened the front door of the house, but before he could walk inside, the yellow cat cut in front of him and darted down the hallway. Robert slammed the door shut behind him and instigated a search of the entire house for the elusive cat. No trace of the cat was ever found, even though it would have been impossible for it to have escaped.

Soon after the Davenport House was turned into a museum in the twentieth century, some of the first tourists swore that they had seen the ghost of a beautiful little girl playing with toys on the fourth floor. The child was dressed in elegant Victorian clothes. Psychic investigators who were called in to examine the haunting activity concluded that the ghost did not mean to scare the visitors intentionally. Evidently, the child did not know she was dead and was looking for a playmate. Sightings of the little girl became so frequent that the fourth floor of the Davenport House was completely closed.

The identity of neither the cat nor the little girl has ever been determined. Still, the staff at the Davenport House are convinced the ghosts are related somehow to the family of Isaiah Davenport. After all, the Davenports did have a daughter. And, with seven children in the house, it is likely that they probably had at least one cat as well.

The Davenport House is located at 324 East State Street, Savannah, Georgia; phone: 912-236-8097.

The Juliette Gordon Low Girl Scout Center

SAVANNAH

uliette Gordon Low (1860–1927) is one of Savannah's most illustrious citizens. Her father, William ("Willie") Washington Gordon II, was commissioned a general in the Spanish American War. Her mother, Eleanor ("Nellie") Kinzie Gordon, was a vivacious woman who refused to honor conventions which she considered to be stuffy or hypocritical. Like her mother, Juliette Gordon refused to be held back by the expectations of other people. Although she was deaf and in poor health much of her life, she was determined to prove that girls too could benefit from scouting, which had originally been created for boys by her friend Robert Baden Powell in Great Britain in 1907. After marrying a wealthy Englishman, William M. Low, Juliette organized a troop of Girl Guides on her estate at Glenlyon, Scotland. On her return to the United States, she began a patrol in Savannah, Georgia, in 1912. The organization changed its name to Girl Scouts in 1913. Juliette's sister, Daisy Gordon Lawrence, became the first registered Girl Scout. Juliette served

73

as president of the Girl Scouts until 1920, when she was named founder.

Construction on the Savannah home in which Juliette grew up began in 1818 and was completed in 1821. It was built originally for Judge Moore Wayne, who later became an associate justice of the Supreme Court. When the Gordon family bought the house in 1831, the interior furnishings were still incomplete. The Gordon family enlarged the house in 1886. Descendants of the Gordon family continued to live in the house until 1953. The Girl Scouts acquired the house a few years later.

Even though the house bears Juliette's name, it is her mother and father who left the most lasting impression on the Regency townhouse. The love shared by Juliette's parents, Nellie and Willie, was noteworthy for its intensity. According to Juliette Gordon Low's biography, *Lady from Savannah: The Life of Juliette Gordon Low,* her mother made no effort to conceal her belief that she was a wife first and a mother second. When her husband urged her to take the children to safety during Savannah's yellow fever epidemic of 1876, leaving him behind to help fight the disease, Nellie is reported to have said, "If you won't go, they can stay here and get yellow fever! What do I care for them in comparison with you, Willie Gordon?" (111). Their love for each other was so passionate that it was later immortalized in a novel by Shirley Sufert entitled *Look to the Rose.* If the family ghost story is to be believed, General Gordon was so devoted to Nellie that death itself could not prevent him from demonstrating his love for her.

Toward the end of her life, Nellie Gordon was beset by problems. Her beloved husband died in 1912. By 1917 when she was eighty-one years old, Nellie was being asked to pay income tax on an income of five thousand pounds a year, of which she actually received only a few hundred pounds (342). When one of Nellie's granddaughters produced a girl child instead of the boy she had her heart set on, she flew into a rage which brought on a fearful attack of angina. In February of 1917, Nellie went into a coma. Although she rallied soon after her daughters Daisy and Mabel arrived from England, Nellie suffered a heart attack, and then another. On February 22, 1917, her five children were gathered in the library. Suddenly, the door flew open, and Nellie marched into the room. When one of her daughters told her that she should not have walked down the stairs in her weakened condition, Nellie replied, "I didn't walk down the stairs. I slid down the banister!"

After Nellie returned to her bedroom, one of her daughters-in-law, Mrs. Margaret McGuire Gordon, walked down the hallway and saw the ghost of General Gordon standing in the doorway. She started to scream, but the specter put his finger to his lips, signaling her to be quiet. Then he opened the door and walked into the room where Nellie lay dying. Margaret's husband, Arthur Gordon, was in the bedroom at the time. A few minutes later, Arthur emerged from the room and said, "Mama's gone, and it's the strangest thing. When the wind blew the door open, she sat up in bed, stretched out her arms, smiled like a bride, and died." Margaret replied, "But it wasn't the wind. It was your father. I saw him!"

When Margaret and Arthur walked down the stairs, the butler, who was standing at the foot of the stairs, asked, "Old Miss is gone?" Arthur replied, "Yes, she has." The butler's eyes grew wide, and he said, "I knew so! I saw General Gordon walk in the door, and he told me he'd come to get Miss Nellie." According to family tradition, General Gordon and Nellie have been together ever since.

The general has not made another appearance in the house since 1917, but other strange things have happened since then. In the early 1980s, a tour guide who was leaving the house late one Sunday afternoon suddenly remembered that she had left a book upstairs. Without turning the lights back on, she reentered the house and rushed up the stairs. As she neared the top of the stairs, she heard the rustling of skirts. There, in the middle of the center hall, stood a familiar figure. The tour guide recognized her as Nellie Gordon from a painting hanging in the library. Alarmed by the mysterious manifestation, the tour guide headed back down the stairs without retrieving her book. For just an instant, she glanced back over her shoulder toward the center hall. The figure of the woman had vanished. While riding back home, it occurred to the tour guide that Nellie may have come back to reclaim her home, thinking that all of the staff had left for the day.

A maintenance man at the center named Eddie has also had strange experiences inside the house. He said that he often encountered the spirit of Nellie Gordon at the dining table when he first came into the house in the mornings. She was usually wearing a blue robe with flowers on it. Eddie also heard the faint sound of a pianoforte playing. The instrument inside the house is missing 80 percent of its keys, yet the pianoforte that he heard was perfectly in tune.

Whenever an object is misplaced, the staff usually blames its disappearance on the resident ghost. The most persistent phenomenon, though, involves the door of a bookcase that has a tendency to swing open when the guides walk past it. The curator, Steve Bolin, has a rational explanation: "If you step on a certain board on the floor, the door opens. This sort of thing often happens with some old houses that just aren't balanced very well. On the whole, it is a very peaceful house."

The pink stucco building is downtown on the corner of Bull Street and Oglethorpe Street at 142 Bull Street, Savannah, Georgia; phone: 912-233-4501.

The Pirate's House

SAVANNAH

Perched upon a bluff overlooking the Savannah River is one of the most historic spots in Savannah, Georgia. When Georgia was founded in 1733, this spot was called Trustees Garden, and it was the first experimental plot in America. A variety of cash crops, including indigo, hemp, cotton, and fruit trees, was planted in small numbers to see if they would thrive in Georgia. The first building constructed here was the Pirate's House, an inn for sailors, smugglers, and pirates. Standing in what is now a fashionable residential area, this rambling, two-story frame structure is an anachronism, a throwback to a time when cutthroats wearing brightly colored clothes and gleaming cutlasses swaggered through the streets of Savannah. Down through the years, many of the guests and employees of the Pirate's House have claimed that the spirits of these colorful individuals have never truly departed from the old building.

The Pirate's House, which was built in 1754, is certainly one of the oldest buildings in Savannah. However, the Herb House, which originally served as the abode of the royal gardener and is now part of the Pirate's House complex, is actually twenty years older than the Pirate's House. In 1754, John Reynolds, the first governor of the colony, converted the garden into a residential area. In 1948, the Savannah Gas Company acquired the property. Soon thereafter, Mrs. Hansell Hillyer transformed the Pirate's House into a museum. It is now a fine restaurant.

Testimony given by guests and employees at the Pirate's House indicates that ghosts from the building's notorious past still walk the dark passageways. Strange noises and eerie lights coming from the upper storage room suggest that some unearthly presence lurks in the shadows. Ghosts can also be found wandering through the Pirate's House's twenty-three dining rooms. Former owner Herb Traub said that one night while he was working in his office, the night manager walked in, visibly shaken. When Traub asked what had happened to him, the night manager replied that he had a horrible experience while closing up one of the dining rooms. He was in the process of closing it up, and when he walked past the door, he saw a strange man sitting in a chair by the table. The night manager turned around to see if he had been imagining things, and the man was gone. He swore that the figure he saw in the room looked like a flesh-and-blood human being.

The most haunted room in the Pirate's House is the Captain's Room, which is reputed to have a literary connection with Robert Louis Stevenson's classic novel *Treasure Island*. Most editions of the book contain a map that clearly shows Savannah, Georgia. Therefore, it is possible that the Captain Flint who died in this room was the inspiration for the Captain Flint in Stevenson's novel. Some of the waiters at the Pirate's House believe that Captain Flint's personality made an indelible impression on the Captain's Room. They say they have heard weird musical sounds and the rattling of dishes in this room. In addition, strange shadows, such as those made by a moving figure, have been seen flitting around the old captain's bedchamber.

The most mysterious feature of Pirate House is a secret tunnel running from the rum cellar to the river less than a mile away. In the eighteenth and nineteenth centuries, the legends say captains in need of crew members got unsuspecting sailors drunk and then arranged to have the unconscious men carried through the tunnel to ships anchored on the river. Supposedly, a Savannah police officer stopped off at the Pirate House, fell unconscious, and awoke on a schooner sailing to China. He did not return home for two years.

Doors leading into the tunnels from the rum cellar were bricked up long ago. However, residents of Savannah still tell a story about one bold young man who tried to explore the tunnel decades ago. Legend has it that he was walking through the dark tunnel when he tripped over something embedded in the dirt floor. He bent down and picked it up. It was a human skull. Despite his revulsion, he continued on his way. Finally, he came to a dead end, the result of a cave-in. Suddenly, he heard the sound of approaching footsteps. Pressing himself against the wall of the tunnel, he stared in amazement as a group of shadowy figures walked by. He could feel the cold blast of air that accompanied them. The young man watched breathlessly as the ghostly crew walked straight through the wall. Convinced that he had seen enough, he turned around and made a hasty retreat.

Aside from its comparatively modest appearance, the Pirate's House can be distinguished from other buildings in the area by its blue shutters. Students of folklore immediately recognize the color as "haint blue," which has the power to repel spirits. Judging from the ghostly activity at the Pirate's House, one must conclude that the blue shutters have not done their job.

The Pirate's House is located at the corner of East Broad and Bay Streets. The address is 20 East Broad Street, Savannah, Georgia; phone: 912-233-5757.

Telfair Museum of Art

The Telfair mansion was designed by renowned nineteenth-century architect William Jay around 1818. This "little palace," which is noteworthy for its curved walls and doors, is now a museum, thanks to the efforts of Mary Telfair, the daughter of the original owner of the house. Mary knew that her father, a former governor of Georgia, wanted the Telfair name to continue to be connected with the house, so in her will she gave it to the city of Savannah to be used as an art museum. After Mary died in 1875, the will was contested by her cousins, who took the case to the Supreme Court. The Supreme Court upheld the will, and Savannah became the site of one of the oldest art museums in the entire South. Former president of the Confederacy Jefferson Davis cut the ribbon during the opening ceremonies.

Mary Telfair's influence can still be felt in Savannah, mostly because of her endowments. In accordance with Mary's wishes, the Pavilion for Women still has a women's board of directors. Independence Presbyterian Church owes its present appearance to Mary Telfair. After the church was destroyed by fire, Mary dictated in her will that it was to be rebuilt to look exactly the same as it had before. Mary also oversaw the completion of Hodgson Hall in memory of her late brother-in-law, William Brown Hodgson, who lived with her and her sister Margaret in the house on Telfair Square.

As one would expect, though, Mary Telfair's continuing presence is most evident at her former home, the Telfair Art Museum. Ghostly manifestations began to occur shortly after the extensive remodeling of the house. Local author Margaret Wayt DeBolt describes Mary Telfair as a "possessive spirit" who makes her displeasure known whenever changes are made in the house that violate her wishes. The museum staff reports that Mary becomes very upset whenever her huge oil portrait is moved. When the painting was moved from its usual position in the dining room, part of the rotunda ceiling crashed through the newer ceiling below it. One of the other paintings in the room was damaged in the process.

Mary's ghost has also enforced one particular stipulation in her will: that "no eating, drinking, smoking, or amusements of any kind" would be held inside the museum. As a rule, receptions after museum events are held in the new lower western wing, where the Telfair's carriage house and stables were once located. One evening, refreshments following a meeting of the historical society were being served on the lawn behind the building. However, a sudden thunderstorm forced the staff to move the food and drink inside the building. The reception had just resumed when a sudden gust of wind blew through the building, rattling the windows and breaking a glass. Some guests claimed to have heard mysterious voices in the room. To prevent the recurrence of a similar incident, the staff now holds all of its parties and receptions in the new annex.

An actress working as a tour guide at the Telfair became personally acquainted with Mary Telfair's inflexible rules. To lend more of a period flair to a special event being held at the museum, she decided to greet people in the type of dress that Mary would have worn in the 1870s and then escort them around the building. For several nights after going to bed, the tour guide dreamed that Mary Telfair was standing in her bedroom, shaking the bed and saying, "Read the will! Read the will!" The next morning, she looked at a copy of the will in the museum and realized that her performance probably fell under the heading of "amusements," which were prohibited inside the mansion. She decided then and there to stop dressing up like Mary Telfair inside the museum. Her nightmares ceased as well.

Sometimes, visitors and staff get the impression that the spirits occupying the house are oblivious to the fact that their time has passed. Spectral sounds have resonated throughout the old house on occasion. Footsteps walking around the building have been heard after the museum is closed. Some have told of the sound of harp music emanating from the vacant front parlor after closing hours. At times, the reverberations have been so intense that they have set off the electronic alarm system. In the 1970s, an art student who was taking classes there apparently caught a glimpse of the spirits responsible for the strange sounds. One quiet afternoon, while walking through the front hall after hours, he was surprised by the sound of music. When he walked into the large front drawing room, he was surprised to see a group of people dressed in nineteenth-century attire moving about and talking. The art student left the room and walked to the library to ask a staff member about the costume party across the hall. The staff member, who was unaware of any parties scheduled in the museum at that hour, accompanied the young man back into the drawing room. The room was deathly quiet. Dust covering the tables and furniture indicated that no one had used the room for quite a while.

The Telfair Museum of Art is located at 121 Barnard Street on Telfair Square, Savannah, Georgia; phone: 912-232-1177.

KENTUCKY

Bobby Mackey's Music World

WILDER

Owners of old mansions that have been transformed into bed and breakfasts have known for years that advertising the presence of a ghost can be good for business. Some unscrupulous owners of "haunted" hostelries have even been known to fabricate a ghost legend simply to attract customers. However, a sign posted at the entrance to Bobby Mackey's Music World in Wilder, Kentucky, implies that the ghosts in this bar do not always welcome visitors: "Warning to our patrons: This establishment is purported to be haunted. Management is not responsible and cannot be held liable for any action of any ghosts/spirits on these premises." Many customers and employees who have experienced the supernatural activity in Bobby Mackey's Music World are convinced that the bar is not only haunted, but evil as well.

The building which Bobby Mackey's Music World occupies has a long, bloody legacy. Built in the 1850s, it was first used as a slaughterhouse. Blood and other bodily fluids drained into a deep well in the basement. After the slaughterhouse closed down in the late 1800s, the building was taken over by a cult of Satanists, who used the old well to catch the blood spilled in their ritualistic sacrifices. In 1896, the cult's sinister activities came to the public's attention when two young men with ties to the Satanists, Alonzo Walling and Scott Jackson, decapitated Pearl Bryan during a sacrificial rite. Bryan, the daughter of a wealthy farmer, had asked Jackson to abort her five-month-old fetus. When it became apparent that the skills Jackson had acquired in dental school were inadequate, he and Walling took her to a secluded spot near Fort Thomas, where they decapitated her with dental instruments. Evidence at the scene suggested that she was alive at the time. Her severed head, which was dumped in the well in the slaughterhouse, was never found. Even though both Walling and Jackson were offered life sentences in exchange for revealing the location of Bryan's head, they said that they preferred to be hanged because they feared retribution from Satan. As he stood on the gallows before a crowd of five thousand onlookers outside the courthouse in Newport, Kentucky, Walling swore that his spirit would return from the grave. A reporter covering the hanging reported in an article published in the March 21, 1897, edition of the *Kentucky Post* that an "evil eye" had gazed upon everyone connected with the murder.

In the 1920s during the Prohibition era, the building was used as a "speakeasy" known as the Bluegrass. Bootleg whiskey was smuggled through the well from the nearby Lucking River. Several unsolved murders, probably mob related, occurred here during that period. Even a domestic tragedy has left its mark on the old building. A young woman named Johanna poisoned her father after discovering that he had murdered her lover in the speakeasy. Shortly before poisoning herself, Johanna predicted in her diary that her spirit would haunt the speakeasy until her boyfriend, Robert, returned to her.

Over the years, the building continued to serve as a nightclub. In the 1940s and 1950s, it was a casino called the Primrose. The owner, E. A. Brady, was brought to trial in 1946 for the attempted murder of a mobster named Albert "Red" Masterson, but he was acquitted September 24, 1946. Then in 1978, the country-western singer Bobby Mackey purchased the old nightclub, which had been operating under the name "The Hard Rock Cafe." After repairing the damage caused by several unexplained fires, Mackey finally opened his "new" nightclub in September 1978.

For over twenty years, patrons and staff have experienced disturbances in the bar that can best be described as bizarre. One commonly reported phenomenon involves unexplained sounds. In the late 1980s, a patron was joking about the ghost when the P.A. system shorted out. At times, the ghostly strains of music have been heard in Bobby Mackey's Music World. The jukebox has come on by itself, sometimes playing "Anniversary Waltz" and music popular in the 1930s and 1940s. In the late 1980s, the band had just taken a break when they heard someone strumming a guitar on the P.A. system. When they looked over at the stage, no one was there. The sound man said that the strumming could not have been caused by feedback in the speakers. A man who gave guitar lessons inside the nightclub after closing hours was waiting for a student to arrive one afternoon. He picked up a guitar from the stage and began walking back to the ballroom when he heard a radio come on. He walked over to the bar where the music was coming from so that he could turn it off. However, after he got there, he could not find a radio anywhere. A man who was helping remodel Bobby Mackey's nightclub during the day heard a large arcade machine come on by itself and play music. As far as he could tell, no one had put any coins in the slot. In the early 1990s, a man who worked for a company specializing in live sound was doing a microphone check when a voice whispered into the microphone and came through the monitor. Within a few seconds, the whispering changed to eerie moans. No one was standing near the microphone at the time. An employee of the bar said that many times she has heard a strange voice call her name from behind the stage, beckoning her to come to the basement. Customers have also heard the sound of toilet seats slam down in the men's restroom and ghostly footsteps.

Ghostly manifestations have also appeared in Bobby Mackey's Music World. In the late 1980s, a customer who was walking toward the men's room glanced into a large mirror at the back of the nightclub and saw a headless woman walking through the crowd. In 1991, a woman named Sandra Murray said that she once saw a woman with long, light-colored hair walk through a room and vanish. Another customer saw the shadowy form of a woman with long black hair. When he approached her, she disappeared into a wall. The same ghost may have actually helped save the lives of some people injured in an automobile accident in front of the nightclub. Wilder police officer Steve Seiter was tending to the victims when a woman with long, light-colored hair came out of the bar, walked over, and offered him some red tablecloths to use as bandages. After the ambulance drove the victims to the hospital, the officer turned to thank the woman, only to discover that she was gone and the bar was closed. Whenever the lady is seen, she always wears a very troubled expression and appears to be looking for someone.

Two other ghosts have been seen inside the nightclub as well. In the late 1980s, a customer had just entered the men's room when he saw a large black dog resembling a mixed-breed Doberman. He continued walking toward the dog when he heard a man's voice say, "Don't be afraid. It's my dog." When the customer spun around, he found himself staring into the smiling face of a man with a handlebar mustache. The customer turned around and walked toward the door to leave. As he looked over his shoulder, he noticed that the mysterious man and the dog had vanished. The black dog has been seen by other customers as well. Every time, the dog appears for a few seconds and then disappears.

Some of the customers claim to have had actual physical contact with the ghost. Many people have felt a cold hand touch their shoulder and neck when no one else was near. Others standing alone have felt something breathe on their neck. Several people have actually sensed something very cold passing directly through their bodies. In 1993, J. R. Costigan of Newport sued Bobby Mackey's Music World because a ghost had supposedly attacked him in the men's room. The lawsuit prompted Bobby Mackey to install the sign at the entrance to his nightclub absolving him from liability if an apparition assaults another patron. Carl Lawson, who lived in an apartment in the nightclub, claimed that the ghosts of Walling and Jackson tried to drown him in his bathtub. In the late 1980s, Carl had taken a box down to the basement when he felt himself being hugged by an unseen presence. He had two dirty hand prints on his back as proof.

The ghost of Bobby Mackey's Music World may have also found ways of indirectly inflicting physical harm. Bobby Mackey's wife was almost crushed to death by a falling ladder several years ago. Not long after that, Carl Lawson attempted to seal up the well in the basement. Afterward, he came down with a case of hemorrhoids so severe that he almost died.

Apparently, the ghosts haunting Bobby Mackey's Music World occasionally leave with the customers. In 1989, a young woman who had felt something cold pass through her in the bar was driving her car back to Cincinnati, Ohio, back from Bobby Mackey's Music World, when she smelled the same perfume that had accompanied the old feeling the night before. Then, without warning, something grabbed her steering wheel, forcing the car to crash into a wall. She survived the accident with a deep gash on her chin, but her car was totally demolished. Other drivers heading home from the bar on northern Kentucky's lonely back roads have smelled a foul stench coming from the back seat. One patron of the bar was driving home late one night when a pair of bulging eyes appeared in the rearview mirror. When the driver turned around, a man with a handlebar mustache was sitting in the back seat. He was wearing nineteenth-century clothes and a noose around his neck.

A series of miscellaneous events that defy explanation have also taken place at Bobby Mackey's Music World. In the late 1980s, a plumber was working on some old pipes inside a wall of the nightclub when he looked up into the darkness of two overhead rafters and saw two disembodied blue eyes staring down at him. Another workman was doing some general maintenance on the old building when he heard a noise coming from the ballroom. He walked over to investigate and was shocked to see an entire row of chairs fall over themselves, as if they were dominoes. The distinct fragrance of rose or lavender perfume is often detected in the nightclub, usually before something bad happens, like the time a man was shot to death inside the nightclub. In the late 1980s, a waiter taking a break was seated at the end of the bar when a drinking glass sitting in front of him turned over on its side and rolled down to the other end of the bar. A retired policeman who found a back door cracked open walked inside the nightclub with his partner and began looking around. As they neared the stage area, they heard the sounds of a man and a woman talking, but they found no one inside the building. Suddenly, the door they had come through slammed shut. On at least two occasions, patrons riding the mechanical bull were injured when it accelerated to full speed by itself.

Despite the inconvenience and trauma caused by the haunting of the nightclub, Bobby Mackey has turned the ghostly intrusions to his advantage. The bar sells an entire line of souvenirs, including T-shirts emblazoned with lettering that says, "I partied with the ghosts at Bobby Mackey's" on the front and "Damn silly, ain't it?" on the back. Bobby Mackey's Music World has been featured on such syndicated television programs as *Sightings* and *Encounters*. He has appeared on national talk shows and plans to produce a movie based on his famous establishment. Mackey would probably agree that there is definitely money to be made on "spirits."

Wilder, Kentucky, is 1.5 miles south of Covington on Highway 9. Bobby Mackey's Music World is located at 44 Licking Pike, Wilder, Kentucky; phone: 606-431-5588.

Headless Woman Rock

LEITCHFIELD

Strange geological formations have tantalized the imaginations of Americans for generations. Some of these rocks have even inspired classic works of fiction, such as Nathaniel Hawthorne's "Great Stone Face." In a gorge in western Kentucky is a very large, shapeless boulder known throughout the county as "Headless Woman Rock." Many of the stories told about this rock are clearly folk tales. Yet, there is enough factual evidence for one or two of these strange narratives to cause the listener to wonder, "Could this have really happened?"

Headless Woman Rock is located in one of those out-of-the-way places known only to "old-timers," hunters, or teenagers looking for a secluded place to neck and party. The rugged terrain is characterized by steep hills, high cliffs, caves, heavily eroded land, and dense forests. Best described as "off the beaten track," Headless Woman Rock can be accessed only by driving down a lonely stretch of two-lane blacktop called "Blowtown Road" and then walking west for a half mile. Understandably, very few people live in this region. Those who do live here reside on a handful of widely scattered farms. The locals still avoid the gorge where Headless Woman Rock can be found, especially at night, when the strange sounds common to such places are amplified and distorted.

Many of the people familiar with the stories have passed on. These days, the best place to find the lore of Headless Woman Rock is the folklore archives of Western Kentucky University in Bowling Green, Kentucky. Most of the stories were collected by Percy Ray Downs Jr. from relatives and neighbors living around Leitchfield. As he talked to his informants, Downs found that the origin of the stories is shrouded in mystery. According to most of the tales, a woman living all alone over by the rock in the early 1800s was murdered one night, either by Indians or outlaws. After she was killed, her murderer left her body but took her head, which has never been found.

Most of the stories revolve around people who encountered the woman's body as it roamed around the gorge in search of its head. People say that the headless corpse can be seen both night and day. On clear, warm nights, some say her screams can be heard echoing down through the gorge. For many years, parents made their children behave by telling them that the headless woman would "get them" if they were bad.

If the stories can be believed, some people actually had first-hand encounters with the headless woman. One man named Charley Taylor said that he was out hunting by the rock one day when he saw the headless woman's body lying on the rock. Without pausing to identify the corpse, Charley turned and ran home. The daughter of another local man named Tommy Meredith also saw the headless woman one day while hunting holly for Christmas decorations. Percy Ray Downs Jr.'s grandfather, Stoy Downs, told Percy, "Tommy Willis's father was riding a horse by the rock one day, and the woman got up on the horse behind him and rode for a while and then got off. He was so scared that he didn't look back, but he knew it was her."

Percy Ray Downs Jr. became so intrigued by one of the stories he had collected that he decided to check it out. One of his female informants told him that she was driving down the road one night when the headless woman stepped out in front of her car. The woman was so frightened by the bloody, headless phantom that she ran off a cliff and wrecked her car. Downs said that after he heard the story, he went to the place where the accident was supposed to have happened and walked around, looking for evidence of a wreck: "To my surprise," he said, "I found a hubcap, steering wheel, and a bumper. How in the world could these things get into such an isolated place? Somehow, the story had some proof behind it."

"Headless Woman Rock" is located about nine miles southwest of Leitchfield on state highway 1133. To get there from Leitchfield, drive west on U.S. 62 to state highway 187. Then take 187 to state highway 1133. From there, head south on Blowtown Road.

Liberty Hall

Female ghosts are a very common motif, or thematic element, in oral ghost narratives. Many of these phantoms wear flowing white dresses of gossamer-like fabric. As a rule, the ghost is the spirit of a beautiful young woman who "died for love," victims of murder or suicide. The stories of these poor women invoke pity and possibly even tears. However, the ghost that haunts Liberty Hall in Frankfort, Kentucky, does not conform to the stereotype of the female revenant. These differences make her story all the more compelling—and believable.

Liberty Hall was built by John Brown. He was born in Augusta County, Virginia, on September 12, 1757, to Reverend John Brown and Margaret Preston Brown, who had emigrated from Ireland. After serving in General Washington's army, he studied law at the College of William and Mary and later with Thomas Jefferson. When Brown came to Kentucky in 1782, he set up a law practice at Danville and quickly became involved in Kentucky politics. After serving as Kentucky's representative to the Virginia Senate in 1784 and as the Kentucky delegate to the Continental Congress in 1787, he was elected to the U.S. Congress to represent the District of Kentucky in 1789 and again in 1791. When Kentucky was admitted to the Union in 1792, he became one of the first U.S. senators.

In 1796, Brown decided to build a large, brick home on a

four-acre site in Frankfort, Kentucky, to serve as a home for his own family and for his aging parents as well. He named his new home after the Virginia academy founded by his father. On February 18, 1799, John Brown married Margaretta Mason, the daughter of a Presbyterian minister. In 1801, he brought his wife to Frankfort from Pittsburgh by flatboat on the Ohio River. According to the legend, Margaretta brought with her from New York cuttings of some old-fashioned roses, the descendants of which are still growing in the garden today. Even though Frankfort was a frontier settlement in the early 1800s, Margaretta turned her home into one of Kentucky's most prominent social and cultural centers. Their guests included such dignitaries as President James Monroe, General Andrew Jackson, and Major Zachary Taylor, who visited Liberty Hall in 1891. In 1825, the Marquis de Lafayette attended a ball given in his honor at Liberty Hall.

After John Brown died at the age of eighty, Liberty Hall was bequeathed to his son, Mason, who lived there until he died in 1867. His wife, Mary Yoder Brown, inherited the property. In 1882, Mary Yoder Brown's children conveyed Liberty Hall to their sister, Mary Yoder Brown Scott, who lived there with her children and her two widowed sisters. When Mary Yoder Brown Scott died, Liberty Hall became the property of her two children, Mary Mason and John Matthew. Mary Mason Scott lived at Liberty Hall until her death on December 10, 1934. On May 1, 1937, the property was deeded to Liberty Hall, Incorporated, by John Matthew Scott. In 1956, Liberty Hall, Inc., turned over control of the property to the National Society of the Colonial Dames of America in the Commonwealth of Kentucky. Mary Mason Scott's will dictated that Liberty Hall was to be maintained as a museum house.

The resident ghost of Liberty Hall is the Gray Lady. Her story began when Mrs. Margaret Varick, Mrs. Brown's aunt, visited Liberty Hall in 1817 to attend the funeral of one of the Browns' daughters. The eight-hundred-mile journey from New York over rough roads and rugged terrain proved to be too much for the sixty-five-year-old lady. Three days after her arrival, she died of an apparent heart attack. Her corpse was buried in the garden for a while. Eventually, though, it received a proper burial in a cemetery.

Sarah Harger, director of Liberty Hall, says that even though her body is no longer on the premises, her spirit still remains: "The first encounter with the Gray Lady took place during the latter part of the nineteenth century. One of the family members, a woman who was very much interested in spiritualism, woke up one night and saw the figure of a woman touching her hand. She was dressed in a grayish-colored outfit, so that's where the Gray Lady got her name."

Stories of the Gray Lady continued well into the twentieth century. Like many ghosts, the Gray Lady was agitated when significant structural changes were made in the house. According to Ms. Harger, one such incident occurred in the 1970s after a fire broke out in the house: "After the restoration, they took some photographs of the main staircase. When they got the photographs back, there was the ghostly image of a woman on the steps. That's our picture of the Gray Lady."

Since then, ghostly phenomena at Liberty Hall have been reported on a fairly regular basis. Often times, staff members have felt her presence when doors open and close mysteriously or when strange lights flicker in empty rooms. Some people have experienced chills while standing in certain parts of the house. Sarah Harger says that the latest bizarre event took place in the summer of 2000: "There is a Windsor chair on the second floor, and it was moved into the middle of the room. None of the staff will admit to doing it. That chair has been moved on several other occasions as well." On one occasion, three gold bracelets not listed on the house inventory were found on a nightstand in the upstairs bedroom. The jewelry was probably made about the time Mrs. Varick visited her niece. In addition, Mrs. Varick is sometimes noticed standing at an upstairs window by passersby.

As it turns out, the Gray Lady is one of three ghosts that haunt Liberty Hall. In 1805, the Browns invited a Spanish opera singer from New Orleans to perform at their home. "She got hot," Harger says, "so she went outside to cool off and she never came back. The house sits right on the river, so she probably fell in. According to the stories, you can see her walking in the garden, but I don't know anyone who has ever seen her, and there is no mention of her ghost in the historical record."

The third ghost at Liberty Hall is also an "outside" spirit. Legend has it that a soldier from the War of 1812 fell in love with a young cousin who had arrived at Liberty Hall for a short visit. Unfortunately, she did not return his affections. The heartbroken soldier returned to war and was killed. For almost two hundred years, his ghost has been seen peeking into an outside window of the house. After a few seconds, the melancholy ghost slowly walks away and vanishes.

As a rule, Sarah Harger does not tell the ghost stories to tour groups unless she is asked. And, it seems, questions about the ghostly manifestations are becoming more and more common, possibly because of the story's tragically ironic twist. Mrs. Varick arrived at Liberty Hall to comfort a bereaved family and, inadvertently, only added to their sorrow through her own death.

Liberty Hall is now a museum run by the Colonial Dames of America. It is located at 218 Wilkinson Street, Frankfort, Kentucky; phone: 502-227-2560.

Van Meter Auditorium

Ghosts seem to have an affinity for large, imposing buildings with an abundance of empty space, such as the Orpheum Theater in Memphis, Tennessee. In many cases, the eerie echoes and dark, shadowy recesses common to most of these buildings play tricks with the minds of susceptible audiences. However, the phenomena witnessed by generations of college students at Van Meter Auditorium defy such an easy explanation. Many members of the academic community at Western Kentucky University truly believe that Van Meter Auditorium is haunted.

Van Meter Auditorium was built in 1910 and dedicated in 1911. It was named for Captain C. J. Van Meter, a major contributor to Western Kentucky University. The generally accepted legend has it that during the building's construction, one young worker was standing on a scaffold when he was startled by the sound of an airplane flying overhead. Craning his neck upward to get a better look, he lost his balance and fell. His body crashed through a skylight and landed directly on the stage. So much blood poured from his shattered body that the bloodstains on the hardwood floor could not be scrubbed away. Some longtime employees of the university believe that if the present flooring were removed, the bloody imprint of a man's body could still be distinguished.

Other explanations have also been offered for the origin of the haunting at Van Meter. According to a variation of the preceding story, the first contractor of Van Meter Auditorium had trouble laying the foundation because the concrete would pour into the caves undermining the university. Before long, his finances ran out, and he became bankrupt. In desperation, he flung himself into the excavation, landing in the wet concrete below. Some people familiar with the history and lore of Western Kentucky University claim that it was the founder of Western Kentucky University, Henry Hardin Cherry, who fell from the lobby staircase late one night and broke his neck inside the auditorium.

Reports of ghostly activity began soon after Van Meter Auditorium was completed. Students alone in the building at night said that they often heard the sounds of footsteps or doors slamming. When the administration of Western Kentucky University moved into the auditorium, the number of unexplained occurrences escalated. Employees returning to work in the morning would find rooms in shambles, chairs overturned, papers reshuffled, and files missing. Custodians working the night shift would lock the front door at closing time, then check it again at night, only to find it unlocked, even though they were the only ones on campus with keys to the door. James Brown, an employee of Western Kentucky University since 1966, claimed that a performance of *Carmen* was interrupted by a very strange occurrence: "While a young girl strolled across the stage, one red spotlight suddenly beamed on the girl. Normally, I wouldn't have given it a second thought. But the fact that it was the spotlight used in the death scene made it rather strange." Brown was not convinced, though, that the building's ghost was somehow responsible for the sudden appearance of the light: "It was not impossible for the light to switch on by itself because at the time, Western had very poor lighting equipment."

Brian Loader, a student from Louisville, Kentucky, claimed that a mysterious blue light was responsible for the eradicable bloodstain on the stage: "When they started to have play rehearsals in Van Meter, one night Dr. Woods seemed awfully upset because a blue light floated out from the vents under the stage. The chandeliers would shake [and] the chairs would rumble. One night, the curtains fell down, and it got so bad no one would stay in Van Meter after the sun went down. They couldn't even have practices. They had to practice in the afternoons. One night, a young lighting technician was up in the scaffolding up above the stage adjusting lights and the blue light came out. He was so frightened that he lost his footing and fell to his death to the stage. Well, naturally, his head and bones and everything were crushed. After that, supposedly, the bloodstain kept coming up through the floor, and they couldn't get rid of it. They tried everything. They sanded the floor. They used everything you could think of on it. As you know, recently, Van Meter has been renovated. A whole new floor and stairs have been added, and the stain is still coming up through the floor."

William Long, technical coordinator at Van Meter Auditorium, became a firm believer in ghosts as the result of a bizarre experience he had there about a month after the Bowling Green Warren County Junior Miss Pageant in 1977. After the pageant, he went through the building turning off the lights and locking the doors. "After I had cut the lights out," Long said, "I went to the rear of Van Meter where my car was parked. When I looked up, the lights were on again. I just thought to myself, 'Hum, the ghost,' and went home." Ever since that night, Long said, he always tried to get out of there as soon as possible after he finished setting up lighting equipment.

The spectral activity at Van Meter Auditorium continued into the 1980s. In 1981, a Mark Twain impersonator visited the university to present one of the writer's famous lectures. The actor asked the faculty member in charge of the program to come to his dressing room to let him know when it was time to go on stage. The faculty member was going over his notes when he saw the actor in full makeup standing in the entrance to the stage. After a few minutes, the faculty member noticed that the actor was gone, so he went to the dressing room to get him. The actor asked him, "Why didn't you come to get me like I asked you to?" The faculty member replied, "Because I thought I saw you standing there in the door." To date, this is the only physical manifestation of the ghost of Van Meter Auditorium.

Most of the students at Western Kentucky University have acknowledged the possible existence of ghosts in Van Meter Auditorium. Senior Deedee Bush dismissed the theory that some of the people who have sensed ghosts in the auditorium have overactive imaginations. "Those who rationalize and try to come up with a solution," she said, "are just copping out." Martha Parks, a senior who was accidentally locked in Van Meter one night, said, "It didn't scare me because I just accept that there are things that just cannot be explained." Parks went on to say that anyone who is skeptical "should go to Van Meter about two A.M., and then see if you don't believe in ghosts."

Western Kentucky University is located at 1 Big Red Way, Bowling Green, Kentucky; phone: 270-745-0111.

LOUISIANA

The *Delta Queen*

When one thinks of bed and breakfasts, steamboats do not, as a rule, automatically come to mind. The *Delta Queen,* the last remaining overnight stern-wheel steampaddler, offers its passengers a taste of the splendor of the golden era of steamboating in New Orleans. From the amply trimmed grand stairway to the Texas lounge with its crystal chandeliers, the *Delta Queen* is a floating museum, a time capsule left over from a more elegant age. Guests are treated in grand style. Many of the suites and staterooms have brass beds, as well as climate control, carpeting, and private baths. Musicians, comedians, piano players, and an organist for the calliope keep passengers entertained until late at night. Even one of the ship's late captains—Captain Mary Greene—is said to make occasional visits to the grand old steamboat.

Mary Greene's husband—Captain Gordon C. Greene—founded the Delta Queen Steamboat Company just as the era of the steamboat was coming to a close around the turn of the century. He started out with a single steamboat, the *H. K. Bedford.* Soon thereafter, he married Mary Becker from Marietta, Ohio. In 1895, his wife, Mary, joined the handful of licensed riverboat pilots in the United States. After Captain Greene died in 1927, Mary assumed ownership of the company, along with her sons Tom and Chris. Following Chris's death in 1943, Tom decided to enlarge the Delta Queen Steamboat Company. In 1946, he purchased the *Delta Queen,* which had been built in 1926. During World War II, it was painted gray and commandeered by the U.S. Army. At a cost of $750,000 the *Delta Queen* was completely renovated by the Greenes. It made its maiden voyage on June 30, 1948. Captain Mary Greene, who was one of only two qualified female pilots on the Mississippi, piloted the vessel in the early months. She loved the life of a steamboat captain so much that she lived in a specially fitted room on the *Delta Queen,* Cabin 109. She died less than a year later after having been a steamboat captain for fifty-five years. Before her death, she told friends and loved ones, "If I were to live over again, I wouldn't miss a day of the life I've enjoyed."

A strict teetotaler all her life, Mary apparently expects her rules prohibiting drinking on board the steamboat to be followed to this day. Soon after her death, a series of unexplained accidents ensued when the first bar was opened in the forward passenger lounge. The most unnerving accident occurred one night in the 1950s when a barge crashed through the forward passenger lounge. Incredibly, the name of the barge was *Mary Greene.*

Mary Greene's spiritual presence has been felt on board the steamboat in other ways as well. In 1982 first mate Mike Williams was sleeping in his bunk during a winter layover when he was awakened at 1:30 A.M. by the sound of someone whispering "psst" in his ear. He had no sooner drifted back to sleep when he was awakened once more by the "psst" sound. Because he was supposed to be the only person on board at the time, he decided to get out of bed and investigate. He was at the bottom of the staircase when he heard a door slam in the cabin room. At the foot of the staircase, he detected a gurgling sound down in the engine room. He climbed down the stairs and discovered water rushing in from a hole that had rusted through a pipe.

Mike is convinced that Mary woke him up that night to prevent her ship from sinking.

Mike's next ghostly encounter aboard the *Delta Queen* took place a few weeks later. Another employee, Myra Fugat, sent Mike a note from the purser's office, indicating that she had just received a note from an elderly lady in the cabin area. According to the note, the lady was sick and wanted someone to check in on her. Mike walked down to the lady's cabin and knocked on the door. When no one answered, he let himself in and found the room to be unoccupied. Thinking that Myra had sent him to the wrong room by mistake, Mike went to the purser's office, where he found Myra in a state of panic. She said that she looked through a window and saw an old lady looking back at her. As Mike and Myra were walking back to her cabin, she stopped in front of one of the historic photos hanging from the wall in the hallway. Pointing to a picture of Mary Greene, she said, "That's her. That's the lady who stared at me through the window." Myra stuck to her story, even after Mike told her that Captain Greene died in the 1940s.

Other people have seen the ghost of Mary Greene as well. Mary Richardson, who was working as a musician on board the *Delta Queen* at the time, was reading in one of the lounges late one night when she saw an older woman walk past her. Richardson said she did a double take and looked back, but the woman was gone. When this happened the third night in a row, Richardson mentioned the incident to the cruise director, who showed her a picture of Mary Greene. "Is this the woman you saw?" he asked. "Yes," Richardson said, "that's who I saw."

Mary's ghost is frequently seen wearing a green housecoat. Captain Gabriel Chengary says that her ghost is frequently sighted in her green housecoat walking through in and around the bars and lounges. Chengary claims that she even opened and closed a door at one of his cocktail parties. Sherry Vetter, a garage owner's wife from Oakland, California, had a very close encounter with the ghost of the *Delta Queen*. During a trip with her mother-in-law, Sherry was stricken with the flu. Unable to rise from her bed, Sherry spent an entire day in their cabin right next to the Betty Blake Lounge. The next morning, Sherry thanked her mother-in-law for giving her an aspirin, mopping her brow, and tucking her in sometime during the afternoon. Her mother-in-law said that it couldn't have been her because she had spent the entire day on shore. Sherry rejected any suggestion that she had dreamt the visit. To this day, she maintains that a mature woman in a green housecoat looked after her when she was sick.

The ghost in the green housecoat also appeared to Phyllis Duke, an entertainer aboard the *Delta Queen*. Duke said that she was on her way to the restroom when she saw a lady in what she described as a "long, green velvet robe." As the ghost turned a corner, she disappeared. Duke told her story to the captain, who replied, "We have a ghost on board. It is the ghost of Mary Greene."

The Delta Queen Steamboat Company is located at Robin Street Wharf, New Orleans, Louisiana; phone: 504-586-0631 or 800-543-7637.

Griffon House

New Orleans may well be the most haunted city in the entire United States. Over the centuries, conflicts between various nationalities and ethnic groups have left behind a legacy of tragedy that is an important element in New Orleans's history and lore. Tales of murder and betrayal abound in the city, especially the French Quarter, where houses like the infamous Lalaurie Mansion are mandatory stopping-off points for the city's ghost tours. Interestingly enough, one of the most haunted houses in the entire city—Griffon House—has received scant attention from writers or tour groups, possibly because it is located not in the popular Quarter, but in the Irish Channel, a neighborhood situated between the Garden District and the Mississippi River. Like many houses in New Orleans, this old home suffered through a period of neglect and decline but was eventually restored by owners who respected the role it played in the city's history. It may be the house's haunted history, however, that has driven off curiosity seekers and, thereby, kept it veiled in obscurity.

The Griffon House was built in 1852 by Adam Griffon. In its original state, Griffon House was an elegant place, suitable for entertaining the city's most prestigious families. At the outbreak of the Civil War, the Griffon family abandoned their fine home, knowing full well that New Orleans's strategic location at the mouth of the Mississippi River would make it a prime target. In 1862, shortly after the Griffons left New Orleans, the Griffon House was one of the buildings selected by Union general Benjamin Butler's troops for the housing of ammunition and supplies. The soldiers assigned the duty of assessing the building's value as a storage facility were greeted by the rattling of chains and ghastly groans as soon as they walked through the front door. Tracing the source of the sounds to one of the upstairs room, the soldiers warily climbed the stairs. They found nothing on the second floor, but in the third-floor attic, they discovered a grisly scene. Several slaves in various states of starvation, their bodies covered with maggot-infested wounds, were found shackled to the walls. The slaves were removed from the attic and taken to another house that was serving as a field hospital.

After the house was scrubbed and cleaned, it was used as a barracks for soldiers and prisoners. Two of the men held as prisoners in the Griffon House were soldiers who had violated General Butler's rule against looting. As it turned out, the prisoners were actually Confederate soldiers who had donned Union uniforms in the hope that the Yankees would not shoot their own comrades. As part of the coverup, the men sang "John Brown's Body" over and over again, usually while drinking whiskey. However, when they learned that Yankees were not exempt from General Butler's anti-looting ruling, the two men hit upon a scheme to cheat the executioners. After bribing a guard to get them a brace of pistols, the two soldiers lay down next to each other on a bed. Placing their pistols against each other's hearts, the two men counted to three and pulled the triggers. Alarmed by the gunfire, the guards rushed into the room, only to find the corpses of their prisoners lying on a mattress so soaked with blood that a large puddle had collected under the bed.

Following the Civil War, the Griffon House was turned into a lamp factory. One night, a black janitor was cleaning up on the second floor after hours when he heard the sound of a pair of heavy boots clomping through a door that opened by itself. He could tell that he was in the presence of another person, even though no one was standing in the doorway. A moment later, he heard the sound of another pair of boots, accompanied by strange laughter. When the laughing voices began singing "John Brown's Body," the janitor dropped his broom, dashed down the stairs, and ran out the front door.

Another morning, the owners of the lamp factory arrived at work earlier than usual. They had just entered the building when a block of cement came tumbling down the stairs, barely missing them. An investigation produced nothing, not even footprints on the freshly painted floor. The proprietors never did find out how the chunk of cement got there.

A short time later, a widow rented an apartment in the Griffon House. She was sewing in her apartment on the second floor, staring out her window at Constance Street, when she noticed a red spot on her arm. She wiped it off and continued sewing. When another spot appeared on her arm, she looked upward and gazed in horror at the blood oozing out of a crack in the ceiling. Screaming at the top of her lungs, the woman ran down the stairs. The next day, as her relatives were helping her move out of the Griffon House, they noticed two blue-clad figures standing in an upper-story window. They could plainly hear a pair of drunken voices singing "John Brown's Body."

The Griffon House went through a series of transformations in the next few years, serving as a mattress plant and a perfume bottling company in the early 1900s. In the 1920s, the house was used as a hiring hall for stevedores. Before it was abandoned entirely, an elderly man rebuilt air conditioners in the house until he disappeared without a trace. Neighbors recalled hearing him talk about seeing "strange things" in the Griffon House, but he never elaborated. After the house had fallen into a state of disrepair, a boy named William Fleming took two of his friends and a pair of dogs there to look for ghosts. They went upstairs where the floor had been ripped up and began walking on the joists. Suddenly, a door blew open. A blast of cold air chilled the boys to the bone and caused one of the dogs to fall off the joists to his death below. The boys immediately beat a hasty retreat out of the Griffon House.

In 1951, a devastating hurricane changed the face of the Irish Channel forever. Two hundred and seventy-five people lost their lives in the storm. Property damage amounted to thirteen million dollars. The old slave quarters behind the Griffon House was completely swept away. When debris was removed from the yard, workers discovered a tunnel leading from the house under the street. An investigation failed to turn up a reason for the tunnel's existence, but workers did find some old uniforms and an old chest bound with chains. For the next twenty years, many of the old houses damaged by the hurricane were abandoned, offering drug addicts an ideal place to "crash." Derelicts never stayed very long in the Griffon House, though. They claimed that they saw two figures they described as "white men wearing police uniforms" walking through the walls and singing "old-timey songs."

Kathleen and Anthony Jones bought the Griffon House in the late 1970s. In an interview conducted by Richard Winer in 1979, they said that they entreated with the ghosts to give them a hand in restoring the house, but they never did. Despite their display of fearlessness, the Joneses worked on the repairs only in the daytime, never at night. Winer also interviewed a black man living across the street who told him that he was mounting a spare tire in front of the Griffon House one night when he heard the unmistakable sounds of laughter and breaking glass.

After that night, he understood why most people in the neighborhood crossed the street when passing by the Griffon House.

Griffon House is a private residence at 1447 Constance Street, New Orleans, Louisiana.

The Myrtles

ST. FRANCISVILLE

Some of the most magnificent antebellum mansions in the entire South can be found in Louisiana. Many of these palatial homes can be found nestled in scenic little towns along the bayou. St. Francisville, known to locals as being located in "English Louisiana," is the home of one of the state's most beautiful—and notorious—plantation houses. The Myrtles was built in 1796 by General David Bradford, famed leader of the Whiskey Rebellion. After George Washington put a price on his head, Bradford fled Pennsylvania for the wilds of Louisiana. Bradford soon settled into the comfortable lifestyle of a southern gentleman farmer. At one time, he owned 650 acres planted in cotton and indigo. Today, the Myrtles' early nineteenth-century splendor has been lovingly restored. Each of the house's twenty-eight rooms is filled with priceless antiques, many of which had once belonged to one of the previous owners, Ruffin Gray Stirling. Visitors to this fashionable bed and breakfast will not only sample the house's period atmosphere, but they might also discover why the Myrtles has been called America's most haunted house by the Smithsonian Institute.

The Myrtles did not begin acquiring its bloody reputation until after it was sold to a law school friend of Bradford's, Judge Clark Woodruffe, in 1817. At age thirty-five, Judge Woodruffe married Bradford's daughter, Sarah Matilda, when she was fourteen years old. They had three daughters: Mary, Jane, and Octavia. He engaged in countless trysts with a wide variety of women during his marriage, including the French mulatto governess of his children, a lovely young woman named Chloe. Before long, the judge's wife found out that Chloe had been sleeping with her husband, and he was forced to end the affair. Now that Chloe was no longer the judge's "favorite," she took advantage of her privileged position as house slave to pick up information regarding other slaves on the plantation, such as impending sales to other plantations. One day, the judge caught Chloe eavesdropping on a conversation he was having in his office with a crony of his concerning a shady business deal. In a fit of rage, he caught Chloe by the arm and cut off her ear. Worried that she would be sent to the fields, Chloe set about to restore herself in Mrs. Woodruffe's good graces. Wearing a green bandanna to conceal her wound, Chloe mixed oleander into a birthday cake, hoping that the poisonous plant would make the family slightly sick so that she could nurse them back to health and thereby prove that she was best suited to manage the domestic duties on the plantation. Judge Woodruffe was away on a business trip and Octavia was in bed, so only Mary, Jane, and their mother ate the cake. Unfortunately, Chloe miscalculated. She put too much oleander in the cake mix; as a result, the two little girls and their mother became terribly ill from eating the lethal dessert and eventually died. When she discovered what she had done, Chloe ran out to the fields and confessed her crime to the other slaves. To keep the judge and other outraged whites from taking vengeance on them, they hanged Chloe from one of the great live oaks beside the house and threw her corpse in the Mississippi River.

However, that was not the end of Chloe's stay at the Myrtles. She seems to have resumed her role as governess of the Myrtles. Guests have seen a lady with a green turban walking around the grounds at night. One former owner of the Myrtles, Frances Kermeen, was sleeping in a downstairs bedroom in 1987 when she was awakened by a black woman in a dark gown wearing a green turban. The specter was holding an "old-time" candlestick. As soon as Frances screamed, the figure vanished. Occasionally, she is seen peeking into a bedroom at night, almost as if she is checking in to see if the sleeping person is all right. Some women report being tucked in a night, just as if they were a small child. Chloe has also been credited with re-setting the thermostats and switching the lights on and off.

The ghosts of the murdered children have also appeared at the Myrtles. The spirits have blond hair and wear white dresses. They are frequently sighted playing together on the grounds. One guest who arrived at the bed and breakfast late at night saw a little girl sitting on the edge of a bed and swinging her legs. Thinking that she was the daughter of friends of his who were also staying at the inn, he remarked that their daughter certainly had grown. When they replied that they had left her at home, he checked around to see if any other families with little girls had checked in. None had. The sounds of giggling and weeping have been heard in the house when no other girls are present. The ghostly girls often show themselves to children, who report to their parents afterward that they have been playing with their "girly friends."

The spirit of the little girls' mother has also been seen, but only rarely. When she does make an appearance, it is usually on the main staircase. Tour guide Hester Eby said that one day she was walking down the main staircase when she sensed that someone was walking right behind her. When she stopped, the other person stopped, too. Hester was certain that it was Sarah's ghost, who had been seen on the staircase before.

The next person to be murdered at the mansion was a lawyer named William Winter, who owned the Myrtles from 1860 to 1871. One evening, he was called outside by a stranger sitting on a horse. Just as Winter opened the door and walked onto the front porch, he was shot in the chest. He staggered back into the house and struggled up the stairs. Hearing the gunshot, his wife hurried out of her upstairs bedroom just in time to see her husband collapse on the stairs. William Winter died in his wife's arms on the seventeenth step. Over the years, Winter's heavy footsteps have been heard plodding across the floor and climbing the main staircase. The sound always ends on the seventeenth stair.

A total of ten people have been murdered here, and one resident committed suicide, so it is small wonder that a host of other spirits are reputed to haunt the premises. A Confederate soldier who was brought to the Myrtles when it was used as a hospital has been seen lying on a bed while his wounded leg is being dressed by unseen hands. Another Confederate soldier marches up and down the front porch. A maid walks through the bedrooms, making up the beds that have been rumpled by a ghostly child. A voodoo priestess hovers over the still form of a young girl. Union soldiers who were shot in a skirmish on the property haunt the grounds. A grumpy ghost hurls a candlestick across the drawing room in a fit of temper. A slender young man in a fancy vest who was murdered over a gambling debt walks around in an upper room where cigar smoke can still be smelled. The youngest ghost is that of a caretaker who was stabbed to death while trying to foil an attempted robbery in 1927. Sometimes, after all of the guests have fallen asleep, they are awakened by the sounds of music, laughter, and clinking glasses, coming, apparently, from a spectral party.

Other strange things have happened at the Myrtles for which there seems to be no rational explanation. In one of the hallways is a mirror with a scratched surface. The mirror has been resilvered many times to remove the defects, but the scratches always return. Some people say that the scratches appear to have been made by someone trapped inside the mirror. Another smudge resembles the hand print of a small child. By way of explaining the mysterious marks on the mirror, the tour guides cite the superstition regarding the necessity of draping a cloth over a mirror during a funeral to keep a living spirit from being trapped inside.

Some female guests have had their sleep interrupted by what seems to be an amorous male spirit. They claim to have felt the presence of someone in bed with them in the middle of the night. Sometimes in the morning, women have found the impression of a figure in the bed where no one slept the night before. Needless to say, these accounts are usually viewed as being funny by everyone except the women who shared their bed with the ghost.

Victor C. Klein, author of *New Orleans Ghosts,* claims that Remy A. Bosio, a medical technician at the Veterans Hospital in New Orleans, actually photographed one of the ghosts at the Myrtles in the summer of 1989. The photograph depicts the spectral form of a young girl in period dress. Bosio says that four members of his tour group saw the girl wave to them from inside the house as they climbed the front steps. He is convinced that the girl is the spirit of Sarah, the little girl who was treated by the voodoo woman.

Apparently, one of the ghosts at the Myrtles is not even human. For years, people who have taken photographs at the mansion have discovered that they captured on film the image of a cat when no feline was present. The cat is clearly visible in several photographs hanging from one of the walls in the Myrtles. According to the historical records, several of the previous owners of the Myrtles had cats as pets.

Not surprisingly, the Myrtles has been the subject of several investigations into the paranormal occurrences at the bed and breakfast. In the mid-1990s, the Office of Scientific Investigation and Researchers looked into the ghosts at the Myrtles. For three days and nights, they measured temperature, radioactivity, and electromagnetic fields. By the third day, they had found nothing more than a few cold spots. But at 1:03 A.M. on their last day there, an alarm clock went off. Then four more alarms went off as well. As far as the investigators knew, the alarm clocks had not been set by anyone in the house. The team left later that morning with plenty of anecdotal evidence but no hard proof that the house was actually haunted.

Probably the most horrifying investigation to be held at the Myrtles involved a camera crew from a Baton Rouge television station. A news reporter who was spending the night in the mansion was joking around on camera, making silly statements such as, "I feel someone picking at my back. Oh, I'm so scared!" All at once, while the cameras were rolling, the reporter's face turned white, and he became completely quiet. Without warning, he jumped out of his chair and refused to go back on camera to finish his report. At his request, the screen went blank. No explanation for the reporter's behavior was ever given.

Another visitor who had a shocking experience at the Myrtles was a famous chef who had come to the Myrtles to prepare a special dinner in the restaurant. Later that afternoon, he told the management that he was going to stay after closing hours to prepare some special sauces. The next morning, the chef failed to report to work. When the manager called him to find out what had happened, the chef refused to discuss it. He swore that he would never set foot on the grounds again. The chef even refused to return long enough to retrieve the cooking utensils he had left there.

The tour guides think they know why the Myrtles has seen more than its share of tragedy over the years. When General David Bradford bought the property for $1.25 an acre, he thought he was getting a real bargain. What he did not realize, though, was that the land was originally taken by the Spanish from the Tunecah Indians, who had used it as their burial ground. Perhaps this is why the spirit of a nude Indian maiden has been seen sitting in the backyard gazebo. And, as everyone knows, it is bad luck to build a house over Indian graves.

This two-story bed-and-breakfast inn lies three miles north of St. Francisville on Highway 61. The address is Myrtles Plantation, P.O. Box 1100, St. Francisville, LA 70775; phone: 504-635-6277.

Oak Alley

VACHERIE

The pavilion formed by the twenty-eight great, intertwined oaks of Oak Alley is not unique in the South, but one would be hard pressed to find a grander entrance to any antebellum home in Louisiana. The plantation's trademark oak trees are so distinctive that its original name—*Beau Sejour*—was changed to Oak Alley in the late nineteenth century, probably because it was the name Mississippi riverboat captains used to refer to it. For locals, the name "Oak Alley" also conjures up images of ghostly visitations. Like so many haunted places in the South, Oak Alley's ghost stories were generated by the tragic fate of a beautiful young girl.

Oak Alley was built by the French sugar planter Jacques Telesphore Roman in 1839. Jacques lived in the house with his wife, Celine, and his daughter, Louise. Returning home from business trips to New Orleans, Roman routinely rode steamboats to his private landing and walked the half mile to his Greek Revival–style home. Jacques Roman died of tuberculosis in 1848, only nine years after his house was completed, initiating a melancholy legacy of pain and suffering that eventually involved his daughter. In the years immediately preceding the Civil War, Louise was courted by a number of eligible young men. One day, one of her suitors rode his horse up the broad avenue of oaks. Standing in the front door, Louise could tell that he had been drinking—a lot! Ever mindful of her status as a refined young Creole woman, Louise ran up the broad staircase. Agitated, no doubt, by the young man's insistent pounding on the front door, she tripped on her crinoline petticoat and fell. As she rolled down the stairs, one of the crinoline wires tore loose from its sheath and gouged her leg.

Despite the ministrations of the servants and the local physician, the cut in Louise's leg failed to heal. Before long, gangrene set in, and her leg was amputated just below the knee. After she recovered from the operation, Louise faced the bitter truth. As a cripple, she could no longer attend the balls held in the other fashionable plantation homes lining the levee. Even worse, she probably would never find anyone willing to marry her. Rather than spend her days shut away inside her beautiful home as a recluse, Louise entered a nunnery in St. Louis. A few years later, she founded her own convent in New Orleans. After Louise died, she was buried along with her amputated leg, which her mother had preserved for her in a small tomb in the garden at Oak Alley.

Oak Alley fell into disrepair early in the twentieth century. It has now been restored and converted into a bed and breakfast. Guests residing in the five beautiful guest rooms inside the main house or in the Creole cottages beside the house marvel at the authentic wallpaper, period furniture, and lacy drapes. The beauty of Oak Alley is a living memorial to the mistress of the house, Celine Roman, whose impeccable taste is evident everywhere.

However, Celine's presence can be felt in other ways as well. Tour guides Helen Dumas and Alma Mitchell have identified her as the veiled lady in black/dark gray who has been seen by tourists for many years. The Lady in Black has also been seen riding on horseback under the plantation's quarter mile of oak trees. People have also seen her walking on the balcony on the second floor and on the widow's walk on the crown of the roof, possibly awaiting her husband's return from New Orleans.

Celine's daughter, Louise, also seems to have returned to Oak Alley. A photograph taken by a tourist in what was thought to be an empty room clearly shows the image of a young blonde girl dressed in a hoop skirt and sitting in a chair. Dumas and Mitchell claim to have had personal encounters with the spirit inside the mansion. Both ladies have been pinched just below the knee as they walk up and down the stairs.

The tour guides have reported other ghostly occurrences at Oak Alley that cannot easily be attributed to a specific individual. They frequently hear footsteps on the second floor and weird noises in the attic as they close down for the night. Helen Dumas has heard a horse-drawn carriage ride up to the front of the house, just as Jacques Roman would have done over one hundred and fifty years earlier when he returned from New Orleans. Alma Mitchell said that one day she was standing in an upstairs hallway when she sensed the presence of someone standing so close to her that she could feel the person's body heat. When she spun around to see who it was, no one was there. Alma was paralyzed with fear, anchored where she stood, until she summoned up the strength to scream and run down the stairs.

The ghostly activity at Oak Alley escalated to the point that a female psychic was summoned to determine if the house was truly haunted. After walking through the mansion, the woman reported that the house contained the spirits of several of the families who had lived there long ago. She singled out one room—the one where one of the owners of Oak Alley, Mrs. Andrew Stuart, died in 1972—as being filled with the ghosts of children and babies. Alma Mitchell and Helen Dumas did not need a psychic to tell them that Oak Alley is haunted. Both ladies carry around a rosary and holy water whenever they go inside the house, just in case they run into one of Oak Alley's former inhabitants.

Oak Alley is located in Vacherie, Louisiana. Take 1–10 southeast across the Sunshine Bridge. Turn left at the end of the bridge onto Highway 18. Drive sixteen miles to the Oak Alley Plantation, 3645 Highway 18, Vacherie, Louisiana; phone: 504-265-2151.

MISSISSIPPI

The Ell Davis Woods

EUDORA

Mississippi abounds with ghosts, but they are by no means confined to houses. Not only are there haunted graveyards in the Magnolia State, but there are also haunted roads, hollows, creeks, fords, rivers, trees, wells, coal chutes, and woodlands. The best-known patch of haunted woods in Mississippi is the Ell Davis Woods. This strip of woodland, located on a bluff about six miles east of Eudora, appears to be just another scenic spot tucked away in the Mississippi backwoods. The large body of lore surrounding the area explains why long-time residents of DeSoto County know better than to pass through it at night.

According to legend, the woods gets its name from a man named Ell Davis, who quarreled with another man over a girl in the early nineteenth century. One day, while Davis was splitting rails, Williams rode up to Davis and declared, "I've come to kill you!" Despite Davis's plea for mercy, Williams gunned him down in cold blood, initiating the woods' haunted reputation. Some people claim that Davis's ghost guards a cache of money that he buried close to his cabin. Others say that his restless spirit still searches for the girl he loved. Regardless of which reason is correct, the ghost that haunts these woods is clearly an uneasy spirit.

One of the first encounters with the ghost of the Ell Davis Woods occurred around the turn of the century. One evening,

Mrs. J. B. Riley of Eudora and two of her sons were crossing these woods when they heard something like a bed tick being dragged through the leaves behind them. She tried to keep them talking to raise their spirits, but the boys could not help looking back over their shoulders. Suddenly, two strange, exotic-looking birds flew down out of the sky and lit on a bush ten yards from the woman and her sons. After a few seconds, the birds flew into the woods and vanished. Their disappearance was accompanied by a low, unearthly moaning sound. Mrs. Riley and her sons wasted no time heading straight home.

A few years later, a man named Braxton Redford was traveling through the Ell Davis Woods about ten o'clock at night when an oddly shaped figure walked into the path ahead of him. Thinking that the man was a friend of his who was trying to scare him, Braxton called out, "Jim, if that's you, you'd better speak!" Braxton waited a few moments for a reply. Receiving none, he called out again, "Jim, if you don't speak, I'll shoot!" Concerned that the man could be someone he knew, Braxton fired his rifle over the figure. All at once, the strange being struck itself on the chest, screamed, and lunged toward Braxton. In the moonlight, Braxton realized, to his horror, that the thing had no head! Braxton began firing rapidly at the shambling thing, but his shots had no effect. Panic stricken, Braxton turned and ran. In his rush to escape the ghost, he tripped over a wire fence. He rose to his feet as fast as he could, ready to run again, but was relieved to see that the phantom had disappeared.

The next reported sighting took place during a midnight 'possum hunt in the Ell Davis Woods a few years later. One September night, the Oswalt, Riley, and Williams boys were chasing a 'possum that their dogs were trailing some distance ahead. Suddenly, a great black dog began chasing the hunters. They fired wildly but were unable to hit him. The black dog chased them for at least a mile. Then, in the moonlight, they saw the dog jump up on a stump, let out a blood-curdling howl, and disappear.

A few months later, the mysterious black dog made another appearance. A man named Williams and his family were coming home from church when the great black dog ran out of the woods. When it reached the Williams's wagon, it stopped, looked at Mr. Williams, barked, and disappeared. Two weeks later, Mr. Williams died.

Another resident of Eudora, Jim McCarver, walked out to a spring in the woods to fetch a bucket of water. As he rose up from filling the bucket, he was shocked to see a headless man standing beside him. A voice from the figure asked for a drink of water. Without dropping the bucket, Jim turned and hurried away. Afterward, Jim said that the thing must have been mighty thirsty, because it followed him all the way to the clearing back of his house. Jim ran into the house and slammed the door behind him. After he caught his breath, he looked out of his window. The headless figure was gone. When he looked in his bucket, there was only a cup of water left in it.

Just outside of the Ell Davis Woods on the old Eudora-Memphis Road stood an old Afro-American church called Johnston Chapel that was the site of a seriocomic incident. One night in the early 1900s, a resident of Eudora named Will Burrus was on his way back to Eudora, riding horseback. To get out of the rain, he took refuge inside the church, where a funeral had been held that afternoon. As Burrus stood inside the door, holding his horse's bridle, he heard a noise from the front of the church. In the enveloping darkness, he could not make out what was causing the noise. All he could tell was that it was moving closer and closer to him. When the noise seemed to be just a few feet in front of him, Burrus was suddenly confronted by someone all in white. Burrus turned and tried to run away, but the thing grabbed him from behind. As Burrus struggled to escape the grasp of the wraith, it began to pray: "Oh! Bless the Lord! Glory be! I knew God would send my son back to me. Come on, I'll take you home!" Finally, Burrus pulled loose and hurried out the door. Burrus immediately jumped on his horse and made it home in record time. The next day, Burrus found out that the ghost was probably the mother of a Negro boy who had been buried at the church that day. She was there praying for the return of her boy, and when Burrus walked into the church that night, she believed, mistakenly, that her prayers had been answered. Burrus later admitted that if this church had been anywhere else but in the vicinity of the Ell Davis Woods, he probably would not have been nearly as scared.

Many other people have had bizarre experiences in the Ell Davis Woods over the years. Travelers riding through the woods have heard strange noises and seen balls of fire rising up from the woods at all hours of the night. By the end of the twentieth century, reports of ghostly activity in the Ell Davis Woods had practically died out, probably because people avoid the place as much as possible, thanks to improvements made in Highway 304.

The Ell Davis Woods is on a bluff six miles east of Eudora, Mississippi, on Highway 304. It is visible from the highway.

King's Tavern

ing's Tavern Restaurant stands on the outskirts of Natchez, Mississippi. Constructed sometime in the 1760s, it is one of the oldest buildings in a city renowned for its antebellum homes. In the late eighteenth and early nineteenth centuries, the structure was a mail run and a tavern where weary travelers on the Natchez Trace sought refuge from the elements. The inn derives its name from Richard King, who acquired the building in 1789 and converted it into a tavern. His guests ranged from the famous to the infamous. Politicians such as Aaron Burr and Andrew Jackson boarded there, but so did a host of outlaws, such as Big Harpe. Like many frontier outposts in that period of history, it was frequently the scene of fierce altercations between drunken guests who settled their arguments with guns and knives. Some residents of Natchez believe that the walls of the old tavern still resonate with elements from its violent past.

Generations of owners, servers, and patrons have had paranormal experiences in the restaurant. Susan Adams, director of a historic home in Natchez called Magnolia, believes that there are at least two ghosts at King's Tavern, both of whom are mischievous. The most playful of the tavern's ghost is the spirit of Richard King's mistress, a woman known only as Madeline. Employees of the tavern claim that she seems to enjoy water.

Water has dripped from the ceiling at spots where there are

no pipes. One of the owners of the tavern, Yvonne Scott, said that when the inn first opened under her management, there was no hot water upstairs. While she was discussing the plumbing with a friend, hot water started running out of a dead pipe. Madeline has been credited with other phenomena in the tavern as well. The heavy door of the waitress station has stopped in mid-swing. Alarms in the restaurant have gone off at 5:00 A.M. and 6:00 A.M. for no apparent reason. After this happens, an inside door on the second floor is always standing open. Lights that have been turned off go back on after the employees have left the building. Waitresses walking into the pantry storage rooms have seen balls of light bouncing off the walls.

Madeline even "gets up close and personal" with the staff once in a while. Beverly Franzen, a Tavern employee in the 1970s, said that one day when she was upstairs alone, she heard a voice say "hello": "I looked around and there was no one there. When she said 'hello' again, I left." Yvonne Scott said that she once felt someone touch her shoulder. When she turned around to see who it was, there was no one there. The attic seems to be Madeline's private domain. In the 1980s, a woman in a restroom was looking in the mirror while putting on her lipstick when her image was replaced by that of a young woman with red hair. She exited the restroom very quickly in an agitated state. Employees have gotten the impression that Madeline is very protective of her privacy in this part of the house. Yvonne Scott said that Madeline expresses her displeasure by blowing the light bulbs. One night, she blew every light in the second floor after a group of people walked into the attic.

A waiter at the restaurant claimed that on one occasion, Madeline actually made his job easier. A customer had entered the restaurant late in the evening and had ordered a bottle of wine with his meal. The waiter explained that the wine was kept upstairs in a locked storeroom and the person who had the key had already gone home. All at once, the upstairs dumbwaiter moved down the shaft and stopped on the ground floor. When the waiter opened the door, he was amazed to find the bottle of wine that his guest had ordered.

According to Beverly Franzen, Madeline usually waits a couple of weeks before revealing her approval or disapproval of a new employee. However, when Grover Moberly became manager in 1977, he found evidence of Madeline's presence on his first day of work. While making an inspection of the restaurant on a Monday morning, he walked up to the third-floor bathroom and was shocked to find small footprints all over the floor. Moberly said, "The prints must have been made sometime Sunday night or early Monday morning because the floor was mopped and waxed Sunday. The strange thing is that no living person was up there, especially with feet that small. The footprints measured only seven inches with six toes showing on one foot. From the placement of the footprints, it appeared that someone had just climbed out of the bathtub onto the wooden floor with wet, bare feet. The tracks led from the tub to the lavatory and then proceeded into the clothes closet. The footprints stopped abruptly at the bathroom door. Chills ran up Moberly's spine when he examined the bathtub and found a spider web stretched across it, indicating that no water had been turned on in the tub. At noon the next day, additional footprints were found in the bedroom. No tracks were visible on the floor between the two rooms. Moberly was particularly puzzled by the appearance of this set of footprints because they were not there when he was in the room earlier in the day. Down through the years, employees have heard the sound of footsteps coming from parts of the restaurant where no one was present.

A waitress working in the fall of 2000 said that she can usually sense when Madeline is around. Some mornings, she has walked into the tavern and felt Madeline's presence. Instead of entering the dining area through the swinging doors of the waitress station on these days, she remains on the other side, getting the salads, napkins, and silverware ready. One morning when she felt uneasy, she waited until the feeling subsided and walked through the swinging doors. Glancing at the fireplace area, she was surprised to find little footprints all around it. The waitress shuddered because the footprints were on a part of the floor under which three skeletons were discovered in 1930 when sewage lines were being installed. Later when a chimney partially collapsed near where the skeletons had been found, a jewel encrusted Spanish dagger was found. The discovery of the skeletons and the dagger gave rise the theory that Madeline had been stabbed with the dagger and buried under the tavern.

A psychic who visited the tavern in August 1977 identified two of the spirits in the tavern as being that of a young girl and an Indian chief. The Indian chief's ghost has been sighted primarily in the part of the building that used to be the post office. One day, a little girl asked her mother to identify the reflection of a man in the mirror of the bar. Her mother replied that there was no man in the mirror. Because the child said that the man was wearing a red hat, employees have speculated that the ghost may be the spirit of an Indian who ran the mail up and down the Natchez Trace.

Probably the most disturbing phenomenon that occurs at King's Tavern on a regular basis is the sound of a crying baby. An employee named Sonia Frost heard the baby crying while she was putting crackers on the tables. She combed the inside and the outside of the building but found no sign of a baby's having been there. The crying sound seemed to come from the wall in the post office or from the dumbwaiter on the other side of the wall. The source of the crying has been traced back to a tragic incident that occurred in the tavern in the early 1800s. An outlaw named Big Harpe was in a room in the tavern one night when he heard the sound of crying coming from the adjoining mail room. He entered the room to find a mother sitting on a bed, cradling an infant. Big Harpe took the infant from the woman's arms and slammed it against a wall, killing it instantly.

Danny Scott, the daughter of the owner of King's Tavern has had several unnerving experiences in the old tavern: "I'll be in the building and know I'm totally alone. Then I'll hear somebody call my name. Other times, I'll go upstairs and feel somebody touch my shoulder. When I turn around, there's no one there. Sometimes, the chains hanging in the dining room that used to be the mail room will swing by themselves. They also say that at midnight during a full moon, you can see the ghost of one of the Indian runners standing by the fireplace in the mail room. He likes to run his fingers through the hair of blond women. The attic really bothers me, though. I hate it. The story goes that years ago, a mother left her baby alone up there, and it suffocated. Sometimes when I'm up there, I have trouble catching my breath, like I'm being suffocated. Then after I've been up there, I'll hear the baby crying for days afterwards, like it's reaching out for help."

Even though King's Tavern has been a terrifying place to work at times, most of the employees do not mind sharing the tavern with ghosts. The spirits may be bothersome at times, but they have never done anything malicious. It could be that they simply want to make their presence known.

King's Tavern is located at 619 Jefferson Street, Natchez, Mississippi; phone: 601-446-8845.

Magnolia Hall

Even in a city renowned for the splendor of its antebellum mansions, Magnolia Hall stands out. It was constructed in 1858 in Natchez, Mississippi, by Thomas Henderson, a wealthy cotton planter and merchant. Even though Mr. Henderson owned several plantations, this Greek Revival–style mansion was intended to serve as his "town house." Magnolia Hall was designed to resemble the "brownstone" row houses of New York and Boston. Built at the then-extravagant cost of $8,000, Magnolia Hall was the last great plantation home built in Natchez before the Civil War. It even featured running water in the bedrooms fed by a large cistern in the attic. After 1870, the house was occupied by the Britton family. In the early 1900s, it was converted into a boardinghouse known as "Magnolia Inn." In the twentieth century, Magnolia Hall underwent several conversions. In the 1960s it housed the Trinity Episcopal Day School. In 1976, the owner of the house, Mrs. George Armstrong, gave Magnolia Hall to the Natchez Garden Club. The building was extensively renovated in 1999.

The haunting of Magnolia Hall has its roots in the death of its builder, Thomas Henderson. In January of 1863, Mr. Henderson suffered a debilitating stroke. In her diary, Mr. Henderson's daughter, Julia, wrote, "About half past seven P.M. a dreadful rattling in his throat came on, and seeming at once to realize that his hour had come, he stretched out his hand to those who stood at his bedside, suffering no one retain it very long. It was evident to all who saw it that he meant, 'Goodbye.'" Julia also recorded that in the weeks before he died, her father was trying unsuccessfully to communicate some sort of message.

The presence of Thomas Henderson was first detected several years ago by hostess Judy Grimsley. On a cold, dreary October morning in 1985, she was going through her daily routine of turning on the lights in the building. When she entered the downstairs bedroom where Mr. Henderson died, she noticed the indentation of a head on a pillow. She showed the indented pillow to the caretaker, Kay McNeil McGehee, who could not believe that the housekeeper would have left the pillow in that condition. After fluffing up the pillow, they proceeded to prepare the house for the day's tours.

On the last day of the pilgrimage of Natchez's historic district, Ms. Grimsley noticed that one of the lamps in the downstairs bedroom was blinking strangely, initiating a chain of even stranger occurrences. As rule, Ms. Grimsley refrained from telling tourists that Mr. Henderson had died in the bedroom because some people found this fact to be very upsetting. However, later in the day, a woman who identified herself as a psychic stated that something tragic had happened in that room. The woman proceeded to narrate the story of Thomas Henderson's last days in the house. She said that in his final moments, he was trying to pronounce a word beginning with the letter "m," which she took to mean "medicine." The psychic then asked Ms. Grimsley to hand her an object that had belonged to Mr. Henderson. Ms. Grimsley gave her the family Bible, which became so hot that neither she nor Ms. Grimsley could hold it.

Ms. Grimsley said that there was no way that the sunlight filtering through the room could had heated the book.

Since then, other strange things have grabbed the attention of various witnesses. Footsteps are occasionally heard throughout the house. Doctors and nurses who have toured the house have smelled laudanum, an opiate derivative that was commonly prescribed as medicine in the nineteenth century. On some mornings, hostesses have found evidence in the kitchen that someone in the house had enjoyed a midnight snack. One of the caretakers reported hearing the sound of pictures sliding down the walls at night. The next morning, none of the pictures in the house were found on the floor. She also said that her two Siamese cats bristled every time they stood in front of the main door of the house. The appearance of rocks about six inches wide on a bedroom floor is one of the strangest occurrences. The hostesses have heard a variety of explanations. One visitor said that Mr. Henderson wants people standing in the room to "sleep like a rock." Another tourist suggested that a spirit in the house was trying to communicate the location of buried treasure. According to Ms. Grimsley, something strange happens almost every year in the house.

Several years ago, Ms. Grimsley and a friend of hers were locking up the house at the end of the day. After they walked into the main hall toward the front door, they turned around and glanced at the main staircase. At the top of the stairs, they saw what Ms. Grimsley described as a "great shouldered, shadowy figure." The two ladies looked at each other and did a double take. The figure on the stairs was gone.

In 1998, the director of Magnolia Hall, Susan Adams, said that she was giving a tour of the house to a group of people, and she guided them into the downstairs bedroom. As soon as she mentioned that Mr. Henderson had died there, the outside shutters attached to bedroom window slammed shut. "Everybody jumped," Ms. Adams said, "including me. All I said was, 'Mr. Henderson. How are you today?'" Even though she pretended to be amused, Ms. Adams was actually deeply disturbed because there was no wind blowing at the time.

An informal investigation of the paranormal activity at Magnolia Hall was conducted by radio station WOKK in Meridian, Mississippi, on the night of October 30, 2000. The investigating team from Meridian included Breakfast Bunch disc jockeys Scotty Ray Boyd and Debbie Alexander, contest-winner Ashley McCleary, and me, who was invited along as the "resident expert" on ghosts. WOKK's sister stations from Jackson, Mississippi, and from Monroe, Louisiana, also sent disc jockeys and contest winners. WOKK employees Scott Shepherd and John David Ainsworth had arrived earlier that day to set up video cameras throughout the home so that visitors to the station's Web site could watch the night's happenings live. Jackson psychic Rosemarie Sellner, who was not able to accompany the WOKK "Breakfast Bunch" because of scheduling problems, had agreed to make herself available all evening via telephone.

At 6:13 P.M., we entered the dimly lit entranceway of Magnolia Hall. After taking a tour of the home with long-time hostess Judy Grimsley, we settled down to the business of waiting for something "spooky" to occur. While some members of the team chatted online with interested listeners, the rest of us walked through the upstairs and downstairs rooms. Nothing out of the ordinary really happened until 7:45 when the lights in the men's parlor began turning on and dimming down. Then at 8:40, one of the video cameras directed toward the bedroom where Thomas Henderson had died picked up a strange orb of light hovering around Jackson DJ Jerry Broadway, who was standing by the bed. At the time, Broadway was only four feet away from the camera. The light was not visible to the naked eye.

At 9:10 P.M., Scotty Ray Boyd called up psychic Rosemarie Sellner, who guided the remainder of the investigation that night. First of all, she informed the group that one of the DJs from Monroe, Louisiana, should change his shirt because ghosts do not like the color red. At 9:22, while she was telling the group what to say to make the spirit of Thomas Henderson happy, the crystals hanging from a chandelier in the hallway began to move by themselves. Next, she informed Scotty Ray that he was standing next to something pertaining to a little boy. Scotty Ray immediately contradicted her, insisting that he was standing by the portrait of a little girl. Then the director of Magnolia Hall, Susan Adams, said, "That's not a little girl. It's a little boy." It turned out that the painting was one of two "death portraits" of little boys with long hair. At 9:29, several members of the group observed that the two paintings were moving slightly. At 9:33, Ms. Sellner surprised everyone by announcing that there were more ghosts in the house.

Ten minutes later, one of the most baffling events of the entire evening took place. The psychic had no sooner announced that a female member of the Henderson family was in the music room and that she loved the piano when two very soft plinking sounds from the piano were heard by all seventeen members of the group. Two people immediately rushed into the piano room to see who was playing the piano, but no one was there. I was struck by the fact that the plinking did not sound as if it were being made by someone who was trying to scare the group by striking one of the keys. If it had been, I believe that the sound would have been much louder.

Later, Ms. Sellner said that Mr. Henderson's spirit was moving out of the bedroom and walking down the hallway. Almost immediately, a red light appeared on the Internet camera. It slowly came down the hall and stopped about a foot behind Scotty Ray's back. The light remained there for several minutes. At 11:39, the red light was detected by a bedroom camera.

At 12:09, Ms. Sellner said that Mr. Henderson's spirit could possibly be lured back to the bedroom by the playing of music, so Jerry Broadway began playing the guitar and singing. Suddenly, the white light that had been in Henderson's room began bouncing all over the room. The light stopped moving soon after Jerry stopped playing.

The psychic activity continued well into the early morning, but to a much lesser extent. At 2:07 A.M., green lights and a small blue "cloud" were captured by the bedroom camera. Three minutes later, the hallway camera revealed more red lights near the stairway. No more phenomena were observed.

The next morning, the general consensus among the members of the group was that they had actually witnessed some sort of ghostly event. Admittedly, several of them, including Scotty Ray Boyd, were already prone to believe in spirits before they arrived at the house. At least one cynic was converted by the strange occurrences of the previous night. Susan Adams, the director, admitted that she had become a believer in the paranormal overnight, despite the fact that she had never had a single encounter during her two years at Magnolia Hall. However, Scotty Ray's co-host, Debbie Alexander, remained skeptical, and so did I, primarily because of the wide variety of "glitches" that could have produced the optical phenomena on the computer screen. I must admit, though, that I have no explanation for the eerie notes coming from the antique piano in the room where no one was present. No living person, at least.

To get to Magnolia Hall, take the South Canal Street Exit

from U.S. 84. Turn right on Washington Street until you get to Pearl Street. Turn left on Pearl Street. Magnolia Hall is located at 215 South Pearl Street, Natchez, Mississippi; phone: 610-442-6672.

The *Meridian Star* Building

MERIDIAN

Next door to the Pigford Building in downtown Meridian is the office of the *Meridian Star,* Meridian's only daily newspaper. Today, the *Meridian Star* occupies almost an entire city block. However, back in the 1920s, the part facing 23rd Avenue was a separate building. There was an alley separating the buildings between 22nd Avenue and 23rd Avenue. The back part of the building facing 21st Avenue used to be an old car dealership. The glass-enclosed section of *The Meridian Star* was the show room, and what is now the press room was originally the shop. According to local lore, a man was killed in the shop years ago when he was crushed under the hydraulic lift. Another man died when he fell from a second story window and landed in the alley. Apparently, the building's tragic history has left its impression in the bricks and mortar.

The strange sightings at the newspaper office have been reported by several individuals at different time. So many stories have accumulated over time that they have become a very interesting body of folklore. In one story told by the former sports editor, Jeff Christian, he and a woman named Rosalind were working together in the building late one night. Rosalind had walked back to the break room to cook some popcorn. When she returned, she was as white as a sheet. She told Jeff that while she was walking across the old part of the building, she was overcome by a feeling of dread. Turning her head to the side, she saw a toddler-sized baby between two and three years old walking across the room just a few feet ahead of her. Rosalind said that it appeared to be a real, flesh-and-blood baby. Concerned that the child could get hurt running around the building with no adult supervision, Rosalind turned around to look for the parents. When she glanced back, the baby had vanished. Rosalind and Jeff searched the entire building but found no trace of the child. No one else has ever seen the baby.

Jeff Christian had a sighting of his own in the pressroom area, which is where most of the bizarre events seem to occur. His own experience took place between the double doors of the newsroom and the double doors of the pressroom. He said that one night he was working in the *Meridian Star* building all by himself. At 2:00 A.M., he was walking through the pressroom when he suddenly felt cold. He glanced up and noticed two filmy-white figures hovering around the pipes that run along the top of the building. The figures were seven or eight feet high with a "bowling pin" sort of shape. They were suspended just above his head, and after a few moments, they rose up and vanished into the ceiling. Reporter Marianne Todd saw the same apparition a few weeks later. Her description matched Jeff's exactly except that she said the two shapes intertwined before they went up into the ceiling.

In October 2000, one of the *Meridian Star*'s photographers, a young woman named Paula, had a very upsetting experience in the darkroom. She was in the darkroom by herself one afternoon. As usual, the door was closed to prevent any light from entering the room. As she was putting the film in the canisters containing the developing solution, she was temporarily blinded by a white light that blazed across the stainless-steel panel. She described the light as being streaked with the sort of lines that appear when the crystal of a wristwatch reflects against a wall. Convinced that her entire film stock had been ruined, she cursed loudly as she scrambled to throw the rest of the film into the canisters. As soon as the canisters were clamped tightly shut, Paula began looking for the source of the light, thinking that someone had left the door open. She also checked the dials to see if anything had been left on. Everything was in place. Paula proceeded to develop the "lead art" for the day's edition, even though she was sure that the film had been ruined by its exposure to the strange light. Miraculously, the photographs turned out fine.

Sheila Blackmon, who has been a reporter for the *Meridian Star*, says that whenever new employees appear for work on the first day, they are warned against going into certain areas by themselves. Sheila has never seen anything unusual so far, but she has experienced weird feelings in the break room: "I have felt things in there, but I can't tell anymore if it's genuine or if I am thinking of those stories that I have heard. I have walked through the break room and felt such a strange urge to start running that it's incredible. I've actually had to clench my fists and force myself to walk slowly through the room without looking from side to side because I have felt so frightened. Somebody better trained in the paranormal than I am could probably talk more authoritatively about the cold spots because there are places in that building that are really cold. That could just be cracks letting the cold in, but the disturbing feelings are something else altogether."

The *Meridian Star* building is located next door to the Pigford Building in downtown Meridian. Take the 22nd Avenue

Exit off Interstate 20/59 and travel north. The *Meridian Star* building is at 814 22nd Avenue, Meridian, Mississippi; phone: 601-693-1551.

Peavey Melody Music

MERIDIAN

irectly across the street from the *Meridian Star* building in Meridian, Mississippi, is a little store with a big history. According to Berry Gray, who has worked at Peavey Melody Music since 1969 and owned it since 1987, people have visited the store from all over the world, even from as far away as Japan, and not just because Elvis Presley visited the store in 1952 when he competed at the Jimmy Rodgers Festival. Peavey Melody Music is widely recognized as the birthplace of Peavey Electronics. Joseph B. "Mutt" Peavey started Peavey Melody Music in 1938 after talking to a local band director who said that there was a need in Meridian for a store that promoted musical instruments and sold popular sheet music. He moved his store to its present location on 22nd Avenue in downtown Meridian in 1946. "Mutt" is probably best known outside of Meridian for having written the Mississippi State University fight song, "Hail State," in 1939. In 1955, his fourteen-year-old son, Hartley, began working at Peavey Melody Music. As rock 'n' roll fever was beginning to sweep the country, Hartley designed his first amplifier from a television power transformer and other spare parts. He continued building his amplifiers while attending Mississippi

143

State University. After graduating, Hartley Peavey opened his amplifier business in his parents' basement, but as demand for his amplifiers grew, he moved it to the second floor of Peavey Melody Music in 1966. By 1968, demand for Hartley's amplifiers was so great that he moved his operation to a new building. Hartley went on to establish one of Mississippi's most successful industries.

However, the history of the building where Peavey Melody Music is housed goes back much farther. Originally known as Wagoner Annex No. 3, it was constructed in 1906. On March 2 of the same year, a tornado described by a local newspaper as a "black funnel cloud of death" swept in from the southwest without warning. The storm destroyed every building between 22nd and 24th Streets, including the New Orleans and Northeastern Freight depot. In addition to razing railroad buildings and two to three blocks of stores, the tornado leveled five city churches, the Meridian Fertilizer Factory, and many homes. Seventeen people who had taken refuge in the Empire Hotel's dining room were killed when the roof caved in. Many of the ruined buildings caught fire, adding to the havoc. After the tornado passed, martial law was passed to prevent looting. Soldiers were posted along Front Street from 26th to 19th Streets. Help arrived a few days later when a train carrying Governor James K. Vardaman, Attorney General William Williams, forty senators and representatives, and dozens of convicts from a Rankin County prison pulled into what was left of the train station. All totaled, the funnel cloud killed or injured up to fifty residents and left more that $400,000 worth of damage.

Many of the victims were taken to the Smith Funeral Parlor, which was located in the Wagoner Annex No. 3. According to the present owner of Peavey Melody Music, the bodies were carrried to the second floor, where they were "stacked up on top of each other like cord wood." Some of the injured people who lay next to the dead eventually died before help arrived. Many of the victims were children. Legend has it that so much blood spilled on the first floor as the victims were carried upstairs that it was swept out of the door with a push broom, staining the wooden floor. Eventually, the stains were covered up with a tile walkway that is still used to this day.

The haunting activity in Peavey Melody Music was first detected in the late 1970s by Berry Gray: "I was keeping the store open on a Saturday with another guy. We'd take turns leaving early, and it was my turn to stay late that day. They used to give kids piano and guitar lessons upstairs. There was also an Arthur Murray Dance Studio up there at one time. I will never forget [what happened] that day. I was puttin' up everything and turning off the lights when I heard some kids sniggering and laughing and running up and down a long hallway where there's an open elevator shaft. I went back to the doorway under the balcony, and I poked my head up the stairway and yelled, 'Be careful of that elevator shaft.' I was thinking, 'Oh, Jesus. Somebody must have left that door [to the long hallway] open. The piano teacher's not looking after those kids.' All I heard was laughing and running. I walked upstairs and found that the lights were off, so I clicked them on and said, 'You guys are supposed to get out of here!' I didn't see anybody, but [I continued] to hear giggling, and it was starting to get colder. When I heard someone moving around one of the rooms, I turned around and said [to myself], 'Feet, don't fail me now!' I went straight out the door, down the stairs, and locked the store up."

Mr. Gray added that other employees as well as repairmen and servicemen working on the organs have also heard laughter coming from upstairs. Robert Holcomb, an employee of Peavey Melody Music, said, "Just about six or seven years ago, we heard noises upstairs, and Mr. Gray said, 'Who's that upstairs?' We could hear the sound of little feet walking back and forth." Virginia Raymond, who was associated with Peavey Melody Music for over five decades, habitually opened the store well before dawn and was well acquainted with the noises coming from the second floor. On more than one occasion, she gave the following warning to people intent upon walking upstairs: "You-all be careful, 'cause they're up there." Mr. Gray has learned to live with the strange sounds: "I think I've made my peace with whatever is causing those noises, but if they get me, I'll come back and haunt them after I'm gone."

Peavey Melody Music is in downtown Meridian. Take the 22nd Avenue Exit off Interstate 20/59 and head north. The address is 813 22nd Avenue, Meridian, Mississippi; phone: 601-483-9215.

The Pigford Building

MERIDIAN

Like so many of the old buildings in Meridian, Mississippi, the Pigford Building has undergone a variety of incarnations over the years. This three-story, red-brick building was originally known as the Pythian Castle Hall and was constructed by the Mount Barton Lodge No. 13, Knights of Pythias. The deed record of June 30, 1915, states that the fraternal organization desired to "furnish a Pythian home for weekly meetings . . . and for club rooms and other conveniences for comfort, pleasure and benefit." In the 1920s, the building was purchased by Pigford Realty and rented out to other businesses. For many years, offices were housed in the second level, and a beautiful ballroom occupied the third floor. Between 1933 and 1976, R. M. Hamil operated the post office/drugstore on the first floor. Over the years, various other businesses have occupied the first floor, including a grocery store. By the year 2000, the two upper levels of the building had been closed up.

Most of the recorded hauntings at the Pigford Building have centered around the only portion of the first level that is still in use, a clothing and gift shop called Alexander's. Almost as soon as the store opened its doors in October 1999, strange things started to happen. By November, employees and customers reported hearing a woman's ghostly laughter. As the weeks passed, other bizarre events began to take place. Jewelry that had been pinned to a display board was found scattered over the floor the next morning. Employees frequently found clothing on the floor when they opened the store, even though it had all been hung up the night before. Before long, footsteps on the roof were heard. Then on May 15, 1999, an employee named J. T. Mohammad actually saw the ghost, which she described as a white woman dressed in a handkerchief-like dress. She had long hair and seemed to glow as she glided effortlessly across the balcony: "I could feel someone looking over the rail down at me. As I looked back, I could see someone walking away in white, dreamy-like." Mohammed added that she was not really frightened by the apparition: "She's more like company. Like a presence."

This is not to say, though, that everyone in Alexander's is happy to be working alongside a ghost. Later that same year, one of the owners was in a little office room after hours one day counting money when the telephone rang. The store has two phone lines, one for inside calls and the other for outside

147

calls. On this particular night, the little light on the phone indicated that the call was from the inside extension. When she picked up the phone, she heard nothing but static and heavy breathing. Because she was the only one in the store at the time, she was understandably unnerved by the strange voice on the other end of the line. To set her own mind at ease, she searched the entire store, thinking that maybe someone had sneaked inside and was playing a trick on her. Once she had made sure that the doors were still locked and that no one else was inside, she returned to the office. A few minutes later, the phone rang a second time, and once again, the strange sounds came over the line. By this time, the woman was too frightened to stay in the store any longer. She convinced herself that whatever work she still had to do could wait until the next morning, and she left.

One of Alexander's customers also had a scary experience in Alexander's. In 2000, a reporter for the *Meridian Star,* Marianne Todd, was trying on clothes in Alexander's just as it was preparing to close. Marianne and a store employee were the only two people in the store. All at once, she heard noises coming from the fitting room next to hers. The employee knocked on the door to see if someone was inside, but there was no response. When she opened the door, no one was inside. Marianne immediately decided that she had tried on enough clothes for the day and went home.

On October 30, 1999, Meridian radio station WOKK conducted an investigation of the hauntings at Alexander's. Breakfast Bunch co-hosts Debbie Alexander and Scotty Ray Boyd, along with several guests, spent the night at the store. Somehow, Debbie managed to sleep through most of the night, but Scotty Ray said that he was genuinely terrified by what he saw and heard: "The spooky stuff began at 8:30 or 9:00, when we began hearing the sound of someone walking. Then some clothes hanging on a rack on the first floor started swinging, like when somebody walks by and brushes them. There was also an office chair without rollers that moved back and forth. One of the girls with us got so scared at this point that she started squalling and hollering. The weirdest thing that happened involved the upstairs door. Scott Shepherd and I had been running cables and cords throughout the building, and I must have been through that door fifty or sixty times. But within a twenty-five-minute period, that door was nailed shut. I mean, you couldn't budge it! And what is really strange is that it had been nailed on the side leading to the roof. Once you get on the roof, there's no way down except through that door. To top it all off, the next morning, Debbie had a pair of earrings lying beside her. If somebody rigged all this stuff up this way to scare us, they did a pretty good job, because it all seemed real to me!"

Employees have traced the beginning of the spectral activity in the Pigford Building back to the displaying of a portrait of a young woman and a series of historic photographs on the wall of the store. One photograph is of Meridian's famed gypsy queen, Kelly Mitchell. Mitchell died in her mid-thirties in 1914 while giving birth. One of the old photographs depicts the gypsy queen's funeral procession passing by the Pigford Building, which was under construction at the time. Ms. Mitchell's black coffin can be clearly seen on the back of a horse-drawn hearse. Whether or not the restless spirit of Alexander's is connected with the portrait of the woman or with Kelly Mitchell has not been determined to anyone's satisfaction. The manager, Debbie Moorehead, has learned to live with the ghost, whoever she is. She even greets the curious spirit in the mornings whenever she feels her presence. One could say that the workers at Alexander's have learned to live with the dead.

To find Alexander's, take the 22nd Avenue exit off Highway 20/59 and head north. Alexander's is located downtown at 818 22nd Avenue, Meridian, Mississippi; phone: 601-693-7463.

Waverley

WEST POINT

Even people who have seen Waverley many times never quite lose their sense of surprise when they encounter it on the little side road leading off Highway 50. Waverley looms like an immense phantom from the dense forest surrounding it, a relic from the South's romantic past. The gentility radiating from its gleaming white Ionic columns stands in stark contrast with the rambling undergrowth that seems poised to reclaim the old mansion at any time. Walking past the ancient magnolia trees down the long sidewalk lined with box elders, one fully expects to see hoop-skirted ladies and Confederate soldiers resplendent in their dress uniforms dancing in the great hall. Undoubtedly, the mansion's antebellum atmosphere must be at least partially responsible for its haunted reputation. On the other hand, the testimony of eyewitnesses makes one suspect that there must be some truth to the strange stories focusing around Waverley.

Waverley, the only pre–Civil War home in Mississippi with a second-, third-, and fourth-story balcony overlooking the main floor, was built in the Greek Revival architectural style over a period of several years by Colonel George Hampton Young of Oglethorpe County, Georgia. Colonel Young designed the mansion himself. The mechanical details of construction were handled by the Italian architect Charles Pond of St. Louis. Richard Miller from Scotland cut and installed the Italian and Grecian marble. The plasterwork created by two Irish artisans from Mobile ranks as some of the finest in the entire South.

By 1852, construction of Waverley was almost completed, and Colonel Young was more than ready to move into his new home. While the mansion was being constructed, Colonel Young, his wife, and his ten children lived in a small complex of log cabins on the grounds. Mrs. Young bided her time by planting the formal boxwood gardens with plants from their home in Georgia. She had just put the finishing touches on her garden when she died, only a few months before the mansion was finished.

Once completed, Waverley became a self-sustaining community. Colonel Young constructed a cotton gin, a gristmill, a marble-lined swimming pool, a tannery, stables, kennels, bathhouses, a brick kiln, and even a ferry. Gas for the beautiful chandeliers was produced by burning chunks of pine in a copper-domed brick retort near the house. Colonel Young even attempted to grow silkworms on his plantations. Some of the mulberry trees that he planted to provide nourishment for his worms are still growing in the back yard.

The Youngs' six sons and four daughters grew up in Waverley, and four of them were married there. Several of the boys attended the University of Mississippi, which their father had been instrumental in founding. Colonel Young's sons also fought in the Civil War. All returned home except Beverley, who died in a Federal hospital in New York from wounds he had received at Gettysburg. Colonel Young died in 1880 and is buried, along with his wife and other family members, in the small family cemetery just about one hundred feet down the road across from Waverley.

After the last of the Youngs' children, Captain William Young, died in 1913, Waverley fell into a state of decline. The once-elegant mansion stood empty for the next fifty years. During this sad period in Waverley's history, it was visited only by occasional hunters, children, vandals, and a variety of rodents. Then in 1962, Waverley was rescued from total destruction by Mr. and Mrs. Robert A. Snow Jr. of Philadelphia, Mississippi. Even though most of the furniture was gone and the floors were littered with refuse, the Snows knew that they had purchased an architectural treasure. Actually, the house was in remarkable condition considering all the years it stood vacant. Only three of the 718 spindles were missing from the staircase banister. The wooden floor and all of the original chandeliers, doors, and doorknobs were still there. In the main hall, they found two beautiful mirrors, one with a large crack in the middle. Later, they learned that the mirror had been broken during the Civil War. One cold night during a dress ball, the heat from a lamp that had been placed too close to the mirror caused it to crack. Amazingly, the original keys had been kept in a safe deposit box in a bank in Columbus. As soon as they moved in, Donna Snow, her husband, and their four children set about restoring their antebellum home. Restoration of the last room had just been completed when Mrs. Snow died in 1991. At the time of this printing, the process of preserving Waverley was still going on.

Donna Snow became aware that she and her family were sharing their home with an unearthly presence from the moment they began sweeping, painting, and repairing the house. The first week after the Snows moved into Waverley, the entire family was awakened by a tremendous explosion. A hurried search of the house failed to reveal the source of the disturbing noise. These explosive sounds continued two or three nights each week. After that first year, the Snows never heard the explosions again.

Nine months after the exploding sounds ceased, Mrs. Snow said that another spirit made its presence known at Waverley. She was walking across the upstairs balcony one afternoon when she heard a child call out, "Mama, Mama!" Thinking that one of her daughters was standing on the main floor, she peered over the balcony but saw no one. For the next five years, Mrs. Snow continued to hear the plaintive voice of a little girl who was no more than four or five years old. As a rule, Mrs. Snow heard the little girl when she walked about the house performing her household tasks. On several occasions, Mrs. Snow also heard the child calling, "Mama, Mama!" at night. Her first impulse was to check in her children's room across the hall to make sure that they were all right. Once she had satisfied herself that her none of her children had called out to her during the night, she told herself that it was just the ghost, and she returned to bed.

The spirit of the little girl also manifested itself in a room on the second floor that has come to be known as the "Ghost Room." On several afternoons, usually in the summer, Mrs. Snow entered the room to find the impression of a small body about four feet long on the freshly made bed. It appeared as if a small child had climbed up into the high bed after playing all day and taken a little afternoon nap.

Mrs. Snow continued to feel the presence of the little ghost girl for five years. Her last encounter with the little girl took place one day while she was working in the kitchen. Suddenly, the tranquillity of the morning was shattered by a child's voice frantically calling, "Mama! Mama! Mama!" Later, Mrs. Snow recalled that the little girl sounded distressed, as if she needed her mother's immediate attention. For the first time, Mrs. Snow spoke to the spirit: "What's wrong? I will help you if I can." There was no reply. Mrs. Snow never heard the voice again.

Although Mrs. Snow appears to have been the focal point of much of the ghostly activity in the house when she and her family first moved in, paranormal phenomena continued to take place after her death. Todd Childs, the caretaker at Waverley, lived there between 1996 and 1999. By the year 2001, members of the Snow family were still living on the first and second floors. The third floor was being used as the attic, and the fourth floor was the observatory.

Although the little girl's voice is not heard in the house anymore, there is evidence that her spirit is still around. The little girl's ghost was seen by both of Mrs. Snow's daughters. Cindy was seven when she first saw the ghost. Then after she married and had children of her own, she returned to the house and saw the ghost again. Todd said that little girl's ghost's afternoon naps in the "Ghost Room" are infrequent, but they do still occur, usually between two o'clock and four o'clock.

The identity of the little girl remained a mystery until 1997 when an investigation of the Burt family records revealed that two little girls died in the house during the same week. In 1862, Dr. Burt left the county to serve at the Battle of Shiloh. While he was away, the older of his two daughters contracted diphtheria. Without any slaves to help her care for the girl, Mrs. Burt believed that the wisest course of action was to take her and her sister to Waverley. The Youngs did all they could to help the girl, but she died on the third day of her arrival at Waverley. The funeral was held in the Young family cemetery. The next day, the younger daughter, who was four years old, woke up before the rest of the family. Apparently, she was playing on the stairs leading from the second to the third floor when her head became stuck between two of the spindles. When her body was discovered a short while later, it appeared that she had struggled to extricate herself from the spindles and, in the process, had broken her neck and died. The evidence would lead one to believe that she is the child whose spirit has never completely left Waverley.

The little girl is not the only female ghost at Waverley. After Mrs. Snow died in 1991, the family hired tour guides. One afternoon, one of the tour guides named Melissa had just taken a group of tourists through the entire house. Just as they were leaving the hallway on the first floor, one member of the group asked, "Who is that on the third floor?" Melissa replied, "Nobody's here but us." "I beg your pardon," the man said. "There's a woman sitting on the stairs on the third floor smoking a cigarette." From the lady's description of the red-haired woman, it became obvious that she was the spirit of Mrs. Snow. People who had known Mrs. Snow recalled that as a rule, she only smoked outside. However, on cold or rainy days, she smoked on the third floor so that her smoke would not be detected on the lower floors.

According to Todd Childs, the most persistent paranormal occurrence at Waverley is the exploding or crashing sound that the Snows heard during their first year in the house. One incident that occurred just a few years ago proved to Todd that the terrible sound that had resonated throughout Waverley since 1962 was real: "One time, a film crew from A & E came here. While they were filming an interview in the hallway, Mr. 'Robert' [Snow] and I were sitting on the porch. It was completely quiet outside and inside. No tourists were present at all that day. Right in the middle of the interview, there was this immense crashing sound. Mr. Robert and I ran inside, thinking that something had happened to the equipment. We searched the entire house but couldn't find anything. When we replayed the video, the sound of the crash was on the film." He went on to say that other sounds are heard at Waverley as well: "There are lots of sounds of glass shattering. Voices are sometimes heard as well. The locals say we're scaring ourselves at night, but 98 percent of the things happen in broad daylight. Ordinarily, I never mention the ghosts unless someone mentions them to me first."

Apparently, not all of the ghosts at Waverley are female, as Todd Childs discovered in 1997: "I'd worked here about a year. I was giving a tour to a large group of about seventy-five people. I had to split them into smaller groups. Well, I had finished the group, and everybody had left. I had the front door locked. The best thing to do when you have a large group like that is to make sure everybody's out of the house [before you lock up]. While I was looking around, I saw a man on the second floor standing in front of the balcony door. He was standing with his hands behind his back looking straight out the balcony door. I thought somebody had been left behind. I said, 'I'm sorry. I thought everybody had gone.' I turned back and unlocked the door and opened it again. And when I turned back, he [the ghost] was not there. So I waited a minute for him to come back, still believing that it was a tourist. These two staircases are the only way down from the upstairs, and he didn't come down either one, so I went up. I thought maybe he'd gone into one of the bedrooms. I searched all four bedrooms and looked down all the balconies. No one could have gotten down without using the stairs."

Four years later, Todd had another encounter with the male apparition: "I had put my coat in here. I laid it on the red sofa. Well, that afternoon, I needed my coat, so I came out of the kitchen and went through the dining room. These two doors were open. I looked out of the corner of my eye, and there was a man standing right by the door looking into this room. So I turned, and just as I looked at him and he looked at me, he turned and walked back toward the staircase. He wasn't out of my view the whole time. As he walked out in the hallway, I ran after him, but he wasn't there. He's the only ghost I've seen. I've never seen the girl's ghost. I've never seen the red-haired woman. I think the man I saw was Colonel Young's son, Thomas Erskine, just based on photographs I've seen."

A medium who visited Waverley in association with a television camera crew determined that one child's ghost was present in the mansion and the ghosts of at least three adults. She added that the name Tom seemed to stand out. It seemed to her that the other ghosts did not care much for Tom. In fact, according to the medium, they seemed to be intimidated by him.

Several of Waverley's ghost legends center around the mirrors. In 13 Mississippi Ghosts and Jeffrey, Kathryn Tucker Windham writes, "Others told of seeing a kaleidoscope of faces in the tall, dusty mirrors in the stairwell, faces, perhaps, of people who had paused to gaze into those mirrors long ago and whose reflections were eternally etched on the silvery surfaces" (107). According to Todd Childs, the mirrors in Waverley still reflect images from times gone by: "A lot of times, you'll catch things out of the corner of your eye. You'll be walking by the mirror, and you'll turn around and you'll catch little glimpses of things. The girl I was talking about said that one evening she was here in an old dress—we have to wear period attire on special occasions—and she was getting laced up in her corset in one of the bedrooms upstairs. She said that she was standing in front of one of the mirrors, and behind her in the mirror, she saw a woman come out of the bedroom. She was in an evening gown. When she turned around, the woman was gone."

In the book Ghosts! Personal Accounts of Modern Mississippi Hauntings, Sylvia Booth Hubbard reported that Waverley's ghost took Mrs. Snow's peach pickle spoon and hid it in a blue bowl on the top shelf of a display case. Todd Childs says that things still turn up missing in Waverley on a fairly regular basis: "This happened six weeks ago. Carolyn Dickert, who worked here, put her canvass bag in a little nook over by the stove. I had to get a haircut, so I put my keys where I had always put them—on the little shelf on the other side of the doorway. I took a shower, shaved, came back downstairs, and my keys were gone! She had a tour group, and she had not even been in the kitchen. I looked for my keys and couldn't find them. We combed the entire house and looked everywhere I had been. I keep a spare set, of course, so I took it. When she finished her tour group, she helped me look. We even moved furniture and looked underneath. Finally, I said, 'Look in your bag.' She said, 'There's no way they're in my bag.' So she dumped out her bag on the table, and the only things in her bag were an apple, a sandwich, a Coke in a can, and a paperback book. That afternoon when she got ready to go home, she opened her bag, and there were my keys. We still don't know how they got there."

The ghostly phenomena at Waverley are not confined to the interior of the house, either. Todd Childs recalls, "Several years ago when a camera crew was photographing the outside of the house, the cameraman was halfway down the yard taking pictures of the front of the house. When the pictures were developed, there was a huge ball of light to the left of the doorway. This is pretty strange, because there are no reflective surfaces in the front of the house. The glass panes around the door frame are red, and they don't reflect light."

For the most part, Todd Childs and the other employees have learned to live with the "other" inhabitants of Waverley. This does not mean, though, that Todd is entirely comfortable in the house: "I've slept in every [other] room of the house and have even stayed here alone for days at a time, but I will not stay in the room to the left of the 'Ghost Room.' I can't explain it. I get a very uneasy feeling whenever I go in there."

Waverley is located just off Highway 50, between Columbus and West Point, Mississippi; phone: 601-494-1399.

NORTH CAROLINA

Fort Fisher

The rallying cry "Never say die!" has been closely identified with the American spirit. Washington's troops at Valley Forge, the defenders of the Alamo, the survivors of the attack on Pearl Harbor—all of these heroes possessed a devotion to duty so powerful that they dared to make a stand against impossible odds. Toward the very end of the Civil War, the Confederate troops at Fort Fisher in Wilmington, North Carolina, also refused to admit defeat until the end was inevitable. Some say that the commander of the fort is still leading the attack against the Yankees over a century after his own death.

After President Abraham Lincoln ordered the blockade of all southern ports in April 1861, blockade running became the lifeline of the Confederacy. Government blockade runners hauled steel, copper, and munitions for the war effort. By 1864, Wilmington, North Carolina, had become the most active port for blockade runners in the South. Wilmington's isolated location twenty-eight miles up the Cape Fear River, combined with ample fortification, helped it become the most active port for blockade runners in the entire South. Fort Fisher, a huge earthwork situated at the tip of a peninsula at the New Inlet passage, was the only thing keeping the supply lines open. Even though the fort's guns had been able to protect blockade runners from Union warships, General William Whiting, the commanding officer in charge of the defense of Wilmington, knew that it was just a matter of time before Fort Fisher was attacked by Federal forces.

On December 23, 1864, the assault on Fort Fisher began in earnest. General Benjamin Butler disguised the *Louisianan* as a blockade runner. Then the ship was loaded with 215 pounds of gunpowder and moved within a few hundred yards off shore. The gunpowder was detonated, and the terrific explosion illuminated the night sky but did little damage to the fort. On December 24, the Union navy pummeled the fort with heavy artillery, but the earthworks held firm. On Christmas Day, Butler launched an infantry attack against Fort Fisher, but it, too, was a dismal failure.

Following his humiliating defeat at Wilmington, General Butler was replaced by Major General Alfred Terry, who sent a great armada of Union warships to Wilmington on January 12, 1865. Fort Fisher took a terrific pounding from the Union navy's blistering barrage. General Whiting was replaced by his superior officer, General Braxton Bragg, who was already making plans to evacuate Wilmington because he believed that Fort Fisher could not be saved. Angered by Bragg's refusal to answer his request for reinforcements, Whiting joined Colonel Lamb at Fort Fisher on the first day of the attack. The popular general, known to his troops as "Little Billy," had decided not to give up without a fight, even though there was little hope of victory.

The land attack against Fort Fisher began on January 13, 1865. About 4,000 Federal troops attacked the northwestern point of the fort, and 2,000 infantrymen moved against the northeast corner. The Union army was facing a Confederate force of 1,900 men with only forty-four heavy guns to defend the fort. The Confederates quickly repelled the smaller force, but before they could even begin cheering, thousands of Yankees poured over the northwestern wall. Holding his dress sword high in the air,

General Whiting led the attack, but he and his troops were completely overwhelmed by the Yankees' sheer strength in numbers. Legend has it that General Whiting was attempting to remove the flag the Yankees had just raised over the fort when he was shot twice. Shortly thereafter, Colonel Lamb was wounded as well. The Confederates continued defending the fort without their commanding officer for several more hours before the Federal victory was secure. Later that evening, Major James Reilly, with flag of truce in hand, formally surrendered the fort to the Union army.

After the battle, General Whiting was taken to a prison camp called Fort Columbus in New York Harbor. Without proper care, Whiting's wounds became infected, and he contracted dysentery as well. Before he finally died on March 10, 1865, he wrote a letter to General Robert E. Lee requesting that General Bragg's refusal to send reinforcements to Fort Fisher be investigated. Three weeks later on April 9, 1865, General Lee surrendered at Appomattox Courthouse.

Fort Fisher's reputation as a haunted place began in 1868 when a Civil War reunion was held there. Three Confederate veterans had just finished greeting old friends late in the afternoon and were walking around the earthworks when one of them spotted a lone figure standing on top of one of the old gun emplacements. Thinking that this might be a comrade of theirs they had not yet talked to, the three veterans waved to the man, but he did not wave back. As they neared the earthworks, the men noticed that the strange man was wearing an officer's uniform and that he was very short. When the officer waved his sword in the air, beckoning them to follow, the man's identity became clear. This was the ghost of General Whiting. Before the shock of their encounter with the supernatural really soaked in, the ghost vanished before their eyes.

In the years following the Civil War, other veterans of the defense of Fort Fisher have also seen the apparition of their former commander, standing along the walls of the fort. More recently, his spirit has been seen poised on top of the sand dunes, preparing to lead his final charge. One cannot help but wonder if maybe this is General Whiting's way of showing his devotion to duty or, possibly, protesting the behavior of his superior officer, Braxton Bragg, which led to Whiting's death, the capture of Fort Fisher, and the fall of the Confederacy.

Fort Fisher is a state historic site in New Hanover County, south of Wilmington. The fort is located where Highway 421 ends at the tip of the peninsula. The address is Fort Fisher, P.O. Box 169, Kure Beach, NC 28449; phone: 910-458-5538.

Gimghoul Castle

CHAPEL HILL

Piney Prospect is one of the most picturesque spots in and around the campus of the University of North Carolina at Chapel Hill. Located in the forests of Chapel Hill's Battle Park, Piney Prospect was once part of the basin that helped form the Atlantic Ocean. Around the turn of the century, former university president Kemp P. Battle led students on a hike up the hill on Sunday afternoons so that they could take in the beauty of nature. To remember that special trip, each student placed a rock at the top of the hill. The resulting pile of rocks, which became known as the Freshman Rock Pile, was eventually used by Waldesian stonemasons to build one of the most mysterious buildings in the entire region, the unique Gimghoul Castle.

The idea for Gimghoul Castle was the product of the fertile imagination of a law student named Edward Wray Martin (Class of 1891). During his nightly walks up Piney Prospect, Martin, a die-hard romantic, imagined an ocean extending below the hill. He envisioned knights and fanciful creatures descending upon a fortress he called Hippol Castle at the top of the hill. Determined to transform his dream of building Hippol Castle into reality, Martin co-founded a fraternity called the Order of the Gimghouls in 1899. For the first few years of its existence, the order was housed in a lodge at the corner of Rosemary and Boundary Streets. After the sale of property owned by the Gimghouls, construction of the castle became a financial possibility. The order began clearing the land in the winter of 1924. Teams of men were hired to haul rock up the hill to the construction site. Two years and several hundred tons of stone later, work on the castle was completed at a cost of $5,200. The Gimghouls finally had their castle by the prehistoric sea.

Few people outside of the fraternity have seen the castle's interior. Some of the friends and relatives who have been invited inside say that the castle has a great hall, three tower rooms, a social room, a reception room, a chapter room, small living rooms, a kitchen, and a long room which opens onto a terrace. Like a real castle from the Middle Ages, it is sumptuously furnished and drafty.

Just behind the castle is an amphitheater-style "seat," called the Battle Seat in honor of President Battle. For years, one could see for twelve miles from this vantage point. Recently, though, the view has been obscured by the encroaching forest.

The history of the Order of the Gimghouls has become intertwined with the tragic story of Peter Dromgoole, who was a student at the University of North Carolina in 1831. A member of a well-respected family from Brunswick County, Virginia, Dromgoole spent more time drinking and carousing than he did studying. After a heated argument with a professor, Dromgoole decided to drop out of school.

Even though Peter was no longer enrolled at UNC, he still attended the Commencement Ball of 1833. Afterward, he exchanged harsh words with a young man whom he suspected was competing with him for the affections of a young woman known only as Miss Fanny. The two students must have said things to each other that would have been impossible to take back because they agreed to a midnight pistol duel near the spot where Gimghoul Castle now stands. Peter had not informed Miss Fanny of his intention of fighting a duel over her honor, but she was warned at the last minute by a slave who had overheard the two men talking. Dressed only in her nightgown and her bedroom slippers, Miss Fanny rushed up Piney Prospect as fast as she could go. She arrived on the scene just in time to hear the gunshot and witness her lover clutch his chest and collapse on a large rock. Peter Dromgoole was only eighteen years old.

Miss Fanny raised Peter's head from the pool of blood that had started to flow around the rock and asked the other duelist to leave. She then sobbed uncontrollably and collapsed to the ground. As she was carried away, the students who had assisted Peter's rival quickly began digging him a shallow grave under the rock to avoid prosecution for violating North Carolina's anti-dueling law. The shock of seeing her lover killed before her eyes proved to be too much for Miss Fanny. For the next few days, she returned to the rock and spent hours weeping there, totally unaware that her lover was buried underneath. Eventually, she died of a broken heart and was buried next to Peter under the same rock. In commemoration of the tragedy, the rock has become known as "Dromgoole's Rock," and the spring flowing at the base of Piney Prospect is called "Miss Fanny's Spring."

Dromgoole's Rock lies on the axis of an imaginary line through the front door of the castle and the round reception room. Its surface is covered with large splotches of rust which, according to generations of UNC students, is an eradicable blood-stain. Despite the efforts of Miss Fanny's suitor and his second to remove the bloodstain, it always returned as a reminder of their heinous crime. Stricken by conscience, they confessed to the murder sixty years later.

Like many legends, the story of the duel at "Dromgoole's Rock" is probably 90 percent folklore. Bruce Cotten, whose mother was a direct descendant of Dromgoole's grandfather, investigated the truth behind the legend in the 1920s. After looking at the family papers at the Dromgoole home place in Brunswick County, Virginia, he discovered that Peter Dromgoole's application for admission to UNC was denied. He studied with a tutor while awaiting future admission. Although Dromgoole's roommate, John B. Williams, described him as a "moody youth and inclined to wildness," there was no proof that he went "wild" during his stay at the university. A letter written on April 22, 1834, by a minister named Thomas P. Hunt suggests that after Peter Dromgoole left Chapel Hill, he took the name of his former roommate, Williams, and enlisted in the regular army at Fort Johnson in Smithville. There is no record of Dromgoole's fate after joining the military.

Exposing the fictional elements of the Dromgoole legend will not really diminish the haunted aura surrounding Gimghoul Castle. Onlookers continue to violate the "Private Property" signs and prowl the castle grounds. Undoubtedly, the building's unusual architecture, as well as the intriguing mystery of the bloody rock and the dark secrets of the secret society, will continue to draw people to the Gimghouls' sanctuary for years to come.

Gimghoul Castle is located just east of the University of North Carolina campus off Gimghoul Road. Visitors are not welcome.

New Hanover County Public Library

WILMINGTON

Wilmington, North Carolina, is a pleasant resort city on the Atlantic Ocean. To the casual visitor, Wilmington does not appear to be the sort of city that ghosts would inhabit. In fact, the most haunted building in Wilmington—the New Hanover County Public Library—does not match the conventional image of a "spooky" place. Yet, this modern-looking, box-like structure ranks as one of the most haunted libraries in the entire United States.

The New Hanover Public Library moved into its present location in 1981. The building, which was constructed in the 1950s by Belks, a regional department store chain, originally served as a department store. It has a basement and four floors, but the fourth floor is not used. Interestingly enough, the building is located on the site of a nineteenth-century mansion that also had a haunted reputation. The beautiful, Italianate-style house was built in the 1860s by one of Wilmington's most respected families, the Wood family. Father and son were both doctors who loved reading. The story goes that before a locally famous duel was fought, one of the duelists spent the night in the Woods' house. Unable to sleep, he paced back and forth across the floor. After he was shot and killed, his spirit supposedly returned to the house where he spent his last night. Eerie footsteps heard at night on the second floor were attributed to this unfortunate young man. Some people believe that after the old place was razed, the ghost may have taken up residence in the building that replaced it. Others feel that the books donated to the library by the Wood family may have carried with them some kind of psychic residue. Not coincidentally, they argue, these books are housed in the same area where most of the hauntings occur, the Historical Wing. Beverly Tetterton, librarian in the Historical Wing for twenty years, added a third reason why the Woods' house may be responsible for the haunting of the library: the Local History Room is thought to be in the approximate location of the haunted room in the Woods' house.

Another theory is that the ghost is the one which haunted the previous location of the library, the old Wilmington Light Infantry Armory on Market Street. Originally a private residence known as the John Taylor House, it was later converted into an armory for the Wilmington Light Infantry, a local military unit. It became the library in 1954. Beverly Tetterton said that when she first started working there a year before the library was moved to its present location, she was told that patrons and staff had seen strange shadows and heard footsteps, usually at night. One evening, after seeing one of these shadowy shapes, she told the girl at the front desk that she thought there was somebody in the building. They closed up early that night.

Ever since the library moved to the old department store building, archivists in the Historical Wing have sensed the presence of something not human. Most librarians believe this to be the spirit of an elderly woman, a genealogist with a keen interest in local history. Before her death in early 1983, she spent hours in the Historical Wing poring over old books and newspaper clippings. Most of the disturbances in the Historical Wing take the form of the kind of noise one makes when conducting research, such as the flipping of pages in a book or the pulling of a book from a shelf: "Early in the morning, I will be reading the newspaper and hear noises—of books moving on the shelf, books falling over. It sounds like someone is there in the back using the room." Pamphlet cases that were locked up at night have been found unlocked the next morning. When Beverly Tetterton first heard the noises in 1981, she thought they were being made by rats from the wharves along Cape Fear. Poison was put out, but the noises continued. For the past twenty years, she has also heard other noises as well, such as the sound of someone bumping against metal shelves or reading with elbows resting on the shelves when no one else was around. She has also heard footsteps in the Historical Wing late at night, although the ghostly sounds are usually best heard in the morning. In the 1980s, the apparition was sighted three times by library patrons. In 1985, a woman who saw the specter as she was walking around a corner of the stacks could not determine if it was male or female because it had already started to fade before she could catch a good glimpse of it. Later, she told librarians that she put her hand out, and the spot where she reached was cold. Two men described her as a short woman who bore a close resemblance to the local historian who had died some years before. One of the men saw the ghost twice, in 1982 and then again in 1983. He told a reporter for the *Raleigh News and Observer,* "I was looking through the top of the shelves, and I could see her over the books. I called her name. She looked at me, then turned real quickly and flew down to the end of the stacks." He followed the apparition to the front of the history collection where Beverly Tetterton was seated at her desk. When she said that she had seen no one walk past her, the man's face reportedly turned "white as a ghost."

In an interview conducted in 2001, Ms. Tetterton said that the staff knows the identity of the ghost for two reasons: "First of all, we open up in the morning, and we sometimes find a book that was hers lying out on a table. It's the last book she was working on when she died. Also her files were donated to the library, and sometimes we will find them lying around, too." As of 2001, the ghost had not been heard from in two years. Despite this fact, the janitorial staff still cleans the Local History Room before dark, just in case the library's ghost decides to reappear.

The New Hanover County Public Library is at 201 Chestnut Street, Wilmington, North Carolina; phone: 919-341-4390.

The Vander Lights

VANDER

T he South has many small towns whose only claim to fame is its connection with the supernatural. Adams, Tennessee, for example, has the Bell Witch. Carrollton, Alabama, has the face in the window of the Pickens County Courthouse. Not to be outdone, Vander, North Carolina, has a ghost of its own. This sleepy little crossroads between Fayetteville and Stedman appears at first glance to be no different than hundreds of other little towns in North Carolina. However, with a little luck and a lot of patience, an intrepid visitor to Vander might get to see the Vander Lights.

The origin of the phenomenon has been the subject of speculation for over seventy-five years. The legend behind the Vander Lights bears a strong resemblance to two other coastline stories—the Elkton-Emerson Light and the Maco Light. According to one story, a brakeman on a chilly October night in the early 1900s lost his grip and fell onto the tracks, where he was immediately decapitated. Another version of the story has it that a man switched the railroad tracks for the next train, but it appeared out of the darkness ahead of schedule without warning. Barely slowing down for the rural crossing, the train startled the switchman, knocking him into its path. In still another story, a switchman was lost in thought one clear, quiet night when a train roared through the crossing, causing the man to fall from his perch onto the tracks. All of the versions have the same postscript. The spirit of the unfortunate man reappears years later, walking up and down the deserted tracks between Vander and Stedman and swinging his trademark lantern in an endless search for his missing head in the swampy mists.

Many people have sighted the ghost near the spot where the railroad bisects the bay between Vander and Stedman. One of the first reported sightings of the Vander Lights took place around 1917. A resident of Fayetteville named A. J. Carter, who grew up very close to the place where the light has usually appeared, claimed to have seen the light once when he was a boy. He was so shaken by the experience that he refused to walk alone at the spot after dusk. "I would walk a long ways out of my way," he said, "to avoid passing the place after dark."

Vander native Maxine Little and her twin sister Allene saw the light in the 1930s and 1940s when they were growing up on Old Vander Road. They saw the light several times as they were walking over the railroad tracks by a cotton field. Maxine said that the light was usually the size of a man's head, but sometimes it was bigger. It always bobbed back and forth across the railroad track. Because the girls saw the light so many times, they learned to live with it. Maxine never called the light a "ghost," preferring instead to think of it as gasses produced by the effects of weather and temperature on the soil. Although she was never really scared by the light, Maxine was perplexed by its behavior. The light always remained in front of them, no matter how far they walked. Maxine added that as word spread about the Vander Lights, hundreds of students from Fayetteville and other towns cruised along Old Vander Road, just to see the lights.

Fayetteville Times photographer Billy Fisher, who grew up along a country road in Stedman, saw the light only once when he was young, but the memory lasted him a lifetime. Billy described it as a ball of fire. It shot out of the woods and then floated just over the tracks and vanished.

Vander firefighter Chris Bradshaw says that in the late 1970s and early 1980s his home was a well-known sighting place for the Vander Lights. Carloads of people drove into the front yard of the Bradshaw home and parked there for hours in the hope of seeing the ghost. Chris's parents were not exactly pleased with all of the attention, though. "The people would knock on the door," Chris said, "wanting to use the bathroom."

Duane Smith, forty-three, saw the ghost along the railroad tracks when he was a teenager. Smith said, "I don't care how far you walk, he keeps his distance." As a young man in his early twenties, Duane saw the light again, this time when he was working in a nearby field with a group of other men. His co-workers were so scared by the apparition, Duane said, that work slowed down dramatically that day.

A variety of alternative explanations for the phenomenon has been offered by those skeptics who refuse to believe in ghosts. The most common explanation is phosphorous gas, more commonly known as "swamp gas." Many other theories have surfaced as well. Some people have said that the lights could be flares dropped by paratroopers from a military drop zone near Stedman. Wesley Carter, whose house is located by the tracks, says that the mysterious light is nothing more than a Stedman streetlight that can be seen on a clear night.

Sighting of the Vander Lights have diminished in number since the 1980s. Some attribute the "disappearance" of the lights to the lifting of the train tracks between Vander and Stedman. Now the tracks are only used to transport cargo from the Monsanto plant. In the 1990s, a lumberyard cleared much of the woods around the area where the lights were seen. Marshall Spain, who works in a lumber company office next to the tracks, says that he has never seen the Vander Lights, even when he has had to work late at night. Many Vander natives are not quite so eager to give up their ghost. Barbara Cashwell, who works at the Stedman Library, which is housed in the former Stedman train, treasures the memory of the Vander Lights. "It's neat to think that maybe it's real," she said.

The Vander Lights have been sighted along Highway 210 between Vander and Stedman, North Carolina.

SOUTH CAROLINA

Hagley Landing

Except for a few touristy shops, paved roads, and subdivisions, Pawley's Island still looks much the same as it did centuries ago. Hagley Estates, one of the island's most upscale residential communities, was developed on the site of a large antebellum farm known as Hagley Plantation. It is difficult to believe now, but in 1918, this area was the site of one of the most dramatic ghostly encounters in the entire Southeast.

Although other versions of the story of the haunting of Hagley Landing exist, the most dramatic is the interview given to WPA supervisor C. S. Murray by one of the primary witnesses, a cabinetmaker named Eugene F. LaBruce from Georgetown, South Carolina. In the summer of 1918, LaBruce drove passengers between Pawley's Island and Hagley Landing on the Waccamaw. As a rule, he made the trip several times a day. Occasionally, a party of young people who were working in Georgetown would go for a drive after the ferry had made its last trip, and he would meet them at Hagley Landing at 11:00 P.M.

One night, LaBruce reached the landing at 10:45, so he decided to lie down on a piece of canvas and rest a bit before the boat arrived at 11:00. It was a clear, moonlit night. LaBruce became so comfortable that he quickly fell asleep and had a dream so vivid that he still remembered it years later: "I was standing with a crowd of people in front of a little church near the wharf.

A wedding was in progress, and it seemed that we were waiting for the bride and groom to emerge from the front door. Everyone was dressed in clothing typical of the Civil War period, and I gathered the impression that peace had just been declared. After a short while, the bridal party appeared on the church porch. I looked at the newly married couple standing there in the moonlight and noticed that the bride was a striking brunette, and the groom a handsome finely proportioned blond. Both were of the landed gentry class, I imagined.

"As the crowd made a rush for the porch, a man dressed in a Confederate uniform dashed up to the clearing astride a horse that had evidently been running at top speed for hours. The figure dismounted and ran towards the place where the bride and groom were standing. When he reached the couple, the bride uttered a little cry and said, 'It is too late. I have just married the other man!'

"The soldier stood frozen in his tracks and listened like a man in a trance while the woman explained that she had waited three years, and believing that he had been killed in battle, had finally consented to marry one of her former beaus.

"The soldier then turned to the groom and said without show of emotion: 'Well, I will fade out of the picture—it is the best solution.' And he started to leave. Then the groom cried, 'No! If anyone must fade from the picture, I will be that one.'

"The soldier made for the wharf, followed by the bride and groom, and when he had reached the end of the pier, jumped overboard and disappeared. Without a second's hesitation, the woman in white followed him, and then the groom. Everyone was in a turmoil. Boats were launched, strong swimmers discarded their clothing and plunged into the water, and a score of men were calling orders in rapid succession. A mighty gale was blowing from the west, lashing the river into foamy waves which broke against the muddy bank with a resounding roar. The search for the bodies was still underway when I awoke, shivering with excitement.

"I rubbed my eyes and looked about me. The church had disappeared, and the crowd of men and women had vanished. I could scarcely believe that I had been dreaming, for every detail of the harrowing scene was stamped on my brain. Suddenly, I became aware that I was not alone on the wharf. For some reason, I did not feel inclined to investigate, but something impelled me to turn my head. Standing a few feet away from my improvised bed, I saw two figures. I realized with a start that they were dressed like the people in my dream and that the woman closely resembled the bride and the man [resembled] the groom!

"'This is nonsense,' I told myself. 'The boat must have come and gone, and the other people are somewhere around. Those two are trying to play a trick on me.' So I said most politely, 'Will you tell me who you are? If you are waiting to go to Pawley's, I have the automobile ready.' They did not answer my greeting, so I tried again. 'Will you tell me who you are? My automobile is waiting.'

"Neither the man or woman replied, but turned around and strolled off the dock. This made me angry, and I called out, 'You had better stop this foolishness and tell me who you are. I will find out soon enough at any rate.'

"But the couple kept walking slowly away from me and seemed to be whispering to each other. Then I became really frightened and started to imagine all sorts of weird things. Could I have been carried back through the years to the time of the Civil War by some mysterious force, or had I passed from this world when I fell asleep? I tried to recall the history of the region but could not remember ever hearing about a church at

Hagley's or recall reading of such an incident or hearing a similar story. Why, then should I have this dream?"

LaBruce was still trying to answer these questions to his satisfaction when the couple completely disappeared right in front of his eyes. He was standing frozen on the spot when the chugging of a motor woke him from his reverie. The ferry docked, and a young man and woman stepped ashore, relieved that LaBruce had not given up on them and returned to the island. He was still thinking about his strange vision while he drove them through the sandy roadbed.

Later on in the season, on another moonlit night, LaBruce returned to Hagley Landing to meet a special boat that was not due until midnight or later. The three men and three women who climbed into LaBruce's car were looking forward to a moonlight ride through the scented woods and a refreshing swim in the surf. LaBruce was traveling about twenty miles an hour along the narrow road lined with gnarled oaks when he saw two figures step out into the road directly in front of the car. Realizing that there was no clearance on either side of the road, LaBruce came to an abrupt stop, throwing his passengers violently against one another.

Ignoring the complaints of his passengers, LaBruce watched transfixed at the two figures slowly walking arm in arm along the road. He recognized them as the brunette bride and the handsome groom of his dream. The couple spoke quietly to each other, completely oblivious to the car. LaBruce took his eyes off the road for just a second, and when he looked again, the couple had disappeared.

LaBruce once again turned his attention to his passengers. He explained that he had come to a sudden stop to throw the boys and their girlfriends together so that they could become "better acquainted." Then he accelerated the engine to forty miles an hour and headed for the beach.

When they reached the beach, everyone left the car except the girl who had been sitting beside him. She told her friends to run along because she had something to say to Eugene: "The girl turned to me. 'Eugene, I want you to tell me why you stopped the car so suddenly by the ferry landing?'

"'Oh, I just wanted to have a little fun,' I replied. I thought it best to stick to my original story.

"'You needn't tell me that. I know why you stopped.'

"My heart was beating faster and faster. Perhaps this young woman had seen the same figures. In this case—why, nothing was the matter with my mind—and probably two real ghosts had appeared. But I would not give myself away.

"'I told you why I stopped. Why don't you believe me?' I countered.

"'Because'—and she averted her eyes—'you know you saw a man and a woman in the road.'

"'I did not see anyone,' I said in what I thought was an indifferent tone.

"'You can't fool me, Eugene. We both saw those people.'

"'If we did, no one [else] in the automobile saw them,' I asserted.

"'That makes no difference. I saw them and you did too, or you would have never slammed on the brakes like you did.'

"There was no use pretending any longer. 'Yes, I saw them,' I said evenly, 'and I barely missed killing them at that.'"

Instead of telling the girl that he had dreamed about the two spectral figures just a few weeks earlier, LaBruce pretended that he had never seen the man and woman before. Although he never saw the ghosts again, LaBruce firmly believed that they still strolled the wooded paths around Hagley Landing on bright, moonlit nights.

Nothing remains of Hagley Plantation except for huge oak trees hundreds of years old and abandoned rice fields by the river. After the Civil War, the plantation chapel was dismantled. The lumber and oak stalls were donated to the Prince Frederick Pee Dee Episcopal Church, and the stained-glass windows were given to the Prince George Winyah Episcopal Church in Georgetown. In fact, the memory of Hagley Plantation is kept alive primarily because of the events of 1918. To this day, some people report sightings of the ghostly trio along Hagley Boulevard and in the woods around Hagley Landing.

Pawley's Island is on the Grand Strand, eleven miles northeast of Georgetown on U.S. Highway 17. Hagley Estates is located opposite U.S. 17 from the south entrance to Pawley's Island.

The Ladd House

CHARLESTON

Charleston, South Carolina, is one of the most romantic old cities in the entire South. Centuries-old mansions, stately oaks dripping with Spanish moss, picturesque churchyards, all of these elements conjure up images of a more-refined time when vestiges of British gentility could still be found in Charleston. For this reason, in the eighteenth century, this thriving seaport was known as the "London of the New World." Dueling was another British custom commonly practiced in Charleston until it was outlawed in 1834. Probably the most famous duel ever fought in Charleston involved an occupant of a house on Church Street now known as the Ladd House. Some say that the tragic consequences of that duel still resonate in that house to this day.

The Ladd House is a Georgian-style mansion built in 1735 by a wealthy landowner named Thomas Rose. With the exception of a few additions, such as a piazza and an upstairs screened porch, the house looks very much the same today as it did back in 1783 when a twenty-two-year-old doctor from Rhode Island, Dr. Joseph Ladd, boarded here with the two ladies who owned it, the Rose sisters. Dr. Ladd's goal was to set up a general practice and earn enough money so that he could marry Amanda, the girl he left behind in Rhode Island. He gave the impression of being very cheerful to everyone he met. Every day after returning from his office, he bounded up the stairs, whistling an English show ballad. His pleasant disposition made him very popular in Charleston society. However, no one knew that Dr. Ladd was a very troubled young man. He had a tendency to act impulsively, especially when angry. He was also very lonely being separated from Amanda. He spent long hours in his room writing poems to his fiancée. The following lines from one of his poems show how despondent he became at times: "My soul distracted still is fixed on you. / Was ever heart so wretched and true?"

Dr. Ladd did manage to form one strong friendship during his stay in Charleston with a local man named Ralph Isaacs. Even though Dr. Ladd and Isaacs had many interests in common, their difference in social status began to erode their friendship. Isaacs, who resented his friend's popularity, frequently spoke to Dr. Ladd in a very sarcastic manner. One October night in 1786, after viewing a production of *Richard III,* Dr. Ladd and Isaacs got into a heated argument about the acting ability of a young actress named Miss Robinson, who played Queen Anne. Afterward, Ladd and Isaacs began publishing their hostility toward each other in articles published in the *Charleston Morning Post and Daily Advertiser.* Finally, Dr. Ladd decided that he could take no more verbal abuse. He challenged his former friend to a duel.

The next morning, they met in a field outside of Charleston. Dr. Ladd had a change of heart and fired his pistol up in the air. Isaacs, however, wanted Dr. Ladd to suffer. He stared straight at Dr. Ladd, raised his pistol, and fired twice, shooting the kneecaps out from under the young man. Without even looking back, Isaacs marched to his carriage and drove away.

Dr. Ladd was immediately carried back to his room, where a physician removed the two bullets and tended to his wounds. Dr. Ladd lingered on for three weeks until gangrene set in. After great suffering, Dr. Ladd finally died. Some would say, though, that his spirit never really left the place where he had felt so comfortable. Not long after the death of their charming boarder, the sisters began hearing strange sounds. Sometimes late in the afternoon, they heard footsteps running up the stairs. At times, they also heard whistling in the garden, usually the same tune that Dr. Ladd loved so much. Some of the later owners of the Ladd House have seen Dr. Ladd's ghost slowly walking up and down the stairs, whistling all the while. When sighted, his ghost always appears to be in a pensive mood.

The present owner had a very "close encounter" with the spirit of Dr. Ladd in the early 1990s. She was in her bedroom reading at about nine o'clock at night when she heard her children talking and laughing in the bedroom across the hall. Concerned that they had not yet fallen asleep, she left her bedroom and was headed toward her children's bedroom when she saw the figure of a man standing on the stairs. He was dressed in late-eighteenth-century clothing and stared straight at her. Then the ghostly manifestation slowly faded away. She has never seen the ghost since, although shortly afterward, the gardener claimed to have seen a male ghost standing outside in front of the house.

Apparently, there is another ghost in the Ladd House. A psychic who visited the house in the early 1980s went upstairs alone to see if she could channel the psychic energy from Dr. Ladd's ghost. When she came back downstairs, she said that she did indeed sense the spirit of the doctor, but she felt the spirit of a little girl in the drawing room even more strongly. The owner of the house was not very surprised because the year before, a workman repairing the roof had discovered the dress of a little girl underneath a section of slate. The dress was at least 150 years old. Not very much is known about this spirit, aside from the fact that she was a member of the Savage family, who lived in the Ladd House in the 1830s. The child died when she was eight years old and is often seen on the second floor and in the garden.

The most-haunted house on Church Street is still a private residence. Oddly enough, few of the residents have ever felt threatened by the ghostly manifestations. In fact, some of the subsequent owners of the Ladd House have felt that the ghosts are protective spirits. This goes to show that while the sudden occurrence of ghostly phenomena may be startling and possibly even frightening, the knowledge that one is sharing his home with a spirit or two can also be a comforting thought for some people.

The Ladd House is located at 59 Church Street, Charleston, South Carolina.

St. Philip's Protestant Episcopal Church Graveyard

CHARLESTON

So many churches have been built in Charleston that it has been called "the holy city." Undoubtedly, the best known of all the churches is St. Philip's Protestant Episcopal Church, which is the first Anglican church organized in the South. St. Philip's is also the oldest congregation in Charleston. Constructed in 1710, the church was modeled after the Jesuit Church in Antwerp. This impressive structure, known during the eighteenth century as "the most elegant religious edifice in America," was one hundred feet long, sixty feet wide, and forty feet high, with a fifty-foot cupola that housed two bells and a clock. The appearance of the church was so striking that it was used as a landmark by boatmen on the nearby docks. Like many of Charleston's old churches, St. Philip's also has an adjoining cemetery, which is the final resting place of some of Charleston's most illustrious citizens, such as Edward Rutledge, a signer of the Declaration of Independence; the fiery nineteenth-century orator and statesman John C. Calhoun; and DuBose Heyward, author of *Porgy*, which George Gershwin used as the basis for his opera *Porgy and Bess*. However, St. Philip's graveyard is also recognized as being the focal point of two ghost stories separated in time by almost two centuries.

The first of these ghosts is that of an Afro-American slave known only as Boney. He was one of hundreds of dockworkers who unloaded indigo and rice, which was then sold and shipped to ports of entry around the world. Boney's job was to unload the rice that was sent down to Charleston by his master, the owner of the Waccamaw River Plantation. Boney was highly valued as a slave because of his keen eyesight. He was able to see and identify one of his master's schooners long before it docked at Charleston. Boney's sharp eye came in handy one night in 1796 when he was waiting for two schooners loaded with his master's rice to arrive. He was on the dock talking to the factor who also served as the banker and stockbroker on his master's plantation when he was distracted by an odd glow coming from the steeple of St. Philip's Church. He stopped talking in mid-sentence and began running in the direction of St. Philip's. Boney scaled the brick wall of the church and then began climbing the wooden steeple. Finally, when he reached the roof of the steeple at the very pinnacle of the church, Boney found the source of the fire: a burning cedar shingle. He pulled the shingle loose from the pegs that anchored it to the roof and tossed it down into the Cooper River. Boney used his one free hand to rip off his shirt and smother the flames that had just begun to spread to the other shingles.

After Boney climbed down from the church, his life changed completely. The factor who had been watching Boney from the ground reported his heroic act to his master when he arrived in Charleston the next morning. Boney's master was so impressed with his slave's bravery that he granted him his freedom. Boney was elated at first, but adjusting to his newfound freedom proved to be much more difficult than he had imagined. With nothing to do, Boney spent most of his time in St. Philip's cemetery, sitting with his back to a tombstone and gazing up at the church steeple. Before long, he wasted away and died. Boney was buried on the grounds of the Waccamaw River Plantation.

The legend of Boney did not end with his death. Soon after the Civil War, a well-to-do Charleston woman was riding past St. Philip's cemetery in her carriage when she noticed something strange. Ordering her driver to stop, she climbed down from the carriage and began walking through the graveyard. Suddenly, her attention was arrested by the form of what she later described as a "gray man." He had dark skin and hair but eyes that were so white that they appeared to glisten. With his back resting against a tombstone, the man was looking in the direction of the church steeple. Amazed by what she had seen, the woman climbed back into her carriage and returned home to tell the story to her children. She was one of the many people who have seen Boney's ghost down through the years. Often times, he is seen leaning against one of the headstones. But his glance is always directed toward the steeple of St. Philip's Church.

The second ghostly sighting at St. Philip's graveyard is much more recent. On June 10, 1987, a Charleston resident named Harry Reynolds was traveling around taking photographs of some of the city's most scenic locations. By the time he reached St. Philip's graveyard, the gate was locked. Harry really wanted a picture of some of the oldest, most picturesque tombstones, so he stuck his camera through the bars of the wrought-iron fence and took a picture of a row of tombstones in the back of the graveyard. After the film was developed, Harry noticed the transparent image of a woman kneeling on a grave in a position of mourning. Harry was puzzled by the photograph because he did not recall anyone else being in the graveyard on the day he was there. He returned the photo and the negative to the lab to see if the ghostly image was the result of some kind of flaw in the film itself or his own error. The lab determined that the photograph was not a double exposure and that the negative had not been tampered with in any way. No explanation was given for the strange form captured on film by Reynolds's camera.

Even more startling was the information obtained by an examination of the tombstone in the photograph. It marks the grave of a young woman who died at the age of twenty-nine on June 16, 1888. She bled to death internally six days after giving birth to a stillborn infant. The baby died on June 10, 1888, the same day almost ninety years later that Harry Reynolds took his photograph.

St. Philip's Protestant Episcopal Church Graveyard is on 146 Church Street, Charleston, South Carolina; phone: 803-722-7734.

Wedgefield Plantation

GEORGETOWN

The Southeast was undoubtedly the most war-torn part of the country during the Civil War. Renowned historians, like James McPherson, and writers, like William Faulkner, tell us that the effects of the American Civil War are etched in the very landscape, buildings, and sensibilities of southerners. In fact, the Civil War is such an overpowering presence in the South that it is easy to forget that another war was fought here as well, the Revolutionary War. In South Carolina, for example, echoes from the War for Independence can still be heard in the history and the lore of some of the state's oldest buildings. At Wedgefield Plantation, located just north of Georgetown, the horrors of that war produced one of the South's grisliest ghost stories.

Wedgefield Plantation, which was in full operation in 1750, was founded on one of the first land grants in South Carolina. The first house on the estate was a small one-and-a-half-story cottage used primarily by the overseers. The second manor house was erected shortly after a prominent planter-merchant named Samuel Wragg bought the 610-acre plantation. The house was a large two-and-a-half-story, rectangular building with a detached kitchen. The exterior of the house was fairly simple in design, but the interior was anything but simple. Several of the rooms were adorned with beautiful plaster moldings created by the renowned craftsman, Pickney of Charleston. It was a fitting residence for a man of Wragg's status.

Because many of his business dealings were with England, Wragg tried to take a neutral position when the American colonies began fighting for their independence. However, after British forces occupied Georgetown, Wragg was forced to admit where his true sympathies lay. Wragg had no sooner announced that he was a Tory than he was branded a traitor by his neighbors.

Wragg's own daughter was ashamed of him as well, but instead of voicing her disapproval of his political affiliations, she kept silent for a very good reason. Not only did she remain loyal to the Colonies, but she had also become a spy for General Francis Marion, who was trying to keep the coastal area of South Carolina out of British hands. Between 1790 and 1781, the "Swamp Fox" routinely left messages for her in the cemetery of Prince George Churchyard. After she picked up the notes, she placed the information she had gathered in the same location. Wragg, who hated Francis Marion, would have been furious to learn that he was harboring one of the rebel general's secret agents under his own roof.

In the early 1780s, Wragg allowed the British to use his manor house as a temporary prison for known rebels in the area. Wragg also permitted twenty British soldiers assigned to guard the prisoners to be interned on his property. One day, Marion learned that the father of one of his soldiers was among the two men and four women being held prisoner at Wedgefield Plantation. Marion was concerned that the senile old man might, inadvertently, reveal plans for local operations that he had overheard in his parlor. Marion got in touch with Wragg's daughter, who confirmed that the old man and several members of his family were being temporarily lodged in her father's servant house under heavy guard. In the message she left Marion in the cemetery, she mentioned that her entire family was going to attend a party at nearby Mansfield Plantation, including most of the sentries. The girl added that only one British soldier would be left behind to guard the prisoners. Marion agreed that this would be an opportune time to free the prisoners at Wedgefield Plantation.

At twilight the following Thursday, a party of Marion's men galloped through the avenue of oaks on Wedgefield Plantation. Assuming that the men on horseback were British soldiers, the sentry walked down the steps to greet them. By the time he realized that the intruders were really rebel soldiers, the men were almost upon him. While one of Marion's men ran past the sentry into the house to free the prisoners, a saber-wielding cavalryman dashed up the steps and lopped off the sentry's head with a sword. The headless body staggered around for a few seconds and then fell to the ground, convulsing like a decapitated chicken. No one who was present that night ever forgot the terrible death of the British dragoon.

The first ghostly sighting at Wedgefield Plantation was reported several weeks later when Wragg's daughter was awakened by the sound of hoofbeats coming down the drive. She ran over to her bedroom window and stared in horror as the figure of the headless sentry stumbled up the steps to the mansion and then vanished. A few months later, other family members witnessed the headless spirit lurching around the yard. In later years, the sentry's appearances were always announced by strange noises, like the clattering of the hooves of many soldiers, usually just before nightfall. Some witnesses said they heard the sound of chains being dragged across the front porch before seeing the ghost. When the spirit appeared late at night, he occasionally wore his head.

The passage of time has wrought many changes in the manor house at Wedgefield Plantation. In the 1930s, the old house was razed and replaced by a more modern mansion. Then in April 1975, a fire nearly destroyed Wedgefield manor house, leaving only the extreme left and right wings and the front facade. When the mansion was reconstructed, great pains were taken to duplicate the former house. Since the 1930s, the headless apparition of the British dragoon has made only very rare appearances. Most likely, the spirit and the old house were so closely connected that when the manor house was removed from the property, so was the ghost. It is also possible, though, that the ghost no longer roams the plantation because he has found what he was looking for: his long-lost head.

Wedgefield Plantation is now part of a residential resort community on the Black River, five miles north of Georgetown off U.S. Highway 701. Wedgefield Plantation is located at 100 Manor Drive, Georgetown, South Carolina; phone: 803-448-2124.

TENNESSEE

Brinkley Female College

Brinkley Female College is just a memory now. It was located in a section of South Fifth Street that was once a prime residential area consisting of imposing mansions and tall oak trees. Now, it is a commercial strip, lined with railroad buildings and warehouses. The site of Brinkley Female College is occupied by a warehouse built by Wurzburg Bros., Inc. If anyone in Memphis talks about the old college at all, it is usually at Halloween, because Brinkley Female College was the setting of what many consider to be Memphis's best ghost story.

The building that housed Brinkley Female College was originally a house built by Colonel Davie before the Civil War. The two-story mansion sported six Ionic columns across the front and was guarded by an iron gate and stood alone on a small hill surrounded by a grove of old trees. After the Civil War, the house was renovated and transformed into Brinkley Female College, a boarding school for forty or fifty students. The school acquired a reputation as a "weird place" almost immediately after it opened its doors, probably because its founder went bankrupt and insane. The school's image suffered even more as a result of the events of February 21, 1871.

That afternoon, a thirteen-year-old girl named Clara Robertson was practicing her piano lesson in one of the upstairs rooms of the college when there appeared before her the form of a young girl wearing a pink dress. Later, Clara described the girl as being a bony figure with a thin covering of skin and green mold. In an interview published in a local newspaper called the *Avalanche,* Clara said that the ghost was "in the shape of a girl about eight years of age, with sunken, lusterless eyes and strikingly emaciated form and features." At first, Clara sat frozen in the piano chair. Suddenly, she let out a piercing scream, ran into an adjoining bedroom, and climbed in bed with a girl who was ill. Clara and the other girl watched in horror as the specter glided across the room after her and placed its hand on the pillow where Clara's head rested. As the creature tugged at Clara's hair, she buried her head in the pillow and attempted to wave the ghost away with her hand. A few minutes later, the ghost backed out of the room, leaving in its wake two little girls, too frightened even to speak.

Clara eventually summoned up the courage to run downstairs and tell her fellow students what she had seen. Even though Clara was the level-headed daughter of a respected Memphis attorney, her classmates found her story difficult to believe. First of all, the apparition appeared in the daytime, not at night. Secondly, they believed that if anyone was going to haunt Brinkley Female College, it would be the ghost of crazy old Mr. Brinkley and not that of a child wearing a pink dress. Clara was mocked so mercilessly that she left the school and refused to go back.

Under pressure from her parents, Clara returned to Brinkley Female College two days later. The morning of her return, Clara was in the upstairs music room with two other students when they were startled by a noise that they later described as sounding "as if someone were dashing water to the floor." The girls turned around and beheld a skeletal form standing in the middle of the room. Clara claimed to be able to see it very distinctly, but the other girls said that they could only make out a shadowy shape moving slowly in their direction. The girls rushed screaming downstairs and bumped into one of their instructors, Jackie Boone. Gasping for breath, they told Miss Boone what they had seen. The teacher followed the girls upstairs and was shocked to discover that their fantastic story was true. Standing in the middle of the room was the shriveled remains of a little girl. All at once, the ghost pointed a thin finger in Clara's direction. In a voice that only Clara and one other girl could hear plainly, the ghost told her that valuables were buried five feet under a stump that was fifty yards from the house. In the newspaper account of the incident, the ghost was reported to have said that "she would have Miss Clara take possession of [the valuables] and use them to great advantage." Miss Boone said that she heard only an indistinct rumbling sound coming from the mouth of the spirit.

After the ghost vanished, Clara was again subjected to ridicule by her classmates. Before long, the teasing became so intense that Clara began to doubt her own sanity. Later that day, Clara's father came to the school, convinced that his daughter was the victim of a cruel joke. The next morning, Miss Boone reported the incident to the headmaster, Dr. Meredith. While the other girls were questioned, Clara stood outside in the garden. Suddenly, the ghost child reappeared. As Clara opened her mouth to scream, the spirit raised its hand and said, "Don't be afraid, Clara. My name is Lizzie Davie, and I will not harm you." The ghost went on to say that the land on which the college stood once belonged to her father. She added that a large glass jar containing the deed to the land and a collection of coins and jewels was buried under a stump. Because all of Lizzie's relatives were dead, she wanted Clara to have the treasure. Before disappearing, the specter told Clara that she must find the jar herself.

When Clara told people what the spirit had said to her, word of the treasure in the school's garden spread like wildfire through Memphis. Older people recalled that the Davie family had indeed lived in the house and that one of their daughters—a beautiful child with long, dark hair—had died in the house twenty years before. They also recalled that she had been buried in a pink dress instead of a white shroud. The *Avalanche* carried the banner headline, "Brinkley Female College Haunted in an Uproar of Terror and Confusion." The accompanying four-column article included a lengthy interview with Clara. Her story so alarmed the citizens of Memphis that some people refused to venture out at dusk. Many women kept their lamps burning all night long.

Even though Clara's father was a skeptic when he first arrived in Memphis, he soon concluded that the best way to investigate the matter was to enlist the aid of a medium, a Mrs. Nourse. After putting Clara in a trance, Mrs. Nourse handed Clara a pen and paper and began asking her questions. Clara responded that her name was Lizzie Davie, and she gave the date of her death. The spirit also presented a much more detailed description of the location of the treasure.

News of the seance touched off a frantic treasure hunt. Within hours, thousands of people descended upon the little campus with shovels in hand. By midmorning, the stump was completely removed from the ground, but nothing was found but some remnants of a long-buried archway. Meanwhile, Clara was safe inside her home, several blocks away.

The next morning, the ghost made another appearance. This time, Clara listened unafraid to what the spirit had to say. The ghost rebuked Clara for not following her orders and digging for the treasure herself. After the ghost vanished, Clara ran over to the neighbors' house and asked them for advice. They told her to disobey her father's orders and go back to the college to look for the treasure. As Clara approached the now extensive hole in the ground, the crowd parted to make room for her. Reluctantly, Clara picked up a shovel and started digging in the hole. After a few minutes, her shovel struck something solid. She threw the shovel down and began digging frantically with her hands. Suddenly, she cried out, "I can see the jar!" and then fainted dead away without producing the jar. She was carried to the porch of the college and revived, but her father, who had arrived on the scene by this time, said that his daughter was too exhausted to dig any more. While Clara was recovering on the porch, the ghost appeared once more and urged her to continue the search. Clara replied that she could not and pleaded with the ghost to allow her father to continue digging where she had left off. The ghost agreed, but only if her father did not open the jar for sixty days.

Robertson carried the jar to his house, followed by a large throng of people who begged him to open the jar in their presence. Finally, he announced that the jar would be opened on the stage of Greenlaw Opera House. Audience members would be charged a $1.00 admission fee. Half of the proceeds would go to Clara as compensation for her ordeal; the other half would be donated to the Episcopal Church Home for Orphans. However, the Episcopal bishop turned down Robertson's offer because he did not want to be connected with a "ghost in any way."

As it turned out, the bishop's concern about the "ghost money" was unnecessary. Three weeks after the discovery of the jar, Robertson was talking to friends at his home one night when he heard a noise outside. Deciding to investigate, Robertson took leave of his guests and went outside. After a few minutes, they became concerned and began a search for him on the grounds. Robertson was found lying unconscious on the ground with a bleeding head and finger marks on his throat. He was revived just as the doctor walked through the door. Robertson explained that while he was walking around the house, he discovered four men in the act of taking the jar from its hiding place in the outhouse, hanging from a rope under the seat. After the thieves retrieved the jar, one of them grabbed him by the neck and struck him in the head with the butt end of a knife.

According to the *Avalanche,* Lizzie's ghost appeared to Clara once more after the stealing of the jar. She gave Clara the name of one of the thieves and described the others. She also revealed the contents of the jar: $2,000 in gold, one set of gold jewelry, and a diamond necklace. At the end of the article, the writer indicated that the authorities were searching for the culprits and expected to make an arrest soon. However, no one was ever brought to trial for the crime.

The story of Clara and the hidden treasure ends here. After completing her studies, Clara married a spiritualist and achieved a small degree of fame for her seances. The fate of Brinkley Female College, though, was not as promising. As a result of the publicity generated by the press, the college lost most of its students. The headmaster, Dr. Meredith, always maintained that the ghost story was a hoax concocted by the headmasters of competing schools to drive Brinkley Female College out of business. A local family rented the building for a few years after the school closed. Then it was divided up into apartments for railroad workers. After all of the other period homes in the neighborhood were torn down, the old building was finally dismantled in 1972. However, stories of the ghost of Brinkley Female College persisted long after the closing of the school. Up until the late 1940s, some of the residents of the apartments claimed to have seen the ghost of a young white girl floating around the old neighborhood. Sightings of Brinkley's pink ghost are still reported throughout Memphis.

Brinkley Female College once stood on the corner of Fifth and Georgia Streets in downtown Memphis. A large warehouse now stands in its place.

Carter House

FRANKLIN

In his novel *A Separate Peace* (1960), author John Knowles dramatized the effects of war on students in a private boarding school in the early 1940s. As anyone already knows who remained at home while wars were being fought overseas in the twentieth century, no one can be totally insulated from the conflict. However, during the American Civil War, many civilians actually witnessed battles being fought on their property. Such is the case with the Carter House in Franklin, Tennessee.

The battle that eventually engulfed Carter House was the culmination of Confederate general John Bell Hood's attempt to prevent Major General John M. Schofield's 23,000-man army from joining General George M. Thomas's 40,000 Federals in Nashville, Tennessee. On November 18, 1864, after Hood effected a delayed rendezvous with General Nathan Bedford Forrest's 5,000-cavalry force in Tuscumbia, Alabama, he began advancing northward with his Army of Tennessee, now 30,000 strong. Hood's plan was to cut off Schofield at Spring Hill. On November 29, after reaching Spring Hill, Hood dispatched a single division under the command of General Patrick Cleburne to break the Union line, but his men were repulsed by Schofield's advance guard. For some reason, the Confederate army went into bivouac for the night, even though the Union army's escape route to Nashville remained open. As a result, Schofield's entire army was able to slip away under the cover of darkness with very little resistance from Hood's troops.

When news reached Hood the next morning that Schofield's entire command had escaped, he was livid with rage. Convinced that his army's defensive mentality was responsible for the fiasco, Hood set off in hot pursuit of Schofield. That afternoon, Hood found Cleburne's men firmly entrenched at Franklin. At 3:00 P.M., Hood ordered the two corps of Alexander Stewart and Benjamin F. Cheatham to attack the Federal line. The Federals were pushed back along the Columbia Pike, allowing the Confederates to pour through the Union line near the Gin House. However, at the Carter House, General Emerson Opdycke was able to rally enough northerners to plug the gap. Hood's forces continued to hurl themselves against the Federal line, resulting in some of the bloodiest hand-to-hand combat since the Bloody Angle of Spotsylvania. At 9:00 P.M., the Battle of Franklin eventually sputtered to a halt. Later that night, Schofield's army pulled out of Franklin and joined Thomas at Nashville on December 1. Hood's losses were 7,000, three times the enemy's total. Among the Confederate dead were five Confederate generals and fifty-four southern regimental commanders. Hood's foolish belief that his troops would prevail if he forced them to fight practically destroyed the Army of Tennessee.

The Carter House, which found itself in the nucleus of a firestorm in the waning days of November 1864, had been built in 1830 by Fountain Branch Carter. On the last day of November, General Jacob D. Cox established his command post at the Carter House in the middle of the night, despite the protests of the Carter family. The next day during the heat of battle, Fountain

Branch's oldest son, Moscow Branch Carter, herded his elderly father, his three sisters, his daughter-in-law, and an assortment of neighbors, slaves, and children into the cellar. Huddling in the darkness, they could only imagine the horrors taking place inside and outside their house. From the screams and the sounds of gunfire, the Carter family could tell that soldiers were killing one another on the porch. One terrified Union soldier, pressing his body against the slightly recessed doorway, kicked out the lower panel of a door and crawled inside. At one point in the battle, a cannonball smashed into the side of the building.

Later that night, the Carter family emerged from their dark refuge, horrified by the carnage left by the two mighty armies. While surveying the damage to his property, Fountain Branch received some bad news. His son Tod Carter, who had taken part in the Confederate's ill-fated assault on the Union stronghold, was one of the thousands of soldiers who lay wounded and dying on the battlefield. As a member of General Smith's staff, Tod could have remained in relative safety on the hilltop overlooking the family farm, but he had felt compelled to help his family defend their house. Moscow Carter grabbed a lantern and immediately began searching for his lost brother. A few hours later, General Smith joined the search for Tod Carter. Before long, Smith found the young man lying in a bloody heap only one hundred yards from his home. Tod's sisters did what they could for their brother in a first-floor bedroom, but his wounds were too severe. Tod Carter died inside the house he loved two days later.

Although the Carter House is not nearly as haunted as nearby Carnton Mansion, some paranormal activity has been reported since it was first opened to the public in 1953. Staff members and visitors have heard many strange noises in Carter House, such as the footsteps coming from empty rooms and the friendly voice of a spectral woman. Poltergeist activity in the house has also been reported. Staff members have lost objects like car keys in the house, only to find them a few hours later in the exact place where they had left them. Once during a late tour of the house, a visitor pointed out to the hostess that a statue was jumping up and down. Staff members have even felt a small child tugging on their sleeves when no one else was present.

Staff members have attributed the ghostly phenomena in the Carter House to three different entities. Several years ago, one staff member saw the spirit of a little girl vanish as she walked down a hallway toward a flight of stairs, leading to speculation that the child could have been Annie Carter, one of Tod's sisters, or a young relative of the Carters who fell over a banister and broke her neck before the Civil War. On several occasions, Tod Carter has also been seen in the house. He is always seen in the bedroom where he died, sometimes sitting on the bed itself. His apparition is never visible for more than a few seconds.

It is a miracle that the Carter House survived at all considering the ferocity of the battle that raged around it. In fact, so many bullets struck the house that the entire south side had to be replaced. Even harder to believe, though, is the fact that it is haunted by only a handful of ghosts.

Carter House is located on U.S. Highway 31 south of Franklin. The address is 1140 Columbia Avenue, Box 555, Franklin, TN 37604; phone: 615-791-1861.

The Orpheum Theater

The stately old Orpheum Theater has been the theatrical hub of Memphis, Tennessee, since it was built in 1928. For over half a century, audiences have thrilled to productions of some of the century's most popular plays and musicals. Nationally recognized actors and actresses have appeared there. And, apparently, so has the ghost of a little girl.

Two explanations have been given for the origin of the ghost. In one story, she is the spirit of a child who died when the old theater, built in 1890, burned in 1923. However, according to Magevney House curator Marjorie Holmes, no one died in the fire. It is generally held by theater personnel that she is the ghost of a twelve-year-old girl named Mary who was involved in an accident on Beale Street just outside the theater. Some say that she was killed in a car accident near the theater in 1921; others say that she was injured in a 1928 trolley accident and carried inside, where she died. She is usually seen in the early morning hours wearing brown pigtails, long, black stockings and what looks like a white mid-blouse or school uniform. Mary appears to prefer to sit in box C-5 in the mezzanine offstage left in the seat closest to the stage. She often appears when someone is playing the organ. Rarely does she appear during a performance.

Vincent Astor, organist, supervisor, and historian for the theater in the 1970s and 1980s, said that dozens of people have seen Mary. "I never have, but I've felt the strange, cold feeling when she is around." In one incident, which occurred in 1972 when Astor was changing a light bulb in the balcony, he sensed that someone was looking over his shoulder. When he looked to see who it was, there was no one there. "Then I felt that cold eerie feeling many have described. It was like getting into a bathtub of cold liver. Once you feel it, you'll never forget it." Technicians working late at night have also had unnerving experiences in the theater. Terrified workmen have reported hearing the crying of a young girl, the sound of doors slamming, and the footsteps of someone walking through the deserted theater. The translucent image of a figure in a white dress has also been seen flashing through the dark halls and roaming around the top aisles of the balcony.

Although Astor never really confessed a belief in Mary, he had heard too many stories about her over the years to dismiss her entirely as the figment of someone's overactive imagination. "People I trust have reported seeing her," he said. One of these people was actor Yul Brynner, who saw the ghost while rehearsing for a production of *The King and I* in the 1950s. In 1977 the New York company of *Fiddler on the Roof* became so certain the Orpheum Theater was home for a ghost that they held a seance in the balcony after the opening performance. Two years later, a Memphis State parapsychology class tried to make contact with Mary's ghost using a Ouija board and seances. Afterward, the class reported that Mary had died in a falling accident that was totally unrelated to the theater. The students also found evidence of at least six other ghosts haunting the theater.

Despite the fact that Mary's spirit has truly terrified some witnesses, she does not seem to be malevolent. In fact, some people associated with the theater have gone so far as to call Mary a "practical joker." Vincent Astor said that Mary is "shy, but she makes little noises and does mischievous things." Supposedly, she has turned lights off and on, unscrewed light bulbs, thrown doors open, and dumped a maid's tools in the toilet.

Several explanations have been given as to why Mary's ghost continues to haunt the Orpheum Theater. Astor said that she seems to enjoy "the crowds, the lights, [and] the make-believe." He has also implied that Mary flourishes on the energy left in the theater by the casts of productions such as *42nd Street* in the 1980s. It could also be, though, that Mary, like so many other ghosts, is a lost soul, a spirit who does not really know that she is dead.

The Orpheum Theater is located on 203 South Main Street, Memphis, Tennessee; phone: 901-525-7800.

St. Mary's Catholic Church

NASHVILLE

In the nineteenth century, St. Mary's Catholic Church was the nucleus of the Catholic community in Nashville, Tennessee. Although St. Mary's is now dwarfed by neighboring skyscrapers in downtown Nashville, it was the most imposing religious building in the city when it was erected in 1847. Generations of priests have nurtured the spiritual life of the faithful at St. Mary's. And, if the stories passed down by the clergy and the church staff are true, one of the priests has become a spirit himself, haunting the dimly lit corridors and dark recesses of St. Mary's.

Up until the late 1960s, a spectral presence periodically interrupted the serenity of the old church. For many years, the stories of the ghost were rarely heard outside of the church walls. Eventually, though, tales told by priests like the Reverend Thomas F. Cashin and Monsignor Thomas P. Duffy at social gatherings began to circulate throughout the community, culminating in the publication of a newspaper article on the haunting of St. Mary's in the *Commonwealth Appeal* in 1973. According to Richard Quick, secretary of the Diocese of Nashville, only two people ever claimed to have seen the "Ghost of St. Mary's." One of these was a housekeeper of Irish descent named Nell Hines, who worked at the church in the 1930s. Quick said that Nell first saw the ghost one day when she was cleaning the kitchen and glimpsed a strange priest walking up the stairs. Thinking that he might be hungry, she walked over to the stairs and called out to him twice, but there was no response. Puzzled by the priest's aloof manner, Nell went over to Richard Quick's office and asked him who the new priest was who had just gone upstairs, and Quick replied that he had not seen anyone. He helped her search for the mysterious priest but found no one. After seeing the apparition a second time, she asked Father Duffy how long the visiting priest was going to stay so that she would know how many to plan on for breakfast. Nell and Father Duffy looked for the priest all over the church but found no one. According to Father Duffy, Nell saw the priest climb those same stairs on several other occasions. Father Duffy said that Nell never saw the ghost anywhere else in the church but in the rectory.

Quick reported that the only other person who actually saw the ghost was a janitor named John Walker, who had worked at St. Mary's during the depression. One of Walker's duties involved shutting up the church late at night. After he turned off all the lights at the main switch, the only light in the church was that which filtered through the windows from the street-light out on Charlotte Avenue. Walker confided to Quick that many times after all the lights had been turned off, he saw a priest walking down the middle aisle in the faint light coming from the window. Walker said that the priest, who was a little over six feet tall, wore a tall hat and carried a stick in his hand. He was certain that the strange figure was not one of the priests at St. Mary's.

Both Father Duffy and Father Cashin were witness to some strange occurrences at St. Mary's. Father Duffy said that many times the door to the library would swing open while he was sitting in there. Then it would close, and in the length of time that it would have taken someone to walk across the room, his bedroom door opened and shut. The year before his death in 1970, Father Cashin said that he often heard footsteps at St. Mary's at all hours of the night. He also was awakened several times during the night by a knocking at his door. Each time, there was no one there. Father Cashin's most bizarre memory of St. Mary's, though, involved the church bell. He said that during the twelve years that he worked at the chancery office and lived at St. Mary's, the church bell rang three times in the middle of the night. To ring the bell, a rope had to be pulled. On the nights when Father Cashin heard the bell ring, the wind was calm. The first time he heard the bell, he was awakened from his sleep and concluded that he had only dreamed that it was ringing. However, on the other two occasions, he was wide awake when he heard the bell. Both times, he rushed to the choir loft to investigate but found no sign of anyone's having been there.

The most horrifying experience at St. Mary's happened to Monsignor John Morgan in 1937. One night, he had been asleep in his room when he woke up to what sounded like a heavy pounding on his door. His first thought was that the telephone had rung without waking him, so the housekeeper was trying to call his attention to it by knocking on the door. He lifted the receiver of the telephone but got only a dial tone. Monsignor Morgan opened the bedroom door and found that the door to the hallway was closed. Finding no one in the kitchen or dining room either, the priest returned to his room, smoked a cigarette, and tried to go back to sleep. Just as he was drifting off into a peaceful slumber, Monsignor Morgan heard the rapping sound again, this time coming from the headboard itself. He jumped out of bed and turned the light back on. Once again, he failed to find the source of the noise. A few days later, Monsignor Morgan went to the Nashville cemetery where he was a director. He had not been there very long before he fell over dead from a heart attack. No one can say for sure whether or not there is a connection between the priest's midnight visitation and his untimely demise.

Three possible identities have been given for the ghost of St. Mary's. One account has it that a priest fell to his death while the church was being built. This story has never been confirmed, but another priest actually did die there right after the Civil War. He died in the rectory, which was not in the same building that is there now but which stood on the same ground. The priest had been a chaplain with Confederate troops from Tennessee. During a particularly fierce battle, he was shot in the head. He survived his wounds but was frequently subject to fainting spells. One sultry night after the war, he was found dead underneath a window in the rectory. Some say that he had opened the window to let some fresh air into the room, fainted, and fell out of the window to the ground below.

The most widely held belief concerning the identity of the ghost is that it is the spirit of Bishop Richard Pius Miles, the first bishop of the Diocese of Nashville. When he first took the post, there were only three hundred Catholics in the area. However, by the time he died in 1860, the number had greatly increased. Richard Quick believed that the ghost is the spirit of Bishop Miles because the figure described by John Walker wore a hat resembling a bishop's miter and carried a staff similar to a bishop's crosier. In addition, Walker described the ghost as being about six feet two inches tall, the same height as the late bishop. It also seemed to Quick to be no coincidence that the ghostly activity in the church ceased after 1969 when workmen broke through a brick wall in the basement of St. Mary's and discovered the coffin of Bishop Miles. Nothing out of the ordinary has been seen or heard ever since the bishop's remains were moved to a place of honor in an alcove just off the entrance to St. Mary's. Apparently, the bishop prefers his new, more visible resting place to the dank confines of the basement.

St. Mary's Catholic Church is located at 330 5th Avenue North in downtown Nashville, Tennessee; phone: 615-256-1704; fax: 615-256-7307.

The Woodruff-Fontaine House

MEMPHIS

One of the most elaborate showplaces in Memphis's Victorian Village is the Woodruff-Fontaine House. The house was built in 1870 for a carriage maker named Amos Woodruff, who had come to Memphis from New Jersey in 1845.

Within a twenty-five-year period, he expanded his carriage business and became president of two banks. He also had interests in railroad, insurance, cotton, hotel, and lumber companies. In 1870 he directed his architects, Mathias Harvey Baldwin and Edward Culliat Jones, to design a house worthy of a successful Memphis businessman. Woodruff paid $12,600 for a lot at the corner of Adams and Orleans and spent $40,000 on his mansion. He lived there from 1870 to 1883 with his wife, Phoebe, and their four children.

The first of the Woodruffs' children to be married in the house was their nineteen-year-old daughter Mollie. Evidently, Mollie's father knew that his daughter was about to marry when he built the house because he planned the second floor accordingly. He and his wife, Phoebe, lived in the master suite, and Mollie and her husband, a young merchant named Egbert Woolridge, moved into the suite across the hall soon after their marriage on December 18, 1871. Beyond Mollie's room was the nursery, and down the hall was another bedroom for the governess.

Unfortunately, the bedroom at the rear of the second floor turned out to be the scene of great sorrow for the Woodruff family. Mollie and Egbert's only child, a son, died immediately after birth in that room on February 13, 1875. Then in May of that year, Egbert contracted pneumonia during a boating accident on a fishing trip and was brought home for treatment. Within three days, he died at the age of twenty-nine in the same room as his infant son. The doctors said that he had "swallowed too much swamp water." The funeral was held in the house.

Mollie lived on at her parents' house as a widow for eight years. On June 14, 1883, she married again, this time to James Hennings, just before Amos Woodruff sold the house to Noland Fontaine. Mollie and James occupied the same suite where Mollie had lived with her first husband. Once again, though, happiness eluded Mollie. Her only child with James died at birth on January 13, 1885. Mollie herself died thirty-two years later on September 20, 1917, while visiting her sister's home on Poplar Street.

Like many spirits, Mollie's appears to have returned to the house where she felt the strongest bond. Mrs. Elizabeth Dow Edwards, the great-granddaughter of Mollie's sister Sarah, heard some blood-curdling stories while coordinating the costumes at the Woodruff-Fontaine House in 1980. She said that she was cataloging the costumes in the house with a friend, Margo Ramsey, when Margo's daughter Michelle came down to where they were working and said that she felt that someone was following her down the stairs. When she turned around, there was no one there. Another time, Margo heard someone behind her say, "My dear," but once again, no one was there. Mrs. Edwards said that on another occasion, while conducting a tour of the house, a woman who identified herself as a medium informed Mrs. Edwards that she had just received a message from Mollie's spirit. The medium was told that the Cabbage Room was arranged incorrectly. The bed belonged on the staircase wall on the east. Mrs. Edwards's personal encounters with Mollie's ghost were limited to hearing a door slam while she and a friend were preparing for a party. Mrs. Edwards called out, but no one answered. Her friend said, "Oh, that's just Mollie. She always comes back when we are getting ready to have a party."

Jeanne Crawford, director of the Woodruff-Fontaine House museum in the 1990s, believes that Mollie is a very active presence on the second floor of the house. She said that volunteers and visitors at the home have heard the sound of a baby's crying and a voice whispering, "Oh, dear, Oh, dear," in the bedroom where Mollie's first child and Egbert died, now called the Cabbage Room. On one occasion, a young woman saw the image of a young woman in a green dress walking back and forth between the bedroom window and the adjoining nursery. Crawford claimed that one of the most horrifying incidents that occurred at the house while she was there involved a professor from the University of Alabama. While taking a tour of the home, the professor and a tour guide were standing in the Cabbage Room when they witnessed the bedsheets being visibly smoothened, as if an invisible hand had ruffled over the ripples in the sheet. No one was standing near the bed at the time. Later that evening after closing hours, the professor and his family returned to the house. As they stood on the sidewalk looking up at the window of the Cabbage Room, the shutters began to flap wildly. The professor and his family climbed back into the car and returned home as fast as they could.

For the most part, Mollie's ghost is a curious and gentle spirit. However, the ghost that haunts the third floor of the Woodruff-Fontaine House is a much more malevolent entity, thought to be a male. Martha Griffith, assistant secretary-treasurer of Elmwood Cemetery and a former volunteer at the Woodruff-Fontaine House, was leading a tour of the third floor when she sensed that something did not want her up there. Several visitors have also been frightened by this aggressive creature.

Despite the fact that the Woodruff-Fontaine House can be a scary place at times, especially on the third floor, most of the staff at the museum enjoy working there. They have come to think of the house as Mollie's domain, the one place in the world that Mollie always thought of as home, despite the tragedies that occurred. As for the scary ghost on the third floor, the workers have no clue as to his identity.

The Woodruff-Fontaine House is located at 680 Adams Avenue, Memphis, Tennessee; phone: 901-526-1469.

TEXAS

The Alamo

The Alamo is not only one of the most immediately recognizable buildings in the United States, but it is also one of the true American shrines. The defenders of the old mission have become martyrs who died protecting the rights of all Texans for self-government. Their gallant thirteen-day stand against a formidable enemy has been memorialized in song, books, and cinema. Unanswered questions relating to such mysteries as the ways in which Davy Crockett, Jim Bowie, and William B. Travis really died have given birth to a host of legends. Not surprisingly, the blood and violence has also produced a large number of ghost stories.

The mission that has come to be known as the Alamo was originally called San Antonio de Valero. It was built by the Franciscan order on the east bank of the San Antonio River at the junction with San Pedro Creek in 1718. When the river flooded the next year, the mission was moved to the west bank farther away from the creek. However, a devastating hurricane from the Gulf Coast convinced the fathers that the mission should be moved upstream and to the east side of the river where it now stands. After twenty years, the adobe walls were replaced with stone to protect the mission from attacks by the Apaches. By 1793, the mission had been abandoned, providing Spanish troops from the city of San Jose y Santiago del Alamo de Pares with a perfect place to stay. The old fortress became known as El Alamo after the cottonwood trees surrounding the mission.

The Battle of the Alamo had its inception in the decision by the people of Texas to sever their relations with Mexico during the winter of 1835–1836. On December 5, 1835, two hundred Texan volunteers attacked General Cos's troops at San Antonio de Bexar, which was four hundred yards from the Alamo. Cos's twelve hundred troops were completely unprepared for the Texans' house-to-house assault and surrendered on December 9. The Texans, who lost only twenty men, thought they had achieved an easy victory.

However, they did not consider how General Antonio López de Santa Anna, would take the news of his brother-in-law's humiliating defeat. Enraged at the audacity of the Texans, Santa Anna mustered an army of 8,000 men. Despite the frigid desert temperatures, muddy roads, and the scarcity of food and water, Santa Anna pushed his men mercilessly toward Texas. On the first day, fifty oxen died. Cannons and wagons that had become mired down in the mud were abandoned. On February 23, 1836, Santa Anna took the Texans defending San Antonio completely by surprise. As the defenders retreated to the Alamo, Santa Anna ordered his men to hoist the scarlet flag of "no quarter" on top of the bell tower of San Fernando Church. Santa Anna had made his intentions clear. He meant to exterminate American influence in Mexican Texas.

The siege of the Alamo proved to be more difficult than Santa Anna had expected. Inside the old mission were about 150 men under Lieutenant Colonel William Barret Travis. Among the defenders of the Alamo were the border heroes Davy Crockett and Jim Bowie. On February 24, Travis sent out a letter, pleading for help: "To the People of Texas and All Americans in the World.... I shall never surrender or retreat.... Victory or

Death!" The only ones who responded to Travis's call for reinforcements was a relief party from Gonzales on March 2, increasing the Alamo forces to about 187 men.

Santa Anna had ordered his men to pound the Alamo with cannon and rifle fire for twelve days and nights, but after the ten days of siege, he became impatient. At four A.M. on March 6, 1836, Santa Anna's men advanced to within two hundred yards of the Alamo's walls to the bugle call of the *Deguello,* sending the same message as the flag flying above the bell tower. The first two charges were repulsed. During the third charge, however, the Mexicans succeeded in scaling the walls. Fighting was hand to hand with knives, pistols, clubbed rifles, lances, and fists. Blood flowed in the barracks, the convent, and the interior of the church. Ninety minutes after the battle began, it was over. Survivors included Mrs. Susanna Dickinson, the wife of an officer; her baby daughter, Angelina; her Mexican nurse; and a black boy. The bodies of the Texans were stacked up like cordwood in three piles, soaked with fuel, and set afire. Only the corpse of Jose Gregorio Esparza was given a Christian burial because his brother Francisco was a member of General Cos's presidio guards.

The ghosts at the Alamo became active a few weeks after the battle, when General Santa Anna ordered a contingent of young soldiers to transport kegs of black powder to the Alamo. The general wanted to destroy the Alamo so that it did not become a rallying point of the Texas revolution. After the soldiers reached the Alamo, they were met by ghosts with flaming swords who barred the doorways. One of the ghosts said, "Depart, touch not these walls! He who desecrates these walls shall meet a horrible Fate. Multiplied afflictions shall seize upon him, and a horrible and agonizing and avenging torture shall be his death." Apparently, the soldiers feared the ghosts more than they feared their superior officers. Throwing the kegs back into the wagon, the men hurried back to camp, where they told Santa Anna that the spirits of the Alamo would not permit them to blow it up. Even though the Alamo's cannons were removed and the pickets were torn up and burned, the building itself was spared. Later, Santa Anna may have wished that he had defied the ghosts and destroyed the Alamo anyway. In 1836, his army was defeated at the Battle of San Jacinto by an army spurred on by their battle cry, "Remember the Alamo."

Sometime after the fall of the Alamo, it was almost sold by the Catholic church for its stone blocks. After Texas joined the Union, the U.S. Army occupied the Alamo. The military repaired the building and added the bell-shaped roof line. In the late 1860s, the spirits of the Alamo surfaced again in the south wall at the main entryway in the low barracks. At this time, the low barracks was used as a jail. Many of the prisoners complained that they had difficulty sleeping because of the racket made by ghosts. The authorities believed that making the prisoners sleep with ghosts amounted to "cruel and unusual punishment," so they decided to tear down the low barracks and build a new jail. However, the threatened destruction of their home awakened the ghosts. For several weeks, guests at the nearby Menger Hotel reported seeing ghosts marching at the low barracks to protest its demolition. In 1871, the low barracks was torn down anyway, despite the objection of the ghosts of the Alamo.

Over the years, ghosts and paranormal events have been seen by visitors, spiritualists, ghost hunters, and employees. As early as 1897, tourists spoke of seeing ghosts in the rear of the building. Spectral figures wearing buckskins or period attire from the early 1880s have also been reported in the Alamo. On a lonely winter night in 1991, one of the Alamo rangers saw a lone figure wearing a long coat and tall hat walking with his head down toward the gift shop. The ranger called out to the man, and when he turned around, the ranger could see that he was wearing a bushy mustache. The stranger then continued walking and disappeared as he passed the rear of the chapel.

Another commonly seen apparition in the Alamo is a soldier wearing a buckskin shirt, pants, moccasins, and a coonskin cap. He is usually seen holding his rifle and standing at attention in the rear of the chapel near the northeast corner. One hot afternoon in the summer of 1997, a couple walking through the grounds saw a man in a full-length, western coat standing near the back entrance to the chapel. He appeared to be soaking wet. Just as they began walking toward the man, he disappeared. Possibly the most terrifying spectral encounter at the Alamo occurred when a ranger was looking for stragglers in the long barracks at closing time. All at once, he came upon a man dressed in buckskins standing with his back against the wall. The man was bleeding profusely from two bullet holes in his chest. A couple of seconds later, the ghosts of two Mexican soldiers appeared with bayonets. They ran over to the wounded man and began stabbing him repeatedly. Within ten seconds, all three figures vanished.

The gift shop has been the scene of several sightings. Many rangers have seen the image of a little boy looking forlornly out of one of the high interior windows. The child has been described as being between ten and twelve years old with blond hair. In February 1994, five gift shop employees had an encounter with another melancholy spirit in the gift shop. They were taking inventory in the basement when they heard the sound of a woman sobbing. When a search of the basement failed to produce the source of the weeping, the women continued counting books and other items for several hours. Finally, one woman became so upset by the eerie sounds that she ran upstairs and refused to go back downstairs. On a different occasion, two women working in the stockrooms in the basement area heard the soft crying of a child. Once again, the source of the crying was never found. Other gift shop employees working in the basement have had the feeling that they were being watched and followed.

Eerie voices have been heard throughout the Alamo. In January or February of 1978, a ranger heard voices coming from the rear or northernmost area of the long barracks. As he walked through the barracks, the ranger heard a series of staccato commands: "No! Stop! Fire!" After a thorough search of the building, he was unable to find the source of the voices. In 1991, another ranger was making his rounds through the north end of the long barracks when he began hearing voices which were barely audible at first but then rose to a murmur. As the ranger approached the south end of the long barracks, the murmuring became louder, but he could not make out any of the words. He turned around and was about to leave the building when he heard a voice call out, "It's too late!" The ranger did not wait to find out the meaning of the words; he exited the building as fast as he could.

Evidently, the storied past of the Alamo is so long and extensive now that even people associated with the old mission have become part of its lore. One of these individuals is actor John Wayne, who produced, directed, and starred in the 1960 film *The Alamo*. Rumors of Wayne's spectral visits to the Alamo began to surface in 1990. A story published in the *National Examiner* claimed that Wayne's ghost returned to the Alamo to protest the publication of Jeff Long's controversial revisionist history of the Battle of the Alamo entitled *Duel of Eagles*. Many San Antonians, including the group that preserves and runs the Alamo, the Daughters of the Republic of Texas, were very upset by Long's unheroic depictions of Davy Crockett and Jim Bowie.

In 1991, the *San Antonio Express Magazine* called on a well-known San Antonio psychic named Joe Holbrook. He was invited to visit the Alamo and see if he could communicate with John Wayne's spirit. During his drive downtown, Holbrook tuned into the ghost of a bootmaker named Buttons Morgan, who distinguished himself by caring for the wounded soldiers during the siege. When Holbrook and the reporter entered the shrine, the psychic immediately sensed the presence of six Mexican soldiers who were killed trying to persuade the defenders to surrender. Holbrook then asked the ghost of one of the Mexican soldiers, a lieutenant named Pedro Escalante, about John Wayne. He was told that Wayne's ghost comes back to visit the Alamo once a month. Escalante added that, to Wayne, the Alamo is "the guts of freedom." Before the lieutenant's ghost vanished, he told Holbrook that the spirits of all of the defenders of the Alamo plan to convene there in 2002.

Although many of the workers have had supernatural encounters at the Alamo, the management prefers to focus on the historical aspects of the old shrine. But some skeptical employees have learned to respect the spirits of the Alamo, even if they do not believe in them. One night several years ago, two rangers went to the chapel at ten o'clock to find out why the lights were on. While they walked through the chapel, they joked around and pretended to scare each other. Finding no one inside the building, the two men were on their way out when they heard chanting and saw a blue light hovering around the monk's burial ground enclave. After they rushed through the door and locked up, they vowed never again to mock the ghosts of the Alamo.

San Antonio is in south-central Texas at the junction of I-10 and I-35. The Alamo, Alamo Plaza, San Antonio, TX 78201; phone: 201-222-1693.

Driskill Hotel

L ike Texas itself, the Driskill Hotel is built on a grand scale. The Traditional Guest Rooms, located in the Driskill Tower, are decorated in the soft color palate of the Texas Hill Country. The sixty-six Historic Guest Rooms feature nineteen-foot ceilings, original works of art, and luxurious draperies. This nineteenth-century palace also offers twelve suites with names such as "Victorian Suite," "Renaissance Bridal Suite," and "Capitol Suite." Guests staying at the Driskill are made to feel that they have been treated like the cattle barons and governors after whom some of the suites are named. For some people, another of the hotel's amenities is the prospect of sharing a room with a ghost.

Jesse Lincoln Driskill, builder of the Driskill Hotel, was born in Tennessee in 1824. He moved to Texas at the age of twenty-five and eventually entered the cattle business in 1857. Earning the rank of colonel during the Civil War, Driskill made and lost a fortune selling cattle to the Confederate army. In 1869, Driskill, his wife, Nancy Elizabeth Jane Day, and their four daughters and two sons moved to Austin, situated in the heart of Texas. In the early 1880s, after Austin had become the capital of Texas, Driskill became a wealthy cattle baron and respected civic leader. In 1884, he drew up plans for a luxury hotel worthy of the capital of the largest state in the Union. He bought the lot at the corner of Brazos and Pecan Streets for $7,500 and commenced building his dream hotel. When construction was completed in 1886 at a total cost of $400,000, the *Austin Daily Statesman* proclaimed the Driskill to be "one of the finest hotels in the whole country." Only two weeks after the grand opening, the inaugural ball for newly elected Texas governor Sul Ross was held at the Driskill. In later years, the Driskill hosted the inaugural balls of other governors as well, such as John Connally and Ann Richards.

Despite the hotel's auspicious beginning, the next few years did not bode well for the Driskill. In May 1887, the general manager and half the staff were lured away by Galveston's Beach Hotel, causing the hotel to shut down temporarily. The hotel reopened under new management in October 1887, but a severe drought killed off most of the colonel's cattle, forcing him to sell the Driskill Hotel in 1888 to Doc Day. Colonel Driskill died of a stroke in May 1890. His portrait now hangs in the lobby.

The Driskill Hotel went through a series of owners in the next few years. In 1893, Day traded the Driskill to an actor named M. B. Curtis for a California ranch and a vineyard plus $14,000. The next year, it was sold at auction for $75,000 to the British holders of its mortgage. In 1895, another cattle baron named Major George W. Littlefield purchased the Driskill for $106,000 in cash. Over the next eight years, Littlefield made substantial improvements in the Driskill, including twenty-eight lavatories with bathtubs, electric fans in every room, and oil painted frescoes on the ceilings. The Driskill was sold again in 1903, this time to Edward Seeling for $80,000 cash.

Over the next sixty years, a series of important historical events took place at the Driskill. In 1904, the Daughters of the Texas Republic met at the Driskill to determine the fate of the Alamo. In 1910, the Driskill hosted Governor William P. Hobby's inaugural ball, the most spectacular event to date, complete with several orchestras playing in stereo behind forests of ferns. In 1934, Lyndon Baines Johnson had his first date with his future wife, Lady Bird, at the Driskill. Johnson's sentimental attachment to the old hotel intensified down through the years. In 1960, he awaited the results of his race for vice president at the Driskill. Then in 1964, he awaited the results of his reelection as president of the United States there. The Driskill also served as the headquarters for the White House Press Corps. During Johnson's term as president of the United States, the Governor's Suite on the fifth floor was permanently reserved for him.

Ultimately, it was the Driskill Hotel's historic past that saved it from destruction. In November 1969, an article in the *Austin American-Statesman* declared that the Driskill was "to meet its end at the hands of a wrecking crew." Spurred on by the news of the fine old hotel's slated demolition, the Heritage Society of Austin designated the Driskill a historic landmark. Then in 1970, a Save the Driskill community effort raised $700,000 through the sale of ten-dollar stock for the Driskill Hotel Corporation. Over the next twenty-five years, ownership of the Driskill changed five more times. In 1995, the Great American Life Insurance Company purchased the Driskill, promising to spend up to $30 million to completely restore the hotel. Finally, on December 31, 1999, the old hotel's new lease on life was celebrated in a grand reopening millennium celebration.

Among long-time employees of the Driskill, the hotel has a reputation for more than opulent furnishings and a rich history. For many years, waiters, maids, managers, and guests have experienced poltergeist-like activity there. People have been in situations where closet lights turned on by themselves. Guests have had their luggage mysteriously moved to different parts of their rooms. Pipes have banged at night for no apparent reason. The most frequently reported phenomena involve elevators which go up and down during the night without passengers.

The hauntings at the Driskill received national attention as the result of a visit by a New York rock group named Concrete Blonde. The group, which was scheduled to back up rock singer Sting on a tour stop at the Erwin Center, checked into the Driskill Hotel in March 1991. One member of the group, Johnette Napolitano, said that her sleep was interrupted by a playful ghost: "He kept turning the lights on and off in my room. I finally unplugged all the lamps. Then he turned on the light in the closet and very slowly opened the closet door, just like a hand was opening it. The light was on in the closet and it shined out into the room onto the bed. Then I knew for sure. I knew he was in there. I just said, 'I knew you're here, but I know that you're not going to hurt me, so I'm going to sleep now.'" A friend of a member of Sting's band had an even more frightening experience at the Driskill when a spirit tickled her feet and then disappeared under the bed. Ms. Napolitano commemorated her experience at the Driskill in a hit song entitled "Ghosts of a Texas Ladies' Man," in which she refers to her strange visitor as her "ectoplasm lover."

Evidence suggests, however, that the ghost, if there is one, is probably not a male. One of the hotel's prevalent legends has it that two women committed suicide in the same room thirty years apart. This story's credibility was enhanced by a Dallas newspaper travel article published in 1986 which reported that a maid saw the ghost of one of the legendary suicides. Tye Hochstrasser, the Driskill's director of sales, dismisses such tales as being nothing more than myth. He points out that there is no record of any suicides having occurred in the hotel's history. He cannot explain, though, why the elevators move at night when no one is around: "We've had Otis (the elevator manufactures) out here, we've had the people who work on the elevators, and they can't figure it out. Those elevators will be opening and closing and going up and down all night long. Is that a ghost? You tell me."

The Driskill Hotel is located at the corner of 6th Street and Brazos Street, Austin, Texas; phone: 512-474-5911.

The Houston Public Library

HOUSTON

Ghosts are perceived by many people to be horrifying entities, bent upon taking revenge upon their murderers or reenacting their own deaths. The ghost lore of the American South also includes stories of gentle spirits whose return is comforting, particularly for those people who knew them before they died. Such a spirit is the custodian of the Houston Public Library.

The Houston Public Library opened in late 1926. The construction of this Spanish Plateresque building was directed by the librarian Julia Ideson. She was also in charge of furnishing the building and keeping it growing. Like a corporate executive, she arrived at work early, stayed late, and worked on weekends. For many years she was the driving force behind the library.

Another fixture at the Houston Public Library was an Afro-American custodian named J. Frank Cramer. Frank, who was born in 1873, spent much of his life at the Houston Public Library. In 1921, he started working at the 1904 Carnegie Library at the corner of Travis and McKinney, where a parking garage now stands. When the new library opened in 1926, he began working there. Even though people who knew Frank remembered him as having a "sweet smile," he lived alone in the basement of the library. His only companions were his German shepherd, Pete, and his beloved violin.

Every day after the library closed, he walked from floor to floor, up the stairs, across the halls, through the stacks, playing his violin all the while. He continued strolling through the library until he reached his favorite spot—the balcony of the rotunda. For hours, he would sit on the balcony, playing Strauss waltzes long into the night. Staff members who knew Frank say that Pete was a music lover, also. After running up the stairs, the exhausted dog would sit by Frank and wag his tail to the music.

Aside from being the library's custodian, Frank also served as the gardener. His love for plants was evident in the bright flowers and trimmed bushes clustered around the entrance. One of his plants has become a living memorial to the smiling custodian. Shortly before he died in 1936 at the age of sixty-three, he took a cutting from the huge 1854 Bagby Oak to the left of the McKinney Street entrance and planted the seeds of the Cramer Oak, the smaller tree to the right.

The Houston Public Library was the only home J. Frank Cramer ever knew, and, if the stories can be believed, it still is. Library patrons and staff claim that on cold, dark days, one can still hear Frank's music. The plaintive strains of his Strauss waltzes always start in the basement, filter through the first-floor corridors, then rise up to the second floor and up to the third-floor balcony, where the music is always the loudest. Then, without warning, the lilting melodies fade away.

Frank's ghostly recitals do not happen every day. In fact, some of the library staff have never heard the music and dismiss the ghost's existence entirely. Disbelievers who have heard the melodies claim that the music comes from nearby skyscrapers. Others say that the pleasant sounds are only the wind blowing through the stately Burr Oaks. This is not to say, however, that the hundreds of students, matrons, and businesspersons who have heard the strange sounds for the past half century can be convinced that it is not the violin music of the library's lonely janitor.

The Houston Public Library is off Main Street in downtown Houston, Texas; phone: 713-236-1313.

The Texas Governor's Mansion

AUSTIN

Haunted places in the American South take many shapes, from the humblest cabin to the most stately Victorian showplace. Records indicate that even the abodes of our nation's leaders have been known to harbor a ghost or two. The most famous example is the White House, where the shadowy form of Abraham Lincoln has been known to walk at night. In Austin, the most historic house in the entire state is not only home to the governor, but to a couple of resident ghosts as well. In fact, the Governor's Mansion is the only historically haunted house remaining in Austin.

The governor of Texas has not always had a permanent place to live. After independence was gained from Mexico in 1836, the governor's residence changed frequently for the next few years. In 1842, a large "President's House" was constructed in

Austin. After a few years, the wooden structure began to fall into disrepair, so it became readily apparent that the governor would need a more substantial home. Before the house was demolished, the furnishings were stored away until the new mansion was built. In 1854, nine years after Texas became a state, the legislature appropriated $14,500 for the construction of a "suitable residence" for the governor of Texas. Austin master builder Abner Cook adapted the popular Greek Revival style of architecture to the frontier. The design for the house included a deep verandah, floor-length windows, and wide hallways. The square plan of the building placed four main rooms on each floor. The rear wing held a kitchen and servants' quarters. Construction on the Governor's Mansion was completed on June 14, 1856. Its first residents were the fifth governor of Texas, Elisha Marshall Pease, his wife, Lucadia, and their daughters.

Like the tales centered around much less prestigious buildings, the haunting of the Governor's Mansion has its origins in a family tragedy. In 1864, it was occupied by Governor Pendleton Murrah and his family, which included his flirtatious young niece. Several young men in Austin were smitten by her charms, including a young man who had been visiting the governor. Hoping that she felt the same way he did, the young man proposed marriage. To his dismay, she threw back her curly head and laughed in his face. Devastated, the young man retired to a small north bedroom in the mansion. At midnight, the family was awakened by a pistol shot. Rushing to the young man's room, family members were shocked to find him sprawled on the cherrywood bed with a gun in his hand. He had shot himself in the head. When it was determined that he was dead, his corpse was removed, and the room was sealed.

Not long afterward, servants talking among themselves reported hearing agonized moans coming from the north bedroom. Their suspicions that the room was haunted were confirmed one night when the governor and his wife were away. The sixteen-year-old daughter of one of the servants and her girlfriend decided to spend the night in the "haunted" room. Around midnight, their excitement was instantly transformed into horror as the room was filled with the wailful moaning of an unseen presence. The terrified girls leaped out of the bed and ran down the hall, convinced once and for all that there was truth in the intriguing stories they had heard about the north room.

The death of the young suitor turned out to be a bad omen for the family. Toward the end of the Civil War, Governor Murrah was stricken with tuberculosis. Determined to die a hero, the governor put on his gray uniform and rode south to Mexico with Confederate governor Joe Shelby's army. Murrah died somewhere along the way, and he was buried in an unmarked grave.

The Union-appointed governor of Texas, Andrew Hamilton, moved into the Governor's Mansion in 1870. When the north bedroom was opened, the governor was shocked to see that the blood splatters on the wall had not been cleaned up. The servants had hoped that the moaning would cease after the blood had been removed, but this was not the case. By some accounts, the moans have continued to this day. The sounds can usually be heard on Sunday afternoons.

The spirit of the rejected lover is not the only ghost in the Governor's Mansion. Sam Houston's forceful personality also seems to have made a lasting impression on the mansion. The hero of the Texas Revolution was elected governor of Texas in 1859. The huge mahogany four-poster bed that he ordered for the sparsely furnished mansion is now located in the southeast bedroom. Sam and Margaret's eighth child, Temple Lea Houston, became the first baby born in that bed and in the mansion. All of Houston's children turned out to be as cantankerous as he was. His five-year-old son Andrew Jackson Houston once locked members of the legislature in their chamber. The feisty little boy refused to turn over the key until his father threatened to have him arrested. Needless to say, the Houstons' stay in the Governor's Mansion will not be soon forgotten.

Some residents of the mansion would argue that Sam Houston never really left. The Governor's Office assistant press secretary said that Texas first lady Linda Gail White had first-hand experience with Houston's defiant spirit. One night, she turned off a light burning above a portrait of Sam Houston. A few minutes later, the light turned back on again. After trying to keep the light off a couple more times, Ms. White let Mr. Houston's spirit have his way.

Living in the state's best-known haunted house does not seem to have affected the number of applicants for the job of governor down through the years. However, the journalist Pete Szilagyi argues that the hauntings just may be the reason why the Texas governor's term has been limited to only two years. "A man can only take so much," Szilagyi says.

The Governor's Mansion of Texas, the fourth oldest governor's mansion continuously occupied in the United States, is open to the public for tours and for virtual tours. It is located at 1010 Colorado, Austin, Texas; phone: 512-463-5516.

The Villa Main Railroad Crossing

In towns and cities scattered across the American South, one can find railroad crossings where accidents have taken place between trains and cars. Some of these crossings have been justifiably labeled "death traps" because of the absence of crossing guards or because of heavy foliage limiting the drivers' vision. In most cases where collisions have occurred, the fault is clearly the drivers'. This fact does not make the death toll any easier to take, especially when the victims are children. In San Antonio, Texas, a tragedy that occurred at a lonely railroad crossing has been transformed into a harrowing legend.

According to most accounts, the accident took place in the late 1930s where the railroad tracks cross Villa Main Street on a small hill. The driver of a school bus had pulled up to a crossing that was unmarked except for two signposts. Instead of stopping a safe distance, opening the door, and looking in both directions, as most school bus drivers are required to do today, the driver took a quick glance and proceeded across the tracks. Without warning, a speeding freight train broadsided the school bus, pushing it down the tracks. After the train finally stopped, the crew rushed over to the bus to inspect the damage. The grisly sight inside the wreckage made even the strongest man look away. The driver was fine, having bailed out of the driver's seat at the last minute, but ten children ranging in ages from five to fifteen died that fateful day. To commemorate the event, streets in the nearby McCreless Meadows neighborhood were named after the victims of the bus crash.

For over sixty years, people in the area have claimed that the Villa Main railroad crossing is haunted. It has been said that if a driver pulls up to within fifty feet of the crossing at the bottom of a slight incline, puts the car in neutral, and steps out of the car, the ghosts of the dead children will push the vehicle across the tracks. People also say that if the motorist stalls at the crossing or refuses to move, the spirits become frustrated and break the windshield. Anguished cries of terror have been heard at the spot as well. Moans have been heard late in the afternoon at about the time the accident occurred. If the motorist's car is dusty when it is "moved" across the tracks, small, childlike hand prints are visible on the trunk.

Skeptics have proposed several different theories to explain away the phenomenon. Some claim that the incline is an optical illusion and that it's really a downhill coast across the tracks. Other particulars of the accident have also been questioned. The tale has been set in different decades, from the 1920s to the 1950s, depending on who is telling the tale. One reader of the *San Antonio Express-News,* Kayra Miller, said that the streets in the McCreless Meadows subdivision are named after the Mc-Creless children and grandchildren, not after the victims of the bus crash. Author and storyteller Docia Williams researched the legend extensively and concluded that there is no truth in it at all. After searching the archives of local newspapers and contacting the San Antonio Police Department, she was unable to find any documentation of a bus accident involving children at this particular crossing. She learned, in fact, that before 1967, no school buses traveled that far out on Villa Main Road. She also secured a report from a surveyor proving that the grade appears to be uphill, but it is actually downhill all the way. The phantom fingerprints that mysteriously appear on the rear of a car that has moved across the tracks, Williams said, could be old fingerprints that did not adhere to the dust. Finally, Williams traces the mysterious cries around the site to a nearby peacock farm.

Williams's well-publicized debunking of San Antonio's official ghost story has hardly diminished the crossing's allure, especially for teenagers hungering for a "cheap thrill." For years, the police have had concerns with traffic and safety in the area, especially around Halloween. There are still no crossing arms or street lights out there, making the area an ideal dumping ground for dead bodies. Media coverage of the phenomena are at least partially responsible for the crossing's continued popularity. In 1995, the syndicated television program *Sightings* sent an investigating team to test the validity of the legend. A car was parked at the "downhill" end of the grade. One member of the team sprinkled baby powder on the trunk. Then the gear shift was set in "neutral." Slowly, the car began "climbing the grade" across the tracks. While the cameras rolled, small hand prints could be seen forming in the baby powder. For those who cannot accept the "easy," scientific explanations, seeing is truly believing.

The Villa Main railroad crossing is located near Villa Main and Shane Roads. The tracks cross Villa Main Street on a small hill near the Stinson Airport, just outside San Antonio, Texas.

VIRGINIA

Eppington

Eppington is probably the best known of Chesterfield's colonial plantation houses. The house is important from an architectural viewpoint because it has seen virtually no substantial alterations. Therefore, any visitor to Eppington would come away with a fairly accurate picture of how a gentleman farmer would had lived in the eighteenth century. However, Eppington's historical value lies primarily in its connection to Thomas Jefferson. The tragic fate of Thomas Jefferson's daughter Lucy has been memorialized in a ghost tale remembed by only a few residents of Chesterfield.

Eppington was built by Colonel Francis Eppes between 1765 and 1775. The layout of the building is unique among early Virginia dwellings. It is a formal three-part house, featuring a rectangular two-and-a-half-story central block. The plan of Eppington's main block is a variation on the traditional hall-parlor scheme, created by adding a narrow stair passage along the north side of the larger room. Its exterior form basically followed the newly fashionable multi-unit "Palladian" scheme. However, the workmanship of parts of the interior is highly unconventional, probably reflecting the limited skills of the craftsmen. For example, the paneled chimney walls are somewhat lacking in symmetry.

Colonel Eppes, a burgess from Henrico, became one of the wealthiest and most influential men in Chesterfield. The first statewide census, taken in 1701, lists him as the owner of 125 slaves, the largest number recorded in the county. Eppes's wealth was due in part to his expertise in farming. His gardens and orchard were so renowned throughout Virginia that Thomas Jefferson called him "the first horticulturist in America." Jefferson also declared Eppes to be a man of sound practical judgment. During his tenure as burgess, Eppington attracted quite a few famous visitors, including the English architect and engineer Benjamin Latrobe, who was instrumental in the construction of the U.S. Capitol in Washington. He was so impressed with the house when he visited it in 1796 that he drew a sketch of Eppington.

Thomas Jefferson also had a strong personal link to Francis Eppes. They married half sisters, the daughters of John Wayles in Charles City County. In 1782, following the death of his wife, Jefferson brought his two young daughters to be raised by Francis Eppes and his wife, Elizabeth. He was certain that his girls would be in good hands with their aunt and uncle while he served as Minister to France. Unfortunately, Eppes and his wife could not protect Jefferson's daughters from the ravages of disease. His beloved daughter Lucy died in the fall of 1784, only one month after her father had left for France. She was only two years old.

Jefferson himself did not receive the news until Lafayette brought letters from Francis Eppes and Dr. James Currie in January 1785. Eppes's letter described Jefferson's daughters Lucy and Mary and Eppes's own daughter, also named Lucy, as having been stricken with whooping cough. Dr. Currie's letter simply stated that Lucy Jefferson and Lucy Eppes had died of the disease. Eager to learn more about his daughter's death, the grief-stricken Jefferson wrote to his brother-in-law, begging him to send letters by a speedy French packet. On May 6, six months after learning of Lucy's death, Jefferson received two letters from

Elizabeth, dated October 13 and 14, 1784. Elizabeth wrote, "It is impossible to paint the anguish of my heart. . . . A most unfortunate Hooping cough has deprived you, and us, of two sweet Lucys, within a week. . . . Your dear angel was confined a week to her bed. Her sufferings were great though nothing like a fit. She retain'd her senses perfectly, called me a few moments before she died, and asked distinctly for water." The death of Lucy made Jefferson more keenly aware that his wife's relations had exerted more of a parental influence on his daughters than he had. Consequently, he sent for Mary to live with him after he became established in Paris. Mary arrived in 1787 over the objections of her aunt and uncle. Even with Mary by his side, though, Jefferson never fully recovered from the death of little Lucy.

Eppington passed into the hand of Eppes's daughter Lucy (named after her deceased sibling, Lucy, as was sometimes the custom) and her new husband, Archibald Thweatt, in 1810. In 1836, Eppington was acquired by Richard N. Thweatt, the husband of Francis Eppes's other daughter, Mary. The farm left the family in 1862 when it was purchased by Henry Cox. Eppington was abandoned in 1862. When William Hines bought the house in 1876, it was in such a sad state of disrepair that hogs were living in the basement.

Descendants of the Hines family occupied Eppington until well into the twentieth century. The last owner of Eppington, Mr. William F. Cherry, was a descendant of the Hines family. In the 1980s, local historian Pattie Grady was having tea with Mrs. Camilla Cherry and another lady when she learned of the ghost of Eppington. Mrs. Cherry told them that ever since she and her husband had begun using the house as a retreat, they had heard the sound of a little girl crying on the second floor. However, when they went upstairs to investigate, the child was nowhere to be seen. Mrs. Cherry went on to say that this had happened over and over again. According to the family legend, the little girl was Lucy Jefferson, who had died so miserably in the house almost two centuries before. Mrs. Cherry was convinced that the story was more than just an old legend. She insisted that the crying that she and her husband had heard was real. They did not imagine it.

The Cherry family donated the house and forty-five acres to Chesterfield County in 1989. The house had been lived in from the 1760s to 1985. The Eppington Foundation was established in 1998 to attract resources for the ongoing renovations, preservation, and restoration. As of this printing, Eppington has been stabilized to prevent the old house from simply falling apart. A new roof has been added, and the foundation has been fortified. Further restoration will have to wait until funding is secured. The public is privileged to walk inside Eppington only once a year during the Eppington Day celebration. No further reports of the haunting have surfaced since the death of Mrs. Cherry. One can only hope that Lucy Jefferson has finally found peace.

Eppington is in the southwestern tip of Chesterfield near the Appomattox River and many miles off the old country road which runs from Petersburg to Amelia County.

Lee's Boyhood Home

Many of the houses lining the cobblestone streets of Old Town, built during George Washington's time, represent the aristocracy of American architecture. The hand-carved moldings, marble fireplaces embellished with cornucopias, parquet floors, and majestic gardens recall a time when names synonymous with the American Revolution visited one another's homes in elegant horse-drawn carriages. Walking through these restored colonial cottages and mansions, one can understand why ghosts have chosen to reside here in the afterlife instead of in the dilapidated, creaky houses found in campfire legends. In the house at 607 Oronoco Street, the spirits of one of America's most illustrious colonial families—the Lee family—are still active and, according to most witnesses, very friendly.

The boyhood home of Robert E. Lee was built in 1795 by John Potts, a business associate of George Washington. Four years later, it was purchased by William Henry Fitzhugh. Considered at the time to be one of the finest houses in the area, it became the home of the Lee family in 1810 when Robert was three years old, primarily because of financial hardship. Lee's father, Richard Henry "Lighthorse Harry" Lee, lost the family's ancestral home at "Stratford," Robert's birthplace, because of an unpaid loan of $40,000 to Robert Morris, who was ruined financing the Revolutionary War. Fortunately, a relative of Anne Carter

Lee offered the Alexandria house for the otherwise homeless Lees. Even though the Lee family's new home lacked the grandeur of Stratford, Robert spent some of the happiest years of his life here. Lee left at age eighteen for West Point and returned forty years later after the end of the Civil War. A neighbor who saw him looking over the wall into the garden asked him why he had returned. He came back, he told them, to see if the snowballs were blooming as they had in his youth.

The first ghostly sighting in Lee's Boyhood Home was reported in the 1930s, when a previous owner saw a small girl giggling by the staircase. People familiar with the history of the house assumed that it was the spirit of a four-year-old child who had died after falling over the third-floor banister many years before. However, most of the hauntings at Lee's Boyhood Home began in the early 1960s, four years before the Lee-Jackson Foundation of Charlottesville acquired the property. At that time, the house was owned by the investment banker Henry Koch and his wife. When the couple and their seven-year-old son, William, first moved in on June 10, 1962, they were startled by the sounds of someone running around the house. Upstairs, they heard childish laughter coming from what seemed to be a four-year-old child. These sounds continued in the weeks that followed. On some days, the Koch family heard the sounds more than once. Oddly enough, they were not really frightened by the sounds. In fact, the noises appeared to be the kinds of cheerful sounds normally associated with a loving family.

Other mysterious occurrences have taken place in Lee's Boyhood Home as well. Mr. Koch said that during a meeting at his home, he and his guests were treated to a serenade of melodies coming from upstairs. The music seemed to have been made by someone playing a stringed instrument. No one was upstairs at the time. Mrs. Koch has also had her share of unusual experiences at the house. One day, she was looking for her missing cigarette lighter when, all at once, it came sailing through the air and landed at her feet. Her first thought was that her son Bill had thrown it at her, but he was later found to be in an entirely different part of the house at the time. Sometimes, the doorbell rings when no one is standing outside the door. On several occasions, people have "sensed" a presence at the house. When Susy Smith, author of *Prominent American Ghosts,* visited the home, she said that she immediately felt a "prickly" sensation in her spine, followed by goosebumps.

Apparently, one of the Lee family's pets has also decided to return home. For years, a small black dog with a long body and long tail has been seen running through the garden and playing in the yard. People have considered this to be exceedingly odd because both areas are walled in, making it impossible for a stray dog to enter the premises. The ghost dog was also seen in the same area as the Kochs' two dogs, neither one of which acknowledged his presence. The archaeologist Keith Barr became convinced of the existence of the spectral animal when he returned one morning to find dog prints covering the area surrounding his dig, which was located in one of the walled-in areas. Even more amazingly, no prints were found leading up to the dig.

The most bizarre incident occurred on a Sunday afternoon when a retired admiral and his wife paid the Kochs a visit. While they sat talking, the admiral's wife suddenly found herself being snowed upon for several minutes while her husband and the Kochs stared at her in amazement. The mini-storm began about one foot above her head. After the snowing stopped, the woman found herself soaking wet. Not surprisingly, she and her husband got up to leave. Just as they were exiting the front door, the snowing started again. It did not stop until the woman had left the house.

The ghostly phenomena continued after Lee's Boyhood Home was taken over by the Lee-Jackson Foundation in 1967. One day, a volunteer tour guide lost her keys. Complaining loudly, she began retracing her steps. Suddenly, her keys floated across the room to the speechless woman. She never again complained about losing anything in the house.

Some people have calculated that Lee's Boyhood Home harbors at least ten ghosts. Although there is no way of determining empirically if that count is indeed true, people who have spent time in the house know that something not of this world still walks the halls. Most people who have encountered the ghosts believe that they are friendly spirits who mean no one any harm. The lady who was snowed upon might disagree, though.

Robert E. Lee's Boyhood Home is located at 607 Oronoco Street in Alexandria, Virginia; phone: 703-548-8454.

Physic Hill

WINTERPOCK

hysic Hill is an old, L-shaped building situated on the crest of a hill two miles east of Winterpock. The house got its name from the two generations of doctors who practiced medicine there in the 1850s. The half-parlor plan structure was built in 1815 by Dr. John R. Walke, a physician from Amelia County. In 1824, a large side-passage wing was added to the north side. The house is set on a high English basement. Of the three remaining chimneys, only one is original. The present basement area of the house was a brick-walled root cellar. According to local legend, Dr. Walke disciplined unruly slaves in the root cellar; he also examined slaves down there prior to their being sold at auction. A "slave auction block" that once stood in the front yard at Physic Hill was moved to the Chesterfield Courthouse in the 1960s.

Dr. John R. Walke was born circa 1790 in Amelia County. His first wife, Martha Branch, was the daughter of Thomas Branch of Willow Hill. She was also the mother of Dr. Walke's children. She died of unknown causes on March 19, 1841, at the age of fifty-two. Dr. Walke married twice more before his death in 1863. The property remained in the Walke family until 1883 when Casper Walke sold the property, which then included 749 acres, to Dr. J. E. Holmes, a Maryland physician. The house was abandoned in the 1930s. The restoration of the property began with Mr. and Mrs. J. Milton Wilkinson and continued with Mr. and Mrs. James R. Hawkins, who bought the estate in 1972. The restoration was completed by Mr. and Mrs. Ellis B. Grady Jr., who purchased the property in 1983 and owned it for fourteen years. They lived there for twelve years.

Pattie Grady enjoyed her years at Physic Hill, despite the fact that she and her family shared the house with a resident ghost. Shortly after the Gradys moved in, they sensed a presence in the house. Pictures inexplicably fell off walls. When they were nailed back up, the pictures would fall again. In one particular room on the third floor, objects such as teddy bears that had been placed on the bed would be on the floor a few minutes later. The Gradys named this room "Martha's room" because of all the strange phenomena that had occurred there. On Christmas Day 1983, there was no hot water in the sink faucet. However, the shower worked fine, even though the same pipe that carried hot water to the sink also carried it to the shower. Later, they began hearing heavy footsteps over the top of the master bedroom.

Although the true identity of the spirit has never been determined, Pattie assumes that it is the ghost of Martha B. Walke, primarily because of an incident that occurred in September 1984. She and her husband hired two young men in their twenties to paint the house. While Pattie and her children were gone for the day, the two men scraped the house. Neither man had been told about the ghost in the house. The next day, one of them asked her if anyone lived in the house besides Pattie, her husband, and her children. She said that no one else lived there. "The painter then replied, 'We saw you drive off, and my partner said he saw an old lady standing up at the window.' I said, 'No. It can't be. The Gradys are gone.' And he said, 'Well, I'm telling you she was there, and she had on this funny-looking outfit.' " When the painter described the woman's dress to Pattie, she recognized it as being almost identical to an outfit Martha's daughter wore in a portrait that she sat for in 1838. Afterward, Pattie envied the painters because they were granted a privileged glimpse of Martha's elusive ghost.

Pattie said that Martha also liked to play little tricks on people. On one occasion, some workmen came over to Physic Hill to put up some siding. After the men had worked for a couple of days, one of them told Pattie that something very strange had been happening to his truck while he was there. "He said that whenever he pulled into the driveway, the truck's radio went off. But as soon as he left our property, the radio went back on."

Martha seemed to have become so attached to the Gradys that she even followed them when they moved: "We were still living at Physic Hill while building our new home, and Martha had gotten really quiet. One evening when coming to check on the progress of our Gates Bluff house from the main road, we noticed that lights appeared to be burning. It was just at dusk, and by the time we got into the driveway of the new house, the lights had gone out. This puzzled us since no electricity was in the house. Another time, a friend and I were at the new house during the day, and the sound of footsteps from the top floor was noticed by both of us, but when we went up the stairs, nobody seemed to be there! All my friends thought that Martha had intentions of 'following' us to the new house, and yet once we moved in, we never saw or heard anything unusual, and the new owners of Physic Hill reported strange happenings. We just surmised that she decided to stay in her old home and not follow us to the new one! We really liked her, and she must have sensed this."

After Pattie and her family moved out of Physic Hill, she discovered a very unsettling fact. When she returned to Martha's grave one day, she took special note of the date of her death: March 19. All of a sudden, it dawned on Pattie that she and her family had moved into Physic Hill on the same day that Martha had died. "There are 364 other days that we could have chosen to move in," Pattie said, "so this has got to be more than just a coincidence."

The couple who purchased Physic Hill from the Gradys— David and Gaye Hay—also had encounters with the ghost. On many different occasions, they would make the bed in "Martha's room" and leave. When they returned, the next day, the covers would be ruffled, even though no one had spent the night in the room.

Pattie Grady never saw Martha's ghost, but she is convinced that she is still there in Physic Hill. "Somebody asked me how I knew it was Martha," Pattie said, "and I said, 'I just knew it. That's all.'" Pattie has spent hours poring over spools of microfilm at the Library of Virginia to try to find any mention of Martha's death in the old newspapers. "I've always wondered how Martha died. But when I get to the issue that I think will help me, the issue is always missing. I guess that we're just not supposed to know the manner of her death."

Physic Hill is located two blocks off Winterpock Road in Chesterfield County, Winterpock, Virginia.

Ramsay House

ALEXANDRIA

Every year, Old Town Alexandria attracts thousands of tourists, eager to visit its picturesque shops and townhouses. Many of them begin their tour by walking through the Information Center of the Alexandria Tourist Council, where they pick up brochures and talk with the staff. Most of these people are probably unaware that the Information Center was originally known as the Ramsay House and that it is the oldest house in the entire historic district. They also are probably not aware that the Ramsay House is haunted.

This stone and clapboard farmhouse stands at the intersection of King and Fairfax Streets. It was built in 1724 by one of the founders of Alexandria, William Ramsay. Ramsay, a Scottish merchant, transported the house upriver by barge from Dufries to the site of what Ramsay hoped would be a great city. One day in 1749, he went forth from his "transplanted" house to carry out an order of the Virginia House of Burgesses. As one of several trustees, Ramsay was authorized to help sell, lot by lot, a sixty-acre tract of land adjoining his home. One of the men who helped him stake out the town was his good friend George Washington, who was still in his twenties at the time. As the years passed, Ramsay became Alexandria's first lord mayor as well as its postmaster. He and his wife, Ann, spent many happy years at their home with their eight children.

The Ramsay House has gone through many changes down through the years. Descendants of William and Ann remained in the house until 1848. For the next one hundred years, it served as a tobacco factory, an antique shop, and, in 1932, a tavern. After a fire rendered the building unusable in 1943, the Ramsay House was abandoned. In 1949, two hundred years after it was moved to its present site, the Alexandria Historical Society initiated a drive to restore the Ramsay House to its former glory.

Staff members at the Ramsay House would argue that John Ramsay, or possibly his son Dennis, never really left his beloved house. In the 1970s, staff members reported seeing Ramsay's image staring out of an upstairs window. In 1986, Barbara Janney, director of the Ramsay House, experienced many things there that she could not explain. She often heard the sound of footsteps where no one was present. Sometimes, a door would open by itself. A door latch has been seen moving up and down. While working late at night, Janney felt the presence of someone near. Many people, she said, witnessed the lights dim inexplicably. One staff member said that on her third day at the Ramsay House in the early 1980s, she was walking down the stairs when she felt as if someone was directly behind her. When she turned around and found nobody there, she hurried out the front door. Robert Connally, director of the nearby Lee-Fendall House, had a very similar experience in the Ramsay House. One night, he was working with a colleague in the Ramsay House when they received the distinct impression that someone had joined them. At almost the same instant, the lights dimmed.

L. B. Taylor Jr., author of *The Ghosts of Virginia, Vol. III*, reported that ghostly activity in the Ramsay House was reported through most of the 1990s. Frequently, staff members preparing to close the Information Center for the day have heard noises upstairs. Thinking that a stray tourist is still in the building, the director sends someone to check it out. Invariably, the search for the source of the noise is fruitless. Once in a while, the sound is more distinct, resembling the crying of a very distraught person. Not only do the lights still dim, but fax machines go off and on by themselves. Peg Sinclair, former director of the Alexandria Tourist Council, says that at times, office workers walking through the building found that furniture had been moved to a different spot. To prove that the furniture had actually moved, the staff have even measured the location of the furniture before they leave and measured it again in the morning. Sinclair said that on one particularly frightening occasion, a man was waiting on the porch to talk to her when a chair rose up off the floor and remained suspended in midair for a few minutes. When she finally walked out on the porch to meet the man, he was "white as a sheet."

Although most people assume that the ghost is the former master of Ramsay House, some staff members believe someone else is haunting the building, a much more tragic figure. William's son Dennis fell in love with a barmaid. Because his father did not approve of his son's love, Dennis was forced to end his romance. Deprived of his true love, Dennis wasted away and died not long thereafter. Whoever's spirit is still roaming Ramsay House, he apparently has some unfinished business that will not let him rest.

The Ramsay House is located at 221 King Street, Alexandria, Virginia; phone: 703-549-0205.

BIBLIOGRAPHY

"About the Driskill Hotel—Historical Timeline." http://www. driskillhotel.com/timeline.html.

Adams, Susan. Personal interview. 31 October 2000.

"Alamo 'Spirits' Are Photographed." *San Antonio Light,* 25 May 1925.

Albrecht, Dana. "Things That Go Bump on the Hill." *College Heights Herald,* 29 October 1987: 1C.

"Allen House to Be Included in Historical Walking Tour." *Advance Monticellonian,* 1 November 1989.

Allen, Paula. "Tracking a Ghost Story." *San Antonio Express-News,* 29 October 1995.

Andrews, James. "The Ghost of St. Mary's." *Commonwealth Appeal Mid-South Magazine,* 25 November 1973: 72–4.

Angers, Trent. "The Spirit of Oak Alley." *Acadiana Profile,* March/April 1981.

Aradillas, Elaine. "Tracks Tale Still Pushes Thrill-Seekers." *San Antonio Express-News,* 31 October 2000: 1F, 10F.

Baggett, Jim. Personal interview. 26 May 2000.

Banks, Marianne. "Have You Seen the Ghost? Alexander's Employees Say Store Is Haunted." *Meridian Star,* 29 May 1999: 1.

Barrett, Matt. Personal interview. 31 October 2001.

Bates, Ron. Personal interview. 10 March 2000.

Beamguard, Jim. "Walls of Gimghoul Castle Guard Their Secrets Well." *Chapel Hill News,* 18 January 1976: 1A–2A.

Belfuss, John. "Alphabet of Evil: Memphis Finds Creepy, Crawly Niche." *Memphis Commercial Appeal,* 31 October 1987, sec. A: 1, 7.

Bell, Elma. "Spirit in the Stacks." *Birmingham News,* 26 October 1997, E-1, E-4.

Bell, Sandra. "Ghost Walks at King's Tavern." *Natchez Democrat,* 31 August 1977.

Bennett, Patricia Thompson. *Lilian Place.* Daytona Beach, Fla.: M. Print, n.d.

Blackmon, Sheila. Personal interview. 14 November 2000.

Block, Harold. "More Light on the Ghost Lights." *Fayetteville News and Observer,* 7 May 1961.

Bolick, Julia. *Ghosts from the Coast: A Collection of Twelve Stories from Georgetown County, South Carolina.* Georgetown, S.C.: The Presses of Jacobs Brothers, 1966.

Bolin, Steven. Personal interview. 14 December 2000.

Boyd, Scotty Ray. Personal interview. 17 May 2001.

Boyles, Barbara. "J. B. 'Mutt' Peavey: The Man behind the Name." *Monitor,* Summer 1990: 66, 68.

"A Brief History of the Texas Governor's Mansion." http://www.txfgm. org/brief.html.

Brock, Kevin. Personal interview. 6 December 2000.

Brodie. Fawn M. *Thomas Jefferson: An Intimate History.* New York: Bantam, 1974.

Brooks, Browning. "Old Jail Is Being Prepared for Some High-Tech Haunting." *Tallahassee Democrat,* 2 December 1984: 1C, 11C.

Brown, Alan. *Shadows and Cypress: Southern Ghost Stories.* Jackson: University Press of Mississippi, 2000.

Callahan, Jody. "Haunted History Leaves This Dude Cold." *Memphis Commercial Appeal,* 27 October 1994, sec. CE-1, CE-5.

Carlson, Charlie. *Strange Florida: The Unexplained and Unusual.* New Smyrna Beach, Fla.: Luthers, 1997.

Chariton, Wallace O. *Exploring the Alamo Legends.* Plano: Republic of Texas Press, 1992.

Childs, Todd. Personal interview. 26 January 2001.

Clemence, Jim. "Haunted House of Books." *Omnis,* 2.3 (1969).

Curry, Ginger Simpson. "Keeping Spirits Up." *Floridian Magazine of St. Petersburg Times,* 14 February 1982: 17–19.

DeBolt, Margaret Wayt. Personal interview. 6 December 2000.

———. *Savannah Spectres and Other Strange Tales.* Norfolk, Va.: Donning Company, 2000.

DeZavala, Adine. *The History and Legends of the Alamo and Other Missions in and around San Antonio and South Texas.* Plano: Republic of Texas Press, 1993.

Downs, Jr., Percy Ray. Student Collection: Headless Woman Rock. Western Kentucky University. Fall 1971.

Durm, Mark. *Stripped of Their Sheets.* Birmingham, Ala.: Seacoast Publishing, Inc., 1999.

Edwards, Jolane. "There Are Ghost Tales in Alexandria." *Mobile Press Register,* 31 October 1970.

Elder, Becky. "Grappling with a Ghost." *Fate,* July 1998: 58–61.

Ewing, James. *It Happened in Tennessee.* Nashville, Tenn.: Rutledge Hill Press, 1986.

Fairley, Laura Nan, and James T. Dawson. *Paths to the Past: An Overview History of Lauderdale County, Mississippi.* Meridian, Miss.: Lauderdale County Department of Archives and History, 1988.

Fausel, Ed. Personal interview. 21 February 2001.

"The Fiddling Janitor." *Texas Monthly,* October 1978: 137.

Finger, Michael. "Ghost Story: What Really Happened to Clara Robertson?" *Memphis Magazine,* October 1984: 27–32.

"Folk Tales/ Ghost Stories." Collected for the W.P.A. by Ruth Bass in DeSoto County, Mississippi, in 1937.

Foreman, Laura, ed. *Discovery Travel Adventures: Haunted Holidays.* USA: Discovery Communications, Inc., 1999.

———. *Haunted Holidays.* New York: Discovery Communications, Inc., 1999.

Fort Zachary Taylor State Historic Site. Available from Southeast Publications USA Incorporated, 4360 Peters Road, Ft. Lauderdale, Florida 33317.

Gardner, Molly. "Ghost of Jilted Lover May Yet Haunt Mansion." *Austin American-Statesman* 31 October 1974.

"Ghost in the Church." Collected for the W.P.A. by Ruth Bass from Mrs. Julia Haraway in Hernando, Mississippi, in 1937.

"The Ghosts at Hagley." Collected for the W.P.A. by C. S. Murray from Eugene F. LaBruce in Charleston, South Carolina, on 17 September 1936.

"Ghostly Noises Haunt Stacks of Library in New Hanover." *Raleigh News and Observer,* 16 November 1986: 48A.

"A Ghoulish Guide to S.A." *San Antonio Express-News,* 29 October 1989: 131.

Grady, Pattie. Personal interview. 24 January 2001.

Gray, Berry. Personal interview. 8 December 2000.

Greene, Amanda. "Local Castle Looms Large in Town Myth." *Daily Tar Heel,* 31 January 1997: 2.

Guten, Keri. "Haunting Tales for Halloween." *San Antonio Light,* 31 October 1983: 1D, 8D.

Hamil, Ms. R. M. Personal interview. 14 December 2000.

Harger, Sarah. Personal interview. 6 March 2001.

Hauck, Dennis William. *National Directory of Haunted Places.* New York: Penguin, 1996.

"Haunted History." *Jacksonville Magazine,* October 1998: 23–4.

Henderson, Kim. "Ghost Making the Rounds at Local Hotel with Strange Goings-On." *Crestview News Bulletin,* 1 November 2000: 13A.

Hensley, Douglas. *Hell's Gate: Terror at Bobby Mackey's Music World.* Jacksonville, Fla.: Audio Books Plus, 1993.

Hines, Perry. "Tales of Horror." *College Heights Herald,* 29 October 1981: G2, G7.

"The Historic Crescent Hotel." www.crescent-hotel.com.

Hubbard, Sylvia Booth. *Ghosts! Personal Accounts of Modern Mississippi Hauntings.* Brandon, Miss.: QRP Books, 1992.

Jasinkiewicz, Bob. "Gimghoul Castle." *Chapel Hill News,* 30 October 1981: 1A, 10A.

Jefferson, Thomas. *The Family Letters of Thomas Jefferson.* Ed. Edwin Morris Betts and James Adam Bear Jr. Charlottesville, Va.: Thomas Jefferson Memorial Foundation, 1986.

Jones, Tina. Personal interview. 24 January 2001.

Kaiser, Rob. "Bar not Typical Haunt." *Cincinnati Enquirer,* 31 October 1996.

Kaye, Ruth Lincoln. *Legends and Folk Tales of Old Alexandria, Virginia.* Alexandria, Va.: Privately published, 1975.

Ketchum, Richard M., ed. *American Heritage Picture History of the Civil War.* New York: American Heritage Publishing Company, 1960.

Klein, Victor C. *New Orleans Ghosts.* Chapel Hill, N.C.: Professional Press, 1993.

Lambroussis, Loretta. "Library Has Legendary Ghost Who Plays Violin." *Houston Post,* 2 March 1961.

"Legend of Dromgoole Haunts Gimghoul Castle." *Town & Gown,* 1985–1986: 46.

Leland, Elizabeth. "A Ghost among the Stacks?" *Charlotte Observer,* 9 November 1986: 1D, 4D.

Lewis, Nolan. "Literary, Musical Approaches Fail to Bring out Library's Ghost." *Houston Post,* 3 November 1987.

Liberty Hall. Pamphlet. Lexington, Ky.: Vistacolor Corporation, 1989.

Lord, Walter. *A Time to Stand.* New York: Harper & Brothers, 1961.

Lovell, Reid. Personal interview. 20 February 2001.

Macy, Edward B., and Julian T. Buxton. *The Ghosts of Charleston.* New York: Beaufort Book Company, 2000.

Magness, Perre. "Memphis Hosts Several Ghosts: Stories Will Be Told." *Memphis Commercial Appeal,* 29 October 1987, sec. E: 1, 9.

Martin, Nancy Rhett. *Charleston Ghosts.* Charleston: University of South Carolina Press, 1963.

McLin, Elva Bell. *Athens State College: A Definitive History, 1821–1991.* Vol. I. Huntsville, Ala.: Crawford & Hicklin Printing Company, 1991.

McPherson, James M. *Battle Cry for Freedom: The Civil War Era.* New York: Oxford University Press, 1988.

Mead, Robin. *Haunted Hotels.* Nashville, Tenn.: Rutledge Hill Press, 1995.

Meyers, Arthur. *The Ghostly Register.* Chicago: Contemporary Books, 1986.

Miller, Laura. "Street Names." *San Antonio Express-News,* 15 December 1984: 276.

Montell, William Lynwood. *Ghosts across Kentucky.* Lexington: University Press of Kentucky, 2000.

Moody, Mark. Personal interview. 12 April 1998.

Moore, Joyce Elson. *Haunt Hunter's Guide to Florida.* Sarasota, Fla.: Pineapple Press, 1998.

Mugno, Marjie. "Spirits among Us." *Texas Parade,* November 1971: 27–30.

Murphy, Drew. "Lilian Place—A Piece of Our History." *Daytona Beach Sunday News-Journal,* 22 October 1978: 1F1.

Myers, Arthur. *Ghostly Register: Haunted Dwellings—Active Spirits: A Journey to America's Strangest Landmarks.* Chicago: Contemporary Books, 1986.

Newmeier, Franz. "The Legend of Steamboatin' in the Grand Old South." www.steamboats.org.

Norman, Michael, and Beth Scott. *Haunted America.* New York: Tom Doherty Associates, 1994.

———. *Historic Haunted America.* New York: Tom Doherty Associates, 1995.

O'Brien, Cyril. "Spirits of Suburbia: Ghostly Accounts Abound around the Beltway." *The Journal,* 31 October 1986: B1, B8.

O'Connell, Joe. "Ghost of a Tale: Spirited Rumors Haunt Driskill." *Austin American-Statesman,* 8 June 1992: A1.

O'Dell, Jeffrey M. *Chesterfield County: Early Architecture and Historic Sites.* Chesterfield, Va.: Chesterfield County Planning Dept., 1983.

Pearson, Dave. Personal interview. 7 March 2000.

Phelon, Craig. "Are the Spirit of John Wayne and a Host of Other Ghosts Haunting the Alamo?" *San Antonio Express Magazine,* 27 January 1991: 1, 10.

Preik, Brooks Newton. *Haunted Wilmington . . . and the Cape Fear Coast.* Wilmington, N.C.: Banks Channel Books, 1996.

Randall, Nancy. "Memphis Ghosts Don't Always Wait for Halloween to Make Appearance." *Memphis Daily News,* 31 October 1985, sec. A: 1, 16.

Randolph, Sarah N. *The Domestic Life of Thomas Jefferson.* Charlottesville, Va.: Thomas Jefferson Memorial Foundation, 1939.

Rhett Martin, Margaret. *Charleston Ghosts.* Charleston: University of South Carolina Press, 1963.

Rhyne, Nancy. *Coastal Ghosts.* Orangeburg, S.C.: Fast & McMillan Publishers, Inc., 1989.

———. *Coastal Ghosts.* Orangeburg, S.C.: Sandlapper Publishing Company, 1995.

———. *More Tales of the South Carolina Low Country.* Winston-Salem, N.C.: John F. Blair, Publisher, 1966.

Roberts, Nancy. *Haunted Houses: Tales from 30 American Homes.* Chester, Conn.: Globe Pequot Press, 1988.

Royalty, Barry A. "Honky-Tonk Devils: Last Stop on the Highway to Hell." *Kentucky Monthly,* October 1999: 34–5.

Sanford, Peggy. "Spirits May Roam Sloss, Library." *Birmingham News,* 31 October 1984, sec. A: 2.

Saxon, Lyle. *Gumbo Ya-Ya: Folk Tales of Louisiana.* Gretna, La.: Pelican Publishing Company, 1987.

———. *Gumbo Ya-Ya: Folk Tales of Louisiana.* Gretna, La.: Pelican Publishing Company, 1991.

Schafer, Daniel L. *Anna Kingsley.* St. Augustine, Fla.: St. Augustine Historical Society, 1994.

Schultz, Gladys Denny, and Daisy Gordon Lawrence. *Lady from Savannah: The Life of Juliette Gordon Low.* Philadelphia and New York: J. B. Lippincott Company, 1958.

Scott, Danny. Personal interview. 31 October 2001.

Shea, William L., and Earl J. Hess. "Pea Ridge." *The Civil War Battlefield Guide.* Ed. Frances H. Kennedy. Boston: Houghton Mifflin Company, 1990: 20–5.

Shearer, Victoria, and Janet Ware. *The Insider's Guide to the Florida Keys and Key West.* Canada: Falcon Publishing Company, 1998.

Slate, Joe H. *Psychic Phenomena: New Principles, Techniques, and Applications.* Jefferson, N.C.: McFarland Co., 1988.

Sparks, Nancy Coons. "The Gurdon Light Phenomenon: You Must See It to Understand It." *Arkansas Gazette,* 22 June 1980: 15F.

Spellman, James David. "They Say It Happens in the Best of Houses." *Washington Post,* 28 October 1977: 1.

"Spine-Tingling Tale of Lizzie Davie's Ghost as Frightening in the Retelling as It Was in 1871." *Press-Scimitar,* 29 October 1977.

Springer, Beulah. "General Lee's Boyhood Home." *UDC Magazine,* May 1967: 11.

Steelman, Ben. "Something Spooky's Going on at the Library." *Wilmington Star,* 18 September 1986: 1D.

Szilagyi, Pete. "Austin's Ghosts and Haunted Houses." *Free & Easy,* October 15–November 15, 1974.

Tate, Pat. Personal interview. 19 April 1998.

Taylor, L. B. *The Ghosts of Virginia,* Vol. I. USA: Progress Printing Company, 1993.

————. *The Ghosts of Virginia,* Vol. II. USA: Progress Printing Company, 1996.

————. *The Ghosts of Virginia,* Vol. III. USA: Progress Printing Company, 1998.

Taylor, Troy. *Haunted New Orleans: Ghosts and Hauntings of the Crescent City.* Alton, Ill.: Whitechapel Productions Press, 2000.

————. *Spirits of the Civil War: A Guide to the Ghosts and Hauntings of America's Bloodiest Conflict.* Alton, Ill.: Whitechapel Productions Press, 1999.

————. *No Rest for the Wicked.* Alton, Ill.: Whitechapel Productions Press, 2001.

Tetterton, Beverly. Personal interview. 6 February 2001.

"Things That Go Bump in the Night." *Jacksonville Magazine,* October 1998: 62–6.

Vivano, Christy L. *Haunted Louisiana.* Metarie, La.: Tree House Press, 1992.

Vosburgh, Grant. "Midnight Mysteries: Frightful Sights Spook Believers." *Fayetteville Times,* 31 October 1979, 6A.

Walker, Karen J. *Volumes in Historical Archaeology.* Columbia: University of South Carolina, 1988.

Ward, Dorothy Y. "The Ghost of Mollie Woodruff." *Press-Scimitar,* 5 May 1982.

Williams, Allison. "Vander Light." *Fayetteville Times,* 31 October 1998, 22–3.

Williams, Docia Schultz, and Reneta Byrne. *Spirits of San Antonio.* Plano: Republic of Texas Press, 1993.

Windham, Kathryn. *13 Alabama Ghosts and Jeffrey.* Huntsville, Ala.: Strode Publishers, 1969.

————. *13 Mississippi Ghosts and Jeffrey.* Huntsville, Ala.: Strode Publishers, 1974.

————. *The Ghost in the Sloss Furnaces.* Birmingham, Ala.: Birmingham Historical Society, 1987.

————. *Jeffrey's Latest 13: More Alabama Ghosts.* Huntsville, Ala.: Strode Publishers, 1982.

Winer, Richard, and Nancy Osborn. *Haunted Houses.* New York: Bantam, 1979.

Wlodarski, Robert, and Anne Powell Wlodarski. *Spirits of the Alamo.* Plano: Republic of Texas Press, 1999.

WOKK Web site. WWW. wokk.com.

Yarbrough, Nancy. "A Spook in the Stacks." *Birmingham Post-Herald,* 29 October 1993, sec. C: 2–3.

INDEX

Adams, Susan, 136, 138
Ainsworth, John David, 137
Alabama River, 10
Alamo, 219, 220, 221, 222, 223, 224, 225
Alamo, The, 224
Alexander, Debbie, 137, 139, 148, 149
Alexander's, 147, 148, 149, 150
Alexandria, Va., 245, 246, 248, 252, 253, 254
Allen House, 33, 34, 35
Arthur Murray Dance Studio, 145
Astor, Vincent, 207, 208, 209
Athens Female Academy, 15, 16
Athens State University, 15, 19
Atocha, 67, 68
Austin Daily Statesman, 227, 228
Austin, Tex., 226, 230, 232, 233, 235
Avalanche, 198, 200, 202

Baggett, Jim, 7, 8, 9
Baker, Norman, 37, 38
Bates, Ron, 24
Baton Rouge, La., 118

Battle, Kemp, 166
Battle of Pea Ridge, 44, 45
Battle of Shiloh, 154
Big Harpe, 129, 133
Birmingham, Ala., 19, 20, 21, 22, 23, 24, 25
Birmingham Public Library, 6
Black River, 194
Blackmon, Sheila, 142
Bobby Mackey's Music World, 85, 87, 88, 89, 90, 91
Bolin, Steve, 76
Bowie, Jim, 219, 220
Bowling Green, Ky., 92, 101
Boyd, Scotty Ray, 137, 138, 139, 148
Bradford, General David, 113, 119
Bragg, General Braxton, 165
Breakfast Bunch, 137, 148
Brinkley Female College, 197, 198, 200, 202, 203
Broadway, Jerry, 138
Brown, James, 99
Brown, John, 94
Brynner, Yul, 208
Burns, Abigail, 16, 17, 18, 19

Burrus, Will, 127
Bush, Deedee, 101
Butler, General Benjamin, 110, 164

C., Sylvia, 12
Calhoun, John C., 188
Carter, Fountain Branch, 204, 205
Carter House, 203, 204, 205, 206
Carter, Moscow, 205
Carter, Tod, 205, 206
Cashin, Reverend Thomas F., 210
Chan, Robert Chung, 71, 72
Charleston Morning Post and Daily Advertiser, 186
Charleston, S.C., 66, 184, 185, 186, 187, 188, 189, 190, 191
Chengary, Captain Gabriel, 107
Chesterfield County, 241
Childs, Madame Jane Hamilton, 16
Childs, Todd, 154, 155, 156, 157, 158
Chloe, 114, 115, 116
Christian, Jeff, 141
Clanton, Dr. Stacy, 35
Cleburne, General Patrick, 203, 204
Coke, Sandra, 17
Colonial Dames of America, 97
Columbus, Miss., 159
Commodore, 64
Commonwealth Appeal, 210
Concrete Blonde, 229
Cox, General Jacob D., 204

Cramer, J. Frank, 230, 231
Crane, Stephen, 64
Crescent Hotel, 36, 37, 38, 39, 40
Crestview, Fla., 54, 55, 59
Crockett, Davy, 219, 220, 224

Daughters of the Republic of Texas, 224, 227
Davenport House, 71, 72, 73
Davenport, Isaiah, 72
Davis, Ell, 125
Daytona Beach, Fla., 63, 64, 65, 66
DeBolt, Margaret Wayt, 81
Delta Queen, 105, 106, 107, 108
Dickert, Carolyn, 158
Dickinson, Susanna, 221
Doherty, Colonel Jerry, 11, 12
Downs, Percy Ray, 92, 93
Driskill Hotel, 226, 227, 228, 229, 230
Driskill, Jesse Lincoln, 226, 227
Dromgoole, Peter, 167, 168, 169
Duffy, Monsignor Thomas P., 210, 211
Duke, Phyllis, 108
Dumas, Helen, 121, 122
Duncan, Frances, 61, 62

Eby, Hester, 115, 116
Elkhorn Tavern, 45, 47
Elkton-Emerson, 174
Ell Davis Woods, 125, 126, 127, 128
Encounters, 91
England, Howard, 52, 53
Eppes, Elizabeth, 242, 243

Eppes, Colonel Francis, 241, 242, 243
Eppington, 241, 242, 243, 244
Eudora, Miss., 125, 126, 127, 128
Eureka Springs, Ark., 36, 37, 38

Fate Magazine, 8
Faulkner, William, 191
Fausel, Ed, 67, 68
Fayetteville, Ark., 47
Fayetteville, N.C., 174
Fayetteville Times, 175
Fiddler on the Roof, 208
Fisher, Mel, 67
Forrest, General Nathan Bedford, 203
Fort Fisher, 163, 164, 165, 166
Fort George Island, Fla., 59, 63
Fort Zachary Taylor, 51, 52, 53, 54
Frankfort, Ky., 94, 95
Franklin, Tenn., 203, 204, 206
Franzen, Beverly, 131
French Quarter, 109
Frost, Sonia, 132
Fugat, Myra, 107

Gardiner, Wendell, 53
Georgetown, S.C., 179, 191, 194
Gimghoul Castle, 166, 167
Gordon, Nellie, 73, 74, 75, 76
Gordon, William "Willie," 73, 74
Grady, Pattie, 243, 249, 250, 251
Gray, Berry, 143, 145, 146
Gray Lady, 95, 96, 97
Great Kaiser, 8
Greenlaw Opera House, 201

Griffon, Adam, 109
Griffon House, 109, 110, 111, 112, 114
Grimsley, 135, 136, 137
Gurdon, Ark., 40, 41, 42, 44
Gurdon Lights, 40, 41, 42, 43, 44

Hagley Landing, 179, 182, 184
Hagley Plantation, 179, 184
Hamilton, Governor Andrew, 234
Hard Rock Café, 87
Harger, Sarah, 96, 97
Hawthorne, Nathaniel, 91
Headless Woman Rock, 91, 92, 93
Henderson State University, 42
Henderson, Thomas, 134, 135, 136, 137, 138, 139
Heyward, DuBose, 188
Hines, Nell, 210
Hobby, Governor William P., 227
Holbrook, Joe, 225
Holcomb, Robert, 145
Holmes, Marjorie, 207
Hood, General John Bell, 203
Houston Public Library, 230, 231, 232
Houston, Sam, 234, 235
Houston, Tex., 230, 232
Hubbard, Sylvia Booth, 157

Irish Channel, 112
Isaacs, Ralph, 185

Jackson, Andrew, 95
Jackson, Miss., 137

Jackson, Scott, 85, 86
Jameson Inn of Crestview, 54, 55, 59
Jefferson, Lucy, 242, 243, 244
Jefferson, Thomas, 94, 242, 243
Johnson, Lyndon Baines, 228
Jowers, Theophilus Calvin, 22, 23, 24
Juliette Gordon Low Girl Scout Center, 73, 77

Key West, Fla., 51, 52, 54
King and I, The, 208
King, Richard, 129
King's Tavern, 129, 130, 132, 133
Kingsley, Anna Madgigaine Jai, 60, 62
Kingsley Plantation, 59, 61, 62, 63
Kingsley, Zephaniah, 60, 61, 62
Klein, Victor C., 117
Knights of Pythias, 146
Koch, Henry, 246

LaBruce, Eugene, 179, 182, 183
Ladd House, 184, 185, 186, 187
Ladd, Dr. Joseph, 185, 186, 187
Lafayette, Marquis de, 95
Lalaurie Mansion, 109
Lawson, Carl, 89
Lee, Richard Henry "Lighthorse Harry," 245
Lee, Robert E., 165, 245, 246
Lee's Boyhood Home, 245, 246, 248
Leitchfield, Ky., 91, 92, 93
Leming, Dr. Charles, 42, 43

Liberty Hall, 94, 95, 96, 97
Lilian Place, 63, 64, 65, 66
Lin Henley Building, 5
Lincoln, Abraham, 163
Loader, Brian, 100
Long, William, 100
Look to the Rose, 74
Louisville, Ky., 100
Low, Juliette Gordon, 73, 74
Lowndesboro, Ala., 9

Mackey, Bobby, 87
Maco Light, 174
Madeline, 129, 130, 131, 132
Magnolia Hall, 134, 136, 137, 139, 140
Mansfield Plantation, 193
Marengo, 10
Marion, Francis, 192, 193
Martin, Edward Wray, 167
McCandless Hall, 15, 16, 17
McCarver, Jim, 127
McCleary, Ashley, 137
McPherson, James, 191
Memphis State University, 208, 209
Memphis, Tenn., 98, 197, 200, 203, 207, 213, 214, 216
Meridian, Miss., 140, 141, 142, 143
Meridian Star, 140
Miles, Bishop Richard Pius, 212, 213
Mississippi State University, 143, 144
Mitchell, Alma, 121, 122
Mitchell, Kelly, 149

Moberly, Grover, 131
Mohammad, J. T., 147
Monroe, James, 95
Monroe, La., 137, 138
Monticello, Ark., 33
Moody, Mark, 12, 13, 14, 15
Moore, Joyce Elson, 62
Moorehead, Debbie, 149
Morgan, Monsignor John, 211, 212
Murrah, Governor Pendleton, 233, 234
Murray, Sandra, 88
Myrtles, The, 113, 114, 115, 116, 117, 118, 119

Napolitano, Johnette, 229
Nashville, Tenn., 203, 204, 209
Natchez, Miss., 129, 133, 134, 135, 140
Natchez Trace, 129, 132
National Examiner, 224
New Hanover County, N.C., 166
New Hanover County Public Library, 170, 173
New Orleans, La., 97, 105, 108, 109, 121

Oak Alley, 119, 120, 121, 122
Opdycke, General Emerson, 204
Ofeldt, Frank, 54
Office of Scientific Investigation and Research, 118
Ogelthorpe County, Ga., 150
Old Exchange Building, 66
Old Leon County Jail, 66, 67, 68

Omega Quest, 18
Order of the Gimghouls, 167, 170
Orpheum Theater, 207, 208, 209

Parkman, John McGee, 25, 26, 27, 28, 29
Parks, Martha, 101
Pawley's Island, S.C., 179, 184
Pea Ridge National Military Park, 44, 46
Pease, Governor Elisha Marshall, 23
Peavey, Hartley, 143, 144
Peavey, Joseph B. "Mutt," 143
Peavy Melody Music, 143, 146
Peoples, Johnny, 8
Physic Hill, 248, 249, 250, 251, 252
Pigford Building, 140, 142, 146, 147, 149
Pirate's House, The, 77, 78, 79
Porgy and Bess, 188
Powell, Kathleen, 11
Powell, L. James, 11
Presley, Elvis, 143
Price, Major General Sterling, 44, 45
Pythian Castle Hall, 146

Rais, Tes, 61
Raleigh News and Observer, 172
Ramsay, Dennis, 253, 254
Ramsay House, 252, 253, 254
Ramsay, William, 252, 253, 254
Red Badge of Courage, 64, 65
Redford, Braxton, 126
Reese, Dr. Charles Edwin, 10, 11

Reynolds, Harry, 190, 191
Richard III, 185
Richardson, Mary, 107
Riley, Mrs. J. B., 126
Robertson, Clara, 197, 198, 199, 200, 201, 202
Roman, Celine, 121
Roman, Jacques Telesphore, 120, 122
Rose, Thomas, 185
Rutledge, Edward, 188

San Antonio Express-News, 237
San Antonio River, 219
San Antonio, Tex., 219, 220, 225, 236, 237, 238
Santa Anna, General Antonio Lopez de, 220, 221, 222
Savannah, Ga., 71, 73, 77, 78, 79, 80, 82
Schofield, General John M., 203, 204
Scott, Danny, 133
Sellner, Rosemarie, 137, 138, 139
Selma, Ala., 25, 26, 27, 28, 29
Shepherd, Scott, 137, 149
Sightings, 91, 238
Sinclair, Peg, 254
Slate, Joe, 18
Sloss Furnaces, 19, 20, 21
Snow, Donna, 152, 153, 154, 155
Snow, Richard, 152, 155
Spanish American War, 53
St. Francisville, La., 113, 119
St. Louis, Mo., 121, 151
St. Mary's Catholic Church, 209, 210, 212, 213

St. Philip's Protestant Episcopal Church Graveyard, 188, 190, 191
Stedman, N.C., 174, 176
Stevenson, Robert Louis, 78
Sting, 229
Sturtivant Hall, 25, 26, 27, 28
Sufert, Shirley, 74
Szilagyi, Pete, 235

Tallahassee, Fla., 66, 68
Tate, Pat, 27, 28, 29
Taylor, Charley, 92
Taylor, L. B., Jr., 254
Taylor, Zachary, 95
Telfair, Mary, 80, 81, 82
Telfair Museum of Art, 80, 81, 82
Tetterton, Beverly, 172, 173
Texas Governor's Mansion, 232, 233, 234
Thornley, Fant, 5, 6, 7, 8
Todd, Marianne, 148
Traub, Herb, 78
Travis, William B., 219, 220
Treasure Island, 78
Turchinov, Colonel Ivan Vasilevitch, 16
Tuscumbia, Ala., 203

University of North Carolina (Chapel Hill), 166, 169, 170

Vacherie, La., 119
Van Dorn, General Earl, 44, 45, 46
Van Meter Auditorium, 95
Vander Lights, 173, 174, 175, 176

Vander, N.C., 173, 174, 175, 176

Vardaman, Governor James K., 144

Varick, Margaret, 95

Vaughn, Joan, 46, 47

Villa Main Railroad Crossing, 236, 237, 238

Wagoner Annex No. 3, 144

Walke, Dr. John, 249

Walke, Martha, 249, 250, 251, 252

Walker, John, 210, 213

Walling, Alonzo, 85, 86

Washington, George, 9, 113, 245, 253

Waverly, 150, 151, 152, 153, 154, 155, 156, 157, 158, 159

Wayne, John, 224

Wedgefield Plantation, 191, 192, 193, 194

West Point, Miss., 150, 159

Western Kentucky University, 92, 98, 99, 100, 101

Whiskey Rebellion, 113

Whiting, Marvin, 6

Whiting, General William, 163, 164, 165, 166

Wilder, Ky., 85, 88, 91

Williams, Docia, 237, 238

Williams, Mike, 106, 107

Wilmington, N.C., 163, 164, 166, 170, 171, 173

Wilson, Carolyn, 35

Wilson, General James T., 10, 11, 20

Windham, Kathryn Tucker, 27, 157

Winer, Richard, 112

Winter, William, 116

Winterpock, Va., 248, 253

Woodruff, Amos, 213, 214

Woodruff, Mollie, 214, 215, 216

Woodruffe, Judge Clark, 114

Woodruff-Fontaine House, 213, 215, 216

Wragg, Samuel, 192, 193

Young, Colonel George Hampton, 150, 151